Therapists At Risk

Perils of the Intimacy of the Therapeutic Relationship

Lawrence E. Hedges
Robert Hilton
Virginia Wink Hilton
O. Brandt Caudill, Jr.

JASON ARONSON INC.
Northvale, New Jersey
London

Director of Editorial Production: Robert D. Hack

This book was set in 11pt. Goudy by Alpha Graphics of Pittsfield, N.H. and printed and bound by Book-mart Press of North Bergen, N.J.

10 9 8 7 6 5 4 3 2 1

Library of Congress Cataloging-in-Publication Data

Therapists at risk : perils of the intimacy of the therapeutic
   relationship / Lawrence E. Hedges . . . [etc.].
      p. cm.
   Includes bibliographical references and index.
   ISBN 1–56821–827–3 (hc)
   1. Psychotherapists—Professional ethics.   2. Psychotherapists—
Malpractice.   3. Psychotherapists—Legal status, laws, etc.
4. Psychotherapists—Job stress.   5. Psychotherapy—Moral and
ethical aspects.   6. Psychotherapist and patient.   I. Hedges,
Lawrence E.
RC455.2.E8T46 1996
616.89'14—dc20   96–11819

Manufactured in the United States of America. Jason Aronson Inc. offers books and cassettes. For information and catalog write to Jason Aronson Inc., 230 Livingston Street, Northvale, New Jersey 07647.

Contents

Part I
Risks and the Changing Face of Psychotherapy

Part II
Touching, Sexuality, Dual Relationships, and Countertransference

Part III
Legal and Ethical Considerations

Part IV
Therapists at Risk

About the Authors

Robert Hilton, Ph.D., is widely known as a "therapist's therapist." He has been in private practice in Orange County for 28 years and has taught courses at the University of California–Irvine and –San Diego, and the United States International University in La Jolla. In 1972 he cofounded the Southern California Institute for Bioenergetic Analysis where he continues to be a senior trainer. He is also a member of the faculty of the International Institute for Bioenergetic Analysis, and in this capacity lectures throughout the United States and Europe. His relevant publications include "Touching in Psychotherapy," and "Countertransference: an Energetic Perspective."

Virginia Wink Hilton, Ph.D., has been a practicing psychotherapist for 20 years. In addition, she has taught and trained psychotherapists in the United States and numerous European countries. Her particular interests have been in sexual issues in the therapeutic process, professional ethics, and the relationship between sociocultural issues and personal process. Dr. Hilton has been the Director of Training for the Southern California Institute for Bioenergetic Analysis. She is also the Executive Director-Elect of the International Institute for Bioenergetic Analysis. Her publications include "Working With Sexual Transference," "Sexual Countertransference," "On Being Fully Alive: The Masculine and Feminine Principle," "When We Are Accused," and "The Devil in America."

Lawrence E. Hedges, Ph.D. is the founding Director of the Newport Psychoanalytic Institute where he currently serves as Supervising and Training Psychoanalyst. He is the Director of the Listening Perspectives Study Center and is in private practice specializing in training psychotherapists in Orange, California. Dr. Hedges is an instructor in psychology and psychoanalysis at the California Graduate Institute. He holds a faculty appointment at the University of California at Irvine Medical School, Department of Psychiatry. He is author of numerous papers and the following psychotherapeutic texts: *Listening Perspectives in Psychotherapy*; *Interpreting the Countertransference*; *Remembering, Repeating, and Working Through Childhood Trauma*; *In Search of the Lost Mother of Infancy*; *Strategic Emotional Involvement*; and *Working the Organizing Experience*.

O. Brandt Caudill, Jr., J.D., is an attorney who has been in practice since 1976 and is a graduate of Georgetown University Law Center. Mr. Caudill specializes in the defense of psychotherapists in civil litigation, before ethics committees, and before licensing boards. Mr. Caudill has made numerous presentations to divisions of the American Psychological Association, California Psychological Association, and Arizona Psychological Association. He has written extensively on issues of interest to psychotherapists, including administrative hearings, repressed memory, dual relationships, and note taking. Mr. Caudill is co-author with Kenneth S. Pope of *Law and Mental Health Professionals*.

Introduction

Lawrence E. Hedges

One lazy Sunday afternoon Virginia, Bob, and I were bemoaning the terrible fate of psychotherapists these days. All three of us have been involved in training therapists for over twenty years and have witnessed striking and alarming changes in the profession during that time. Many therapeutic practices considered common two or three decades ago are now seen by many as potential lawsuit material. Many ways of handling professional and ethical dilemmas that have been widely accepted in the field and are still being taught in graduate schools are rapidly becoming the basis for ethical and legal complaints as well as disciplinary procedures. Changing demands in the psychotherapy marketplace with increasingly tight insurance utilization review procedures and managed care regulation are further putting therapists into jeopardy. Mental health professionals working in such settings are no longer allowed to practice according to tried and true standards of care that are theoretically and clinically sound, but must provide services according to what the insurance and managed care industry is willing to pay for. It seems that the more therapists attempt to adjust to the changing times and conditions, the more the dangers that seem to appear out of the woodwork in our increasingly litigious society.

In our roles as teachers, supervisors, and psychotherapy consultants, Virginia, Bob, and I have each watched the unfolding of numerous tragedies in which the lives of therapists, their colleagues, and their families have been turned upside down or destroyed entirely by faulty and/or misplaced complaint procedures to which they had fallen victim. We began comparing notes about our various experiences and the many cases we had each consulted on, only to find ourselves increasingly shocked at the appalling and unpredictable vulnerability therapists are subject to today. Yes, there have been a number of therapists over the years who have stepped out of line in various ways and have been disciplined accordingly. But the escalating risk exposure that therapists have come under in recent years has meant that many tragedies have happened to therapists that have in no way been of their own making.

What began as a seemingly simple afternoon conversation soon turned into a full-blown, multifaceted interchange that has expanded with increased intensity and concern into the present book. Our first realization was that the vast majority of therapists are not aware—and worse, have no means of becoming aware—of the magnitude and nature of the changes that are occurring in the legal and ethical complaint arena. Therapists do not have the slightest idea of the nature of the dangers they are facing or where these dangers are coming from. Therapists are sitting ducks in the midst of the current lethal cross fire. They are only slowly waking up to the treachery around them that, sooner or later, is highly likely to strike directly or indirectly.

But worse than a simple lack of knowledge, we began to realize that most of the professionals we know and work with are living in massive denial about the truly horrifying things that can easily happen to any practicing therapist—no matter how good, how ethical, or how experienced he or she may be. It is shocking to realize how many professional therapists are being sued and disciplined for doing things that have been and continue to be such widespread practices as to be clearly within a broad national standard of care.

But the people making judgments or rendering opinions against therapists generally have no training or experience in intensive, long-

term, dynamic psychotherapy. So they are not in a position to determine what kinds of interactions frequently do occur in a therapy process. Even a professional well trained in time-limited, behavioral, or
cognitive interventions is unlikely to be able to appreciate the subtleties and complexities involved in the transferences, resistances, and
countertransferences of intensive transformational work. Seasoned psychotherapists are acutely aware of variations of standard technique that
they frequently feel pressed into using for the purposes of working with
a particularly difficult client toward bringing some unusual issue or
image into the light of day. Every experienced psychotherapist can point
to many things she or he has done and continues to do on an almost
daily basis that they would not like to be held accountable for. What
judge, jury, or licensing board can possibly understand the strange limits
to which we often have to go to show a person something about themselves and the operation of their unconscious activities? Ethics committees made up of practicing professionals generally tend to be more
tuned into the exigencies of therapeutic techniques—but even ethics
committees can fall into the routine of employing simplifying and/or
narrow moralizing tactics rather than facing the complex and difficult
task of comprehending the demands of unusual and trying therapeutic
circumstances and unconventional tactics and techniques.

Our initial conversation led to many further conversations on this
important topic. Until we began exchanging experiences and formulat-
ing dilemmas, we had not realized how many facets of our social, professional, and personal lives the accumulating dangers encompassed. Most
complaint cases are settled quietly and confidentially since lawsuits and
disciplinary actions endanger the privacy and reputation of both therapist and client. *Because of the atmosphere of secrecy that enshrouds accusations against therapists, the grim truth of what is happening to psychotherapists
is seldom discussed or given public forum.* Rumors and confidential whis-
pers that reach the ears of most therapists cannot possibly expose the
breadth and depth of the many problems and issues involved. Even we,
as long-time practitioners and trainers of psychotherapists, were surprised
at how little appraised we each were as individuals of the numerous subtleties and implications we discovered when our collective information was
pooled. New issues and questions were raised that, in turn, were put to
our mutual friend and legal colleague, Brandt Caudill, an attorney well
known and respected for his defense work with therapists. Numerous

other colleagues were consulted and other case material gathered as we strove to bring to light the full range of risks facing therapists today as a result of the intimate nature of our work.

Changes in social and cultural conditions seemed to us to account for much of the witch-hunt atmosphere that pervades the complaint processes therapists are currently involved in. Fears of dire consequences to the therapist are seen to be driving many expectable uncertainties of the therapeutic process underground, so that it has become more difficult and risky for therapists to acknowledge errors and mistaken tactics that are a necessary part of the trial-and-error process of psychotherapy. Further, the accusatory atmosphere has become so frightening that responsible therapists are reconsidering whether they want to work with a client who presents a severe personality disorder or a history of abuse.

The scope of psychotherapy has steadily widened over the years from its original goal of treating neurotic conflicts to the transformation of narcissistic vulnerability, borderline personality functioning, and all types of character disorders. More recently it has come to include the psychological treatment of psychotic or "organizing" personality features; thus, patients and psychic constellations previously believed to be untreatable by psychotherapy are now being engaged in the treatment process by professional therapists. No one could possibly have foreseen the multitude of hazards that this extension of treatment to the more deeply disturbed would eventually present to the professional and personal life of therapists. Even a decade ago no one could have imagined that the symbiotic, psychotic, and organizing transferences that we have finally learned to elicit in the treatment process could produce dangerous accusations of a false nature against an unwitting therapist. No one could have guessed that the 1973 concept of *dual relationship*, coined by the American Psychological Association (APA) Ethics Committee to curb sexual acting out by therapists, would uncritically be misused as a moral accusation to be hurled against therapists so that the APA Ethics Committee had to abolish the term completely in its 1992 Code of Ethics. Therapists have tended to believe that if they acted sincerely and in good faith, did a good job, and behaved ethically, they would be safe from blame. Little have we expected the epidemic of false accusations and faulty discipline procedures that now plague us, threatening our peace of mind, our professional life, the welfare of our families, our right to work, and the safety of our personal financial assets.

So alarming were our findings that Virginia, Bob, and I decided to organize a symposium on this issue at the Listening Perspectives Study Center in Orange, California. As we discussed these issues and our fears with Caudill, he added to our growing alarm about therapist vulnerability by pointing out legal and ethical exposures that we as therapists had never even imagined! The range of concerns was expanding well beyond what we could hope to accomplish at a symposium. Ray Calabrese, a Certified Financial Planner, who has worked in cooperation with therapists in their practices for many years and who has watched a series of similar tragedies unfold, then agreed to join us as coordinator of a day-long conference on therapists at risk that was held on April 25, 1994. This book examines the many ideas and issues that emerged at that conference and that have continued to develop in our deliberations since. Jason Keyes managed the actual conference days and compiled the manuscripts for publication.

The conference was as exhilarating as it was packed with concerns. Audience response was overwhelmingly enthusiastic. Therapists expressed thanks for at last being pushed into considering a host of difficult and unpleasant topics that could affect their quality of life for the rest of their lives, so dangerous are the many implications. The therapists shared our shock and dismay at the issues that have been submerged in the secrecy of the accusatory process and expressed gratitude for our having finally exposed them. Audio and video tapes of the conference are available.[1]

The conference also served as the genesis of this book. Part I contains the proceedings of the conference. In Part II we expand on related areas of special interest to each of us—touching, sexuality, dual relationships, and countertransference. Part III contains a series of timely considerations on the legal and ethical front contributed by Brandt Caudill. Part IV is a reprise of many of the dynamic concerns throughout the book, specifically focused on false accusations against therapists.

---

1. *Therapists at Risk*. Conference held at the Anaheim Sheraton Hotel, Anaheim, CA. Contact the Listening Perspectives Study Center, 1439 East Chapman Avenue, Orange, CA 92666.

We hope you find this book to be strong, clear, compelling, and timely. The perils that we face due to the deeply personal and intimate nature of the psychotherapeutic relationship are clearly spelled out, along with some of the ways in which we, as therapists, can limit our personal and professional liability while remaining true to the task of helping people discover their innermost selves.

The dialogue that we hope to stimulate in the community of practicing psychotherapists is long overdue. And it is much more difficult and encompassing than might be imagined. But the dialogue is a vital one, to be approached with care, thought, humility, and a certain trepidation. Over a century of experience, insight, and expertise has gone into developing psychotherapy as a discipline for personal growth and healing. Its contribution to the welfare of humans has been and will continue to be formidable. It is important that we not allow those who nip at our heels to destroy any of the valuable gains in human understanding that have been so painstakingly accomplished. It is important that we not allow our creativity and spontaneity as human beings to be diminished as we pursue this most personal and intimate form of professional life.

Credits

PART I

RISKS AND THE CHANGING FACE OF PSYCHOTHERAPY

The Devil, the Shadow, and the Therapist's Dilemma[1]

Virginia Wink Hilton

Not long ago, a student at the University of California at Irvine sought treatment for an eating disorder. While in therapy with—as the *Los Angeles Times* later put it a "caring Orange County therapist," the young woman recovered memories of having been sexually molested by her father when she was a child. As a result of her confrontation with her father, Gary Ramona, he was divorced by his wife, alienated from his children, and lost his job as an executive in a winery. He sued the therapist, the consulting psychiatrist, and Western Medical Center for more than $8 million (Warren, 1994). According to the *New York Times* version of this story, the therapist now practices in Virginia, and the psychiatrist has given up psychiatry and moved to Hawaii (Gross, 1994). The same article cited a case pending in the state of Minnesota

---

1. This chapter was adapted from a presentation given at the Pacific Northwest Bioenergetic Conference, Whistler, British Columbia, August, 1993, and was previously published, in slightly different form, in the *California Therapist*, Volume 6 Issue 1, Jan/Feb 1994.

where five women were suing a psychiatrist for implanting memories of satanic ritual abuse, and a case in Texas where a woman treated for bulimia successfully sued two former therapists for allegedly persuading her that she had been sexually abused by her mother, brother, grandfather, and a neighbor.

As therapists, we used to believe that if we were adhering to our ethical code, and were doing the best job we knew how, we didn't have to worry about having a suit filed against us, or of being brought before a licensing board. But cases like the ones cited and dozens of other claims and suits that haven't been reported in the media leave us bewildered and terrified!

We know that in the past in our profession there have been instances of serious malpractice that have gone unreported; we know that sexual offenses by therapists have been too long swept under the rug. That many such offenders have been prosecuted means that justice is finally being done. We know that serious dual-relationship issues, boundary crossing, and boundary blurring have been all too common and too often ignored. That such issues have been brought to light and clarified, and that a rigorous dialogue continues about ethics in general is of great benefit to the profession, and certainly to the client population as a whole.

But justifiable complaints and suits are not what worry us. What causes so much anxiety and even panic among psychotherapists are the accusations that are unfair and unfounded—accusations about therapists' behavior that have been taken out of context, exaggerated, skewed, or simply fabricated. In addition we are confronted with the danger of being sued by a family member of a client because we did our job.

Many practitioners know of at least one fellow therapist who is believed to have been the victim of a false accusation or an unfair process. We have listened to the horror stories of the stress of protracted legal processes, of giving depositions, of being cross-examined by a prosecuting attorney, of being investigated by a licensing board, or of losing malpractice insurance—all because of unfair or unfounded claims.

These stories and the fear they generate in us have, to use a biological metaphor, helped to bring about a *contraction* in the profession. When an organism is in danger, it minimizes its exposure to impingement by contracting, and thus constricting its behavior in response to fear. We therapists have become afraid to do many things that formerly would have been standard acceptable practice. For example, many whose practice methods include some form of touch now question whether or not to *ever* touch at *all*. Many others are afraid to deal with sexual issues and avoid them whenever possible. And now some therapists say they try to stay away from issues of childhood abuse and trauma. It's not uncommon for therapists to ask themselves when interviewing a prospective client, "Is this the kind of person who would one day take me to court?"

One unfortunate consequence of what I'm calling a professional contraction is that for many therapists it means a loss of spontaneity, of creativity, and a resulting loss of joy and satisfaction in their work. But the current situation within our profession is reflective of a much larger cultural reality.

During the last decade we have been involved in a deeply painful, long-overdue process of exposing to the light of day sexual abuse behavior that has infected every level of our society. During this period thousands of courageous women and men have come forward, in spite of the pain and humiliation involved, to tell their stories of abuse and violence on the part of parents, priests, teachers, therapists, and other trusted adults. These crimes have been far more prevalent than ever would have been imagined a generation ago.

In recent years charges of sexual abuse have become major media events: we have watched as celebrities told their personal stories of childhood molestation and incest, accused others, and were accused of sexual crimes. Meanwhile, across the country the numbers of victims and accusations have grown enormously. Many of these accusations have been based upon recovered memories.

Along with the accusations of victims there have been the increasingly vociferous responses of those, like Gary Ramona, who say, "I am being falsely accused."

In May of 1993 the *New Yorker* published a two-part article entitled "Remembering Satan," by Lawrence Wright, which was later published as a book (1994). The author tells the story of the Ingram family of East Olympia, Washington. In 1988, two daughters, aged 22 and 18, accused their father of sexual abuse. At first the father, Paul Ingram, denied the charges. But then, after many hours of interrogation and the urging of his pastor to confess, he began producing memories of abusing his daughters. As time went on, the daughters began remembering more and more horrors, including satanic ritual abuse. After being informed of the charges, Ingram would gradually confirm the stories with detailed accounts of the scenes. He implicated two other men who were his friends and colleagues in the sheriff's department. Eventually the mother was accused of being a part of the cult as well. The problem was, the stories didn't always match, no evidence was ever produced of dismembered infants or dead bodies, and there were no scars on the daughters where burns or cuts were said to have been inflicted.

Before the trial, the prosecution brought in a social psychologist, Richard Ofshe, to interview the Ingram family. Ofshe decided to test Paul Ingram's credibility by fabricating a scenario. He told Ingram that two of his children had sworn that their father had forced them to have sex while he watched. Ofshe deliberately encouraged him and prodded him in much the same manner as had the investigators on the case. At first Ingram said he did not remember, as he had done initially with the other charges made. But then, after a time, he produced a signed confession with graphic details of a scene that never happened (Ofshe 1992).

Paul Ingram was convicted, even though, as the Lawrence Wright article made clear, there was no evidence of satanic ritual abuse and no certain evidence of sexual abuse. But this case set off what the author described as a "raging debate over satanic ritual abuse, sex-crimes investigation, and criminal accusations made on the basis of 'recovered' memory" (Wright 1993, part II, p. 54).

Stories like this led many of us to ask: What is going on in our culture? Do devil-worshiping cults exist on a very broad scale and across generations as many claim they do, or are seemingly sane people producing horrifying fantasies that they experience as fact? Which option is more frightening?

Do numerous fathers and mothers not only sexually molest their children and adolescents, but commit lewd acts upon babies in diapers? Or are such "memories" produced by a person struggling to find a reason for dysfunction or a focus for anxiety? Are parents who claim they are falsely accused the innocent victims, or are they denying, misremembering, or lying? Do nursery school teachers commit multiple sexual atrocities upon the children who are their charges, or do children make up stories under the repeated suggestion of their investigators and the pressure of hysterical parents? Are there people who are periodically abducted by aliens, as nearly three million Americans claim, or is this a metaphor for an inner experience of suffering? These are the kinds of perplexing questions that are being raised in the literature these days, and the kinds of questions that face us as clinicians in our work with clients. These questions become crucial to us who are potential witnesses and defendants in suits and countersuits.

The attempt to deal with these disturbing matters has resulted in numerous articles and highly charged discussions on the issues of recovered memory, the concept of repression, how memory works, and the use and misuse of hypnosis and chemically induced interviews. The result has been a polarizing of our profession. The Ramona case was a clear example.

Gary Ramona accused the therapist and the consulting psychiatrist of prompting his daughter to produce memories of events that never took place. The defendants saw Ramona as a manipulative man who molested his daughter over many years, and who then spent over a million dollars to discredit the therapists who rescued her. According to the *New York Times*, a prominent forensic psychiatrist who Ramona hired testified that the conclusions of rape reached by the therapist was "an outrageous misrepresentation," and he said that both therapist and psychiatrist had failed to follow standards for acceptable therapeutic practice (Warren 1994).

That dubious and irresponsible practice methods have led to the inducement of false memories is the charge levied by the critics of the so-called recovered memory movement. Chief among them is the False Memory Syndrome Foundation. This is an organization formed several years ago that includes educators, mental health professionals, and accused parents. Many members are currently in litigation, and there are many more lawsuits to come.

Among those on the opposite side of the fence are sexual abuse and trauma experts and writers (some of whom have themselves been victims), multiple-personality disorder specialists, and some memory researchers. Concerns expressed by these people include that the false memory issue is an indication of the widespread resistance to the recognition of sexual abuse, and that it is another example of the blaming and discrediting of victims (Masters and Johnson Report 1993). Some practitioners express deep concern that the highly publicized activities of the False Memory Syndrome Foundation will intimidate the profession into abandoning its work with victims (Kluft 1992). Some fear that the False Memory Syndrome Foundation is becoming a haven for perpetrators.

So the debate over recovered memories rages on. Meanwhile, clients are suing their parents, and parents are suing their children's therapists. Brandt Caudill has commented that this deeply painful and divisive situation is becoming another kind of Civil War (personal communication).

Once again to the question: What *is* going on in the culture—and how did we get here? As I ponder that question and try to gain some kind of understanding, it seems useful to review our recent history.

The 1960s and 1970s were a time of cultural expansion—of exploration and movement. There were the civil rights movement, the women's movement, and the sexual revolution. In our field there was the flourishing of humanistic psychology and the human potential movement. It was a time of growth and exploration and expansion. By the time the 1980s rolled around we were dealing with sexually transmitted diseases and an AIDS epidemic. The 1980s and 1990s have been a period of cultural contraction, a time of reaction against the excesses of the 1960s and 1970s, in part, but also a reaction against what is *unknown, uncertain, or not understood.* Human beings seem to have little tolerance for the unknown, and even less tolerance for the anxiety created by freedom and the absence of absolutes and answers.

We live in a time when within a few short years the world map has drastically changed: walls have come down, governments and ideologies have collapsed overnight, and within months unimaginable numbers of people have died from starvation and ethnic cleansing. It's too much. Too fast. Too terrifying. We can also add to this list the natural disasters that have taken place. In California we can't even count on the ground beneath our feet! In a time of too-rapid change, of instability, of disintegration, of uncertainty, there is an urgency for black and white, for good and bad, for clear-cut answers.

After reading Wright's (1993) article, I began thinking about the Devil, and I did a little research. I found that he—or sometimes she—has taken many shapes throughout the millennia. (It has only been during the last couple of hundred years that we have had the image of the little red guy with the forked tail and the pitchfork.) When the rational mind concluded that there was no such actual creature, we created devilishness in other forms. It seems we human beings have always required a representation, a personification of the evil and destructiveness we experience in ourselves and in our world.[2]

After the decline of the Middle Ages there were four or five hundred years when witches were considered the representatives of the Devil. It may surprise the reader to know that well in excess of 3 million— some historians say as many as 9 million—females down to the ages of 4 and 5 were burned at the stake or incarcerated and tortured for consorting with Satan (Greene 1992). In certain historical periods the Jews were accused of having the same attributes and activities that are these days ascribed to satanic cults.

In wartime, the enemy easily becomes the devil. In World War II Japanese and German soldiers as depicted in American cartoons and movies were the devils. Hitler came about as close as possible to actually personifying the Satanic archetype. During the Gulf War, the Iraqis called the United States "the Great Satan." During the Cold War communism became our devil. What was wrong with our social order was blamed on the Reds. Even in the early 1980s, Reagan called Russia the "Evil Empire." But then before the decade was over, communism fell apart. There was suddenly no Evil Empire out there. Now what?

I have wondered about the escalation at this juncture of history of reports of satanic ritual abuse on the one hand, and the epidemic of sexual abuse accusations on the other. Are we living in a time when demonic images are being elaborated in order to provide a desperately needed explanation for the brutality of existence? Is there any validity to the assertion that parents have replaced witches as the projection of evil? Perhaps so. And it may be that therapists are becoming the next group.

The problem is, I don't know if there were any real witches among the millions of women who were falsely accused. I do know there are real perpetrators: real parents who have really molested their children, real therapists who have really violated their clients. I personally do not know any Satanists, but I know that history books and newspapers are full of accounts of unthinkable atrocities committed upon women

---

2. I am indebted to Thayer Green, Ph.D., whose unpublished work, *Satan and Psyche*, provided inspiration for much of this chapter.

and children and men, some of them in the name of God, Jesus, and Mohammed. So we are back to a central problem: in spite of a need to find them, there are no easy answers.

As therapists, this is our dilemma: in the face of all the unsettling issues, the conflicting data, and the contradictory expert opinions, some of our most basic assumptions are being challenged. Our credibility as a profession is being seriously questioned, and as individuals we are potentially in jeopardy. What are we to do? What are we to do both to maintain our integrity and to protect ourselves and the clients with whom we work? In response to these questions I have developed several guidelines.

First, I believe we would do well to come to terms with the fact that, according to all the data we have, there *are* no easy answers. I believe we need to resist our temptation to provide them. Easy answers may make us more comfortable with our task, make our job simpler, may give us a sense of power. But they do not help our clients deal with reality. Our critics say that therapists have too uncritically jumped on a bandwagon created by what is sometimes referred to as the sex-abuse industry. "You must have been molested" is too easy an answer to anxiety and dysfunction.

Second, no matter which side of the false memory controversy we are personally on, I believe it is our responsibility as clinicians to attempt to retain our objectivity and our neutrality in relation to what is true and what is untrue. When a person recovers a memory of molest, the data implies that it may or may not be verifiable historical fact. I personally believe that most unrepressed memories of sexual abuse are real, although they may not be remembered accurately. I also believe that some traumatic events may be forgotten and later recovered. But the data suggest that many recovered memories may very well be false.

Does this mean that people who have false memories are either liars or crazy? Far from it. There are many personal possibilities to account for the phenomenon of false memories (Hedges 1994b,d). Or the combined effect of all that is going on in the culture—in the collective psyche—may be acting upon the person to produce a false memory. As human beings we are susceptible to suggestion; our clients may be highly susceptible to *our* suggestions.

We therapists should remember just how much potential authority we carry. The transferential and culturally defined hierarchical nature of the relationship means that for the client there may be enormous power in what we say. I personally feel that we do need to be very careful—in all aspects of therapy, not just around issues of sexual abuse—about inadvertently suggesting or leading the client, about telling the client what to do, and about making pronouncements regarding the truth.

What is the responsible approach to take regarding, for instance, what seems like a dubious recovered memory that the client experiences as the absolute truth? It is my position that our job is not to believe or disbelieve, no matter how bizarre the tale. The person is telling us *something* about his or her experience, and we need to pay attention. Getting involved with the question "Is it true or isn't it true?" may be beside the point.

There are those who point to the client's overriding need to have the therapist validate his or her experience by believing in the truth and accuracy of the memory. When working with couples we often have two distinct sides of an argument, and sometimes two completely different stories about what happened. In such a situation we do not feel the need to validate one or the other as true. The task is to work with the issues, to acknowledge and to be empathically present to the *reality* of the hurt, the anguish, the sense of betrayal, or whatever feelings are evoked. So it is with recovered memories; even if a recalled event of abuse could be proven false as an objective fact, we can validate the emotional experience for which it is the representation. The *feelings* are real, regardless of whether the *event* occurred or not. Some real events in the past that the person experienced as traumatic are being represented in what the person claims to remember.

In the sexual abuse literature, some authors have urged victims to expose and confront the perpetrators, and to take part in civil and criminal suits in order to feel empowered. Such a process may indeed bring about a sense of empowerment. But it can also bring with it enormous pain of exposure and vulnerability. The legal system can be brutally abusive to the victim/plaintiff. Often, even simply confronting parents years after the fact does not produce the desired effects, but creates more pain and deeper alienation. And if the representations of the childhood trauma take the form of false, distorted, or displaced memories, it is unlikely that empowerment will be the effect of a confrontation with an alleged perpetrator who believes him- or herself innocent of the crime as remembered. But while empowerment can certainly be important at times, the paradox is that the ultimate healing of the injury comes when, in the safe and supportive environment of the therapy room, the person reexperiences and accepts the helplessness that was felt when he/she was victimized.

Hedges (1994b,d) suggests that therapists may be inadvertently taking the easy way out when urging clients to file a suit. That is, they may be colluding with the resistance and avoiding the difficult work of dealing with the deep transferences that are emerging in the therapeutic process. The resistance is to having to reexperience in the here and now transference situation the full emotional impact of the original trauma, with the therapist being experienced transferentially as the perpetrator.

A third guideline I find important is that as therapists we have to be absolutely vigilant that we do not use our clients to live out our own unworked-through anger, resentment, rage, vengefulness, or lust toward a parent, a former therapist, spouse, or anyone else. Perhaps a good clue that some of our own stuff is getting into the process is when we find ourselves experiencing intense anger and righteous indignation at what the client has suffered, or when we feel an *urgency* for the victim to do something about it. Then we need to seek out a consultant or perhaps a therapist for ourselves to examine our intense reactions or our need to step out of our ordinary therapeutic stance by suggesting confrontation and/or retaliation.

Finally, we as therapists must be cognizant at all times of a set of inner forces that Carl Jung first chose to call the "shadow." I find this a useful construct, and very important in regard to the issues I am considering. The shadow is defined as the aggregate of all unconscious, undesirable ideas and impulses—all that is incompatible with our conscious attitudes and self-concept. The shadow is that unacceptable part of us that is unclaimed, unintegrated, and gets expressed only in unconscious ways—through dreams, fantasies, or through the mechanisms of denial and projection. The Jungians speak of a personal shadow and a collective shadow. Society, too, has its unconscious, unacceptable side that gets projected onto minorities, ethnic or other definable groups, and other nations.

The projection of the shadow side of individuals and of the collective may explain something about what is going on in our culture on many levels. What we cannot accept in ourselves or in our society becomes the *devil*.

Why does this continue to happen, even after so much enlightenment, so much sophistication, so much personal therapy? It has been suggested that part of what keeps the shadow unintegrated, and projection a powerfully functioning mechanism in our selves and in our society, is the *ethic of perfection* that so permeates the Western psyche (Greene 1992). Our conscious or unconscious desire for perfection finds precedence in the Biblical admonition, "Be ye therefore perfect" (Matt. 5:48). If this is somehow the unconscious goal of therapy, or the unconscious goal of our lives, then repression and projection are the only ways we can get there. John Sanford (1981), a Jungian analyst, says that in the Scripture the word *perfect* was a translation of the Greek word *teleios*, which means "brought to completion." If our goal is not perfection but completion, or wholeness, then the task becomes one of claiming and integrating the shadow—accepting the dark side with the light, the bad with the good. If attaining wholeness is our therapeutic goal and that of our clients, then we can understand the urgency for validation of objective truth by both clients and therapists as a defense against embracing our shadow.

In *Satan and Psyche* Greene (1992) writes:

> There is an Indian tribe in the Southwest who make it a practice to invite Coyote, their equivalent of Satan, to their powwow of the tribal council and provide a place for him. The idea behind this, of course, is that if he is present they can keep an eye on him. If he were ignored, excluded, kept out of sight there is no telling what he might do (W. A. Miller 1981, footnote 34, p. 136). In so many ways the lesson is brought home to us that the denial of the shadow, especially the group shadow, leads to an intensification of the destructive power of evil. . . . It is . . . that alienation and unrelatedness to our own darkness which will inflict unconscious evil upon others and upon ourselves. [p. 125]

Nowhere is this principle more aptly illustrated than in the story of the Ingram family in the Wright (1993) article.

I do not want to be misunderstood to be saying that the bad things that happen are merely the result of projection. Evil is *out there*—and always will be. I want simply to say that these are difficult and dangerous times we live in, and they place a heavy responsibility upon us as therapists and as human beings. What we can do to help heal the real abuse, to calm the imagined hysteria, and to protect ourselves is to attend to the personal and the collective shadow. We would do well to rigorously examine emotionally charged reactions to persons and groups and ideas, to uncover and take responsibility for our projections, and with loving acceptance, to invite into consciousness those unacceptable parts of *ourselves*: the pervert, the perpetrator, the addict, the victim. Walter Wink in *Unmasking the Powers* (1986) sums up the task: "The goal of our striving [is]: To face our own evil as courageously as we can; to love it into the light; to release the energy formerly devoted to restraining it; and to use that energy for the service of life" (p. 40).

The Challenge of Memories Recovered in Psychotherapy[1]

Lawrence E. Hedges

SOME PSYCHODYNAMIC ISSUES INVOLVED IN THE RECOVERED MEMORY CRISIS

Recent shifts in public opinion have led to changes in our society aimed at correcting age-old patterns of abuse. People who have been subjected to damaging treatment have felt encouraged to speak up and seek redress for the wrongs done to them in the past. Memories of painful experiences that individuals have tried not to think about for many years are being revived and abusers are being confronted with the effects of their deeds. This vanguard of the civil rights movement has generated public indignation and a call for more effective laws and judicial procedures to limit widespread abuses of all types.

---

1. Many portions of this chapter were previously published in *Remembering, Repeating, and Working Through Childhood Trauma* (Hedges 1994b). They were first published under the title "Taking Recovered Memories Seriously" in *Issues in Child Abuse Accusations* 6(1):1–30, copyright 1994 and reprinted by permission of the Institute for Psychological Therapies.

But along with the revival of painful memories of abuse that people have done their best to forget, another phenomenon has moved into the public arena—"recovered memories," which emerge with compelling emotional power but exist to tell a story that could not have or did not occur in the exact or literal manner in which the abuse is so vividly remembered. On the basis of such memories, usually recovered in some psychotherapy or recovery group setting, accusations on a large scale are aimed at people who claim not to be perpetrators of abuse. As of August 1994 the False Memory Syndrome Foundation in Philadelphia boasted more than 15,000 member families claiming innocence for the crimes of which they are accused. Highly respected public figures as well as ordinary, credible private citizens known in their communities to lead basically decent lives are having the finger of accusation pointed at them. The controversy is heated and, unfortunately, has become drawn along lines of whether the memories of abuse are "true" or "false."

I believe that childhood memories recovered in this manner are indeed records of actual trauma, but that the representations of early trauma are subject to a variety of confounding sources of variance. To take seriously the people reporting these compelling memories, the images and stories involved cannot be taken literally, but must be considered in the overall context in which they appear and understood to be the product of various kinds of dream-like condensation and displacement, as well as formed on the basis of various unconscious considerations of visual and narrational representation.

Among this group of otherwise credible people who are being accused are numerous well-established individuals in the mental health field and in other helping professions, such as nurses, doctors, lawyers, the clergy, teachers, scout leaders, child care workers, and choir leaders—in short, people vested with caring for others. New laws in more than half the states have changed the statute of limitations to read, "three years from when the abuse is remembered," although it is not yet clear whether such laws will stand up in court. By now accusations based on memories recovered in hypnosis, "truth serum" interviews, recovery groups, and psychotherapy are coming under sharp criticism— partly because so many of the accusations are so outlandish, partly because a sizable number of memories have proved faulty, and partly because of the witch-hunt atmosphere surrounding the recovered memory controversy that threatens widespread injustice if responsible social controls are not forthcoming.

In the midst of all the accusatory clamor psychotherapists today face two major challenges that we must find ways of addressing and controlling. First, there is the plea, if not the demand, from clients that memories recovered in psychotherapy be believed. And faced with a sobbing, shaky, convulsing person relating with horror vivid scenes of childhood abuse demanding to be "validated" by being believed, therapists are in a tough spot. This challenge can be met by the therapist's learning not to collude in the resistance to establish the full emotional impact of the trauma in the deep transference of therapy. Second, the psychodynamics of early childhood trauma mean that it will only be a matter of time before the deep emotional constellation present in the abuse accusations will be transferred onto the person of the therapist in the psychotherapy setting so that the therapist will be experienced as the perpetrator. If the trauma occurred very early, and in most of these cases it did, when the transference comes into place it will take the form of a transference psychosis, and the therapist will be the target of revenge impulses reaching psychotic proportions and in danger of becoming acted out in the public arena. This challenge can be met by the therapist's learning how to meet, manage, and work through the transference psychosis.

The dramatic and at times almost desperate insistence to be believed often *demands* full and literal belief—with this additional claim or veiled threat: "If you don't believe me I won't feel validated in my experience, and I will never be able to feel that I am a real and worthwhile person. These things really happened to me, they must be believed, and if you won't believe me this ends our relationship and I will find someone who will." But this (blackmail quality) demand being issued as a desperate plea or a relationship ultimatum doesn't stop here. "These atrocities happened. You believe me. Now you must support me in my redress of my grievances, my efforts to gain restitution for those crimes committed against me. My 'recovery' of my sanity depends upon my being believed, validated, and aided in my attempts to gain redress. 'They' must be made to confess and to pay for the wrongs they have done to me." In the case of alien abduction memories the final part of the plea is not so clear-cut, but it goes something like this: "People must be made to believe that these things are happening, that lives are being ruined, that my life is ruined by the fears I live with. Until the truth is known and believed we will have no collective way of banding together to protect ourselves from these invading aliens and stopping this use of us like common animals in a zoo or research laboratory."

There is a certain impelling logic in these various claims and demands. And it would seem that this logic, taken along with the passionate persuasion of its absolute truth value, has led therapists to lose their ordinary therapeutic stance.

Therapists are taught in training never to "believe" anything told us in psychotherapy, but to take everything told to us seriously. *To "believe" is to step out of the professional therapist role and get into a dual relationship with the patient that destroys the therapeutic stance, and with it the possibility of ever being able to interpret the illusory and delusional aspects of transference and resistance.* Ever entering the patient's life in a realistic way colludes with unconscious resistance. So we are taught to remain neutral, "equidistant" between the personality agencies of id, ego, and superego and the patient's external reality.

Someone arrives in our consulting room and tells us he has a headache because of too much "stress." The internist says, "It's nerves." We would be out of business quickly if we believed either conclusion. Instead, we learn to receive the complaint along with the proffered interpretations. Then we ask the patient to continue telling us about himself. A woman comes to tell us that she feels pain during intercourse and it is because her husband is so insistent on having sex with her all the time. We hear that the child who is brought for therapy is lying and stealing despite all of the parent's best efforts to raise him correctly. In couple or family work we always hear conflicting "realities." We take each reality seriously as we work, but we refrain from losing our neutrality, our therapeutic stance, and therefore our ability to be of value, by not becoming swept away with the question of whose version of reality is correct or true. We never take at face value what we are told, but we always receive it seriously and ask for more.

In considering the dilemma that arises in regard to believing recovered memories, I began to realize that some of my colleagues are not plagued by this demand to believe the memories told them. I realized that they are the most seasoned therapists, those with the greatest experience and competence in analyzing transference and resistance, regardless of what school of therapy they have been trained in. They take what is told to them seriously and ask for more. Now the trail to the puzzle of recovered memories is getting hotter! Seasoned therapists who understand transference and resistance work, no matter how they label it, feel no need to "believe" the childhood abuse or abduction memories, but take these concerns and beliefs very seriously and work with them. If pressed, these therapists might be inclined to believe that a given person's experience did or did not happen, but that is not their concern. They are aware of the existence of massive abuse and denial in our society (V. Hilton 1993). And without overwhelming objective evidence of specific facts, they have no need to believe or doubt—they know that "believing" simply isn't their job as psychotherapists. One colleague asked, "Whoever gave it to us to be the arbitrators of objective truth? Where but the psychotherapy consulting room are we less likely to be indulged with objective fact?"

FOUR MEMORY MECHANISMS MANIFEST IN TRANSFERENCE AND RESISTANCE

A century of psychoanalytic research has produced an understanding of four basic mechanisms of memory. What has emerged is essentially a psychoanalytic theory that inextricably links memory to significant relationships. In *secondary repression*, the 5-year-old volitionally decides not to experience or spell out in consciousness his or her incestual and parricidal urges, which have proven undesirable within the family structure. In *dissociation*, a whole line of personality development, or a whole sector of the personality such as narcissism, is disavowed or dissociated—walled off from being realized as an active part of the central personality of a 3-year-old as he or she relates to others. In *splitting*, various sequences of emotional interaction, 4- to 24-month symbiotic character scenarios, are valued as good and sought out, or devalued as bad and shunned, based upon the person's original experience with the mothering partner. In expressions of searching for and breaking off through *primary repression* of anticipated pain the possibility of contact with others, the early (pre- and postnatal) trauma of the ways the nurturing other ruptured contact are remembered in the various ways the person breaks contact in subsequent attempts to make connections that might lead to bonding.

These four mechanisms of memory account, respectively, for four major categories of transference and resistance memories that are thought to characterize the four varieties of personality organization that have emerged from a century of study of the kinds of memories that regularly appear in the psychoanalytic and psychotherapeutic situation. In *neurotic personality organization*, the subjective sense of a 5-year-old child's instinctual driveness is remembered in transference along with intense fears (resistance) of experiencing sexual and aggressive impulses toward anyone so intimate as the analyst, because such intensity was forbidden in the family triangular structure. In *narcissistic personality organization* a 3-year-old's intense needs for admiration, confirmation, and inspiration in relation to his or her selfothers is central to transference memories. Natural narcissistic needs are enshrouded in shame (resistance) regarding one's desire to be at the center of the universe. In *borderline personality organization* transference remembering (of the 1- to 2-year-old toddler) is rooted in the replication of a set of interpersonal emotional scenarios. Resistance memories militate against living out the positively and negatively charged (split) emotional interactions (scenarios) in the analytic relationship so that they cannot achieve representation and therefore cannot be relinquished. In *personalities living out the earliest organizing processes*, what is structured in transference memory is the continuous rupturing or breaking of each and every attempt to form organizing channels to the other. Resistance takes the form of terror and physical pain whenever sustained contact with a significant other threatens.

What emerges from a century of psychoanalytic exploration of early childhood memory is that no known memory mechanisms and no known forms of relatedness memory can conceivably support the widespread popular belief that traumatic experiences occurring before the age of 4 or 5 can be subject to massive repression, which can later be lifted in such a way as to allow perfect and accurate video camera recall of facts and events. The view that has captured the popular imagination may be a compelling dramatic device but is contrary to all available knowledge. Memories that do occur as a part of a therapeutic process and that have been widely studied are memories that link past emotional experience to the present relationship realities of the psychoanalytic setting. According to the ways in which personalities may be said to organize themselves, there is simply no place in which massive interpersonal trauma resulting in total amnesia that can later be lifted can possibly occur.

The only possible explanations for the existing reports of recovered memories in all of the considerations thus far made are the following:

1. Memories are based upon later hearsay, which has produced pictures believed to be "memories" but are not.
2. Memories of traumatically intense events endure by sheer force of their emotional impact. But such memories, like of the death of a parent or physical or sexual abuse that is known and confirmed at the time, are not "forgotten" but are always accessible to memory—although perhaps not thought about for long periods of time. That is, memories of known and real trauma may be set aside and not thought about for long periods of time, but are not totally lost and are later accurately recovered through hypnosis, "truth serum," or the free association of psychotherapy.
3. Screen or telescoped memories are, like dreams, the products of primary process condensation, symbolization, displacement, and visual representability. As such, these memories can never be considered "fully and objectively real," no matter how vivid or how corroborated by external evidence they may be.
4. Memories of environmental failure have been "frozen" (Winnicott 1954) until a relationship situation presents itself in which the failure can be emotionally relived in a present regressed relational state, so that the empathic failures can be made good. This last prospect might be the most promising for the video camera theory of memory. But the emergence of this type of memory is situation-dependent and relationship-dependent, and therefore a creative amalgamation of certain elements of the past failure with whatever prospects may exist in the present for a more satisfying outcome, so such memories cannot be considered objectively accurate.

The phenomenon of amnesia for events before the age of 3 is attributable to the observation that during that developmental period there is no capacity for verbal, symbolic, or pictorial recall per se that can possibly be operating independently of somatic, affective, interactive relatedness. Therefore, recovered memories from the earliest months and years of life must be constructions, narrations, or "flashback" dream pictures artfully created to fit the current relationship situation, so that the emotional sense of the environmental failure from the past can be relived.

In conclusion, there is no conceivable way that recovered memories as they are being currently touted in the media and in the courtroom could possibly be remembering anything that is objectively real and totally true in the way they are claimed to be.

THE PROBLEM OF "RECOVERY"
THROUGH BEING BELIEVED

In the effort to understand the central puzzle of recovered memories, the insistence (1) on being believed, (2) on having to have one's experiences validated, and (3) on only being able to achieve "recovery" by being supported in seeking realistic redress begins to look more like a symptom of something else. But if so, I wondered, what is the common root to this symptomatic demand?

Almost as if by divine intervention, a deeply distressed and horrified therapist appeared in my next consultation group. Her horror? "Tomorrow a client I have worked with for two-and-a-half years has arranged, with the aid of members of her 'survivor's' support group, a full family confrontation of her childhood molests."

I replied, "Survivors' groups encourage this kind of thing all the time. What's the problem—surely you're not involved in all that?" "No, of course not. But after six months of therapy when all of these abusive memories began coming out during sessions she became quite fragmented and was having a hard time functioning. I sent her to a psychiatrist who put her on Prozac, which helped. She is on a managed health care plan so her psychotherapy benefits ran out rapidly. I continued to see her once a week for a low fee but she clearly needed more. I suggested she check out the Community Women's Center for a support group. At the center she was referred to an incest survivors' group. I thought, 'Oh, well, she is working on those issues so maybe they can help her.' Over the last two years numerous memories have emerged of absolutely terrible things that happened with her father and brothers. She insisted on my believing all of the memories that came up in group and in session."

"And were the things believable?"

"Well, that's hard to say. She is clearly very damaged, borderline at best with organizing pockets around all of this abuse. I don't question whether she has been somehow badly abused. But I have no idea about the actual memories—there are so many of them and they are so grotesque."

"But she insisted on your believing all of them?"

"Yes, she did."

"And how did you handle that?"

"Well, I did my best to get out of it. You know, to tell her that I know some horrible things must have happened to her, that we would do our best to figure things out and find ways for her to face whatever happened and to find new ways to live—I said it all. But she had to *know* that I believed her. Then the memories began to be more explicit, things an infant can't possibly imagine unless they had actually happened to her."

"And so you believed her?" "Well, in a way, yes. I mean, I don't know about all of the memories, but something awful clearly happened to her. I let her know I believed that. But I'm sure she thinks I believe it all, just like her survivors' group does. But what I'm worried about now is she has all of this energy and support gathered for the grand confrontation tomorrow. She wants them all to confess, to say that they did all of these horrible things to her, to say they are sorry, that they are horrible people to have ever done such things, that they can never forgive themselves, and that there is no way they can ever make it up to her."

"Is that what she wants, some form of recompense?"

"I don't really know what she wants. Her dad and her brothers do have money, maybe she wants some kind of payment. And there is a lot of insurance money. Her survivors' group has educated her on that. But that's not the main thing. Or at least I don't think so. It's like her sanity is somehow at stake. She now has amassed all of the believers she needs to validate her experiences and her memories. She now feels absolutely certain that these many things happened. If they don't confess, if they don't grovel, *if they don't agree that she is right and they are wrong, I'm afraid she'll have a psychotic break!* But what's got me scared is that I have somehow colluded in all of this without really meaning to. She is going to confront the family about all of these things, things that I have no way of knowing ever happened. And she's going to say that she remembered all of this in therapy and that her group helped her get the courage to finally speak the truth. You see, it's awful. I don't know how I got into this jam. And just yesterday I read about a group that's helping families fight back. They are encouraging families to sue the therapist for encouraging people to believe false memories. And, of course, therapists have lots of money to sue for. I have three million dollars in insurance this family could come after. And do you know what's scariest? I have all of those memories written down in my notes. Sure enough, with her shaking, sobbing, writhing as she remembered it all—event by event. Her family, at least on the surface, appears ordinary and normal. I don't think they are going to take well to being told they are criminals, and to being threatened with lawsuits for crimes they supposedly committed twenty-five years ago. It's all one horrible mess and I have no protection in all of this. If the family contacts me for information, I am bound by confidentiality. I can't tell them anything or help mediate in any way. The bottom line is, I'm fucked!"

I replied, "Follow me for a minute as I throw out some possibilities. When I hear your dilemma from the perspective of borderline or symbiotic personality organization, I hear the bottom line is that your client has succeeded in molesting you, violating your personal and professional boundaries in much the same intrusive or forceful way she may once have experienced herself as a very young child. According to this way of considering your dilemma, you are telling me that your life is now in as much danger as she may have felt in as an infant or toddler when all of whatever happened took place. The flashback dream memories are vivid and intensely sexual. What she experienced may have objectively looked very different. But the grotesque sexualized memories metaphorically express a certain true sense of how she felt then, or at least how she feels now when attempting to express intense body sensations that do contain a memory. By this view, you are saying that all this time you have been held emotional hostage in a similar helpless and vulnerable position to the one she felt in as a child—without having the slightest idea of how to protect yourself from this violence."

The therapist said, "Oh, God, I'm sick in the pit of my stomach just realizing how true what you are saying is. I'm feeling all of the abuse in the symbiotic role reversal of the countertransference."

Similar versions of this conversation are being lived in therapists' offices wherever psychotherapy is practiced. Talk shows are filled with the same human tragedy. Television audiences are being forced into the same position as this therapist of somehow judging the fate of those who are producing recovered memories. Judges and juries are being asked to decide the fate of family members who stand accused by the emergence of decades-old recovered memories. The therapist I spoke with is bright, well trained, sincere, and well intentioned. Her course was carefully thought out and managed but nevertheless has proven dangerous. Her training, like that of the vast majority of therapists practicing today, did not include how to work with primitive transference and resistance states so as to forestall massive acting out. By the therapist's own report her client was in danger of a mental breakdown.

The source of the powerful energy that fuels the recovery movement is primordial fear, which leads therapists to search for memories that aim the helplessness and rage toward an external source in the past and thereby shift the focus of this terrifying energy out of the present transference situation. If the client were allowed her breakdown, terrifying and primitive body states would emerge in the consulting room and involve her therapist. She would, for that time period, lose completely her ability to observe her own experience, to test reality, and she would experience the therapist as the abuser, the molester. The accusation and demand for confession and empathic understanding would be ideally aimed at the therapist in such a way that the primitive transference and resistance memories could at last be worked through rather than externalized and acted out. Freud (1895b) discovered that hypnotic "remembering" and cathartic abreacting may indeed be intense emotional experiences that are momentarily compelling and tension relieving, but that without the activation of ego and body-ego memories in transference and resistance and without an intense and extensive working through process there is no transformative cure.

When we believe people are we perpetuating a fraud? When we fail to believe people are we refusing to help them with their recovery? What will ethics committees, licensing boards, and malpractice judges and juries be saying about how we conducted ourselves a decade from now when the psychotic transference finally slips into place and it is we who finally, and now publicly, stand helplessly accused of abusing someone in any of a variety of ways—by believing, by not believing, by molesting, by seducing? "It looks like we're all fucked!," was the response of the consultation group who had heard this therapist's story.

THE FEAR OF BREAKDOWN

This therapist's horrifying vignette brought to my attention a second feature (in addition to the demand to be believed) of the recovered memory controversy. She feared that if her client did not get her way in the family confrontation she would have a psychotic breakdown. The therapist herself was afraid of a malpractice suit or disabling ethical complaint. I realized then that people touched in any way by the phenomenon of recovered memories are afraid that something uncertain but catastrophic is going to happen to them in the vague future that is somehow related to the distant, unknown, and unrememberable past.

The key to taking recovered memories seriously came up in a conversation I had with Bob and Virginia Hilton.[2] Virginia was preparing a paper on the topic for delivery to a bioenergetic conference the following week and we were brainstorming, trying to get to the bottom of the recovered memory mystery (V. Hilton 1993). Bob had just written a paper to be delivered at the same conference on a related topic (R. Hilton 1993), and Winnicott's last paper, which was published posthumously, "Fear of Breakdown" (1974), was fresh on his mind.

Winnicott was the first pediatrician to become a psychoanalyst. His understandings of the early mother–child interaction have made a significant contribution to British psychoanalysis and his powerful influence is now rapidly spreading worldwide. As a result of Dr. Margaret Little's (1990) publication of her own analysis with Winnicott, *Psychotic Anxieties and Containment*, we now realize that Winnicott was the first psychoanalyst to learn how to fully and systematically foster a "regression to dependence" in which the most primitive of human psychotic anxieties could be subjected to analysis—even in people who are otherwise well developed.[3]

In "Fear of Breakdown" Winnicott shows that when people in analysis speak of a fear of a psychotic break, a fear of dying, or a fear of emptiness, they are projecting into future time what has already happened in the infantile past. One can only fear what one has experienced.

---

2. Dr. Robert Hilton is Senior Trainer in the Southern California Institute for Bioenergetic Analysis, where Dr. Virginia Wink Hilton is Director of Training.

3. A full review of the psychoanalytic dialogue over the last century on the nature of therapeutic "regressions to dependence" has recently been undertaken by Robert Van Sweden (1993).

Terrifying and often disabling fears of breakdown, death, and emptiness are distinct ways of remembering terrifying processes that actually happened in a person's infancy. This nugget of an idea and all that has followed in its wake has changed the face of psychoanalytic thinking. What is dreaded and seen as a potentially calamitous future event is the necessity of experiencing in the memory of the psychoanalytic transference the horrible, regressive, once death-threatening dependent breakdown of functioning that one in fact experienced in some form in infancy.

The fear of breakdown manifests itself in many forms as resistance to reexperiencing in transference and resistance (memories) the terror, helplessness, rage, and loss of control once known in infancy. Therapists and clients alike dread disorganizing breakdowns and there are many ways in resistance and counterresistance that two can collude to forestall the curative experience of remembering by reliving the breakdown experience with the therapist. *One way of colluding with resistance to therapeutic progress is to focus on external perpetrators or long-ago traumas to prevent having to live through deeply distressing and frightening breakdown re-creations together.*

Bob found a passage in Winnicott's work that relates the original breakdown to precipitous loss of the infant's sense of omnipotence, however that may have occurred—before or after birth. When the environmental provision fails to support the infant's need to control life-giving necessities of his or her world, a massive breakdown of somatopsychic functioning occurs. The break constitutes a loss of whatever body-ego functions the infant may have attained at the time. Rudimentary or developing ego functions are not fully independent of the interpersonal situation in which they are being learned. So when the environment fails at critical moments, the infant experiences a loss of his or her own mind, a loss of any attained sense of control, and a loss of whatever rudimentary sense of self as agency may have been operating. From the point of view of the infant, the loss of psychic control over his or her environment is equivalent to the loss of the necessary life support systems, so that fear of death (as an instinctual given) is experienced as terrifyingly imminent, complete with the frantic flailings we see in any mammal whose contact with the warmth and nurturing maternal body is interrupted. The environment is empty, the environment that is not experienced as separate from the infant's rudimentary consciousness. When the necessary environmental support for ego skills and consciousness is lacking, the infant psyche collapses. In Green's (1986) terms, the mother of primary desire and pleasure dies.

At the level of the infant's primary organizing attempts there is a functional equivalence between disruption or failure of environmental provision and a sense of emptiness, loss of control, loss of omnipotence, total panic-stricken and painful psychic breakdown, and the terrifying prospect of death. Memories of primordial breakdowns are embedded in somatic symptoms and terror. Some such memories appear to be universal because, regardless of how good the parenting processes are, there are unavoidable moments of breakdown that occur in every person's infancy. However, the subjective experience of intensity, duration, and frequency of breakdowns is markedly traumatic in some people and not possible to be adequately soothed or recovered from. This level of memory is guarded with intense physical pain attributable to the process of (quasi-neurological) primary repression. No one wants to go through the excruciating gross bodily pain and terror necessarily entailed in physically remembering the process of early psychic breakdown. A simplified "recovery" approach may foster repeated intense abreactions that bring the body to the pain threshold in an acting out that is then endlessly repeated in the name of "recovery." But a century of psychoanalytic research has repeatedly and unequivocally demonstrated the futility of this abreaction approach, whether it be acted out in the form of screaming, kicking, accusing, confronting, switching personalities, generating yet more flashbacks, or whatever.

Acting outside or acting inside the therapeutic situation is *never* seen by psychoanalysts as therapeutic, although at times it may be unavoidable or uncontrollable. Analysts and all responsible therapists—whether they work with psychoanalytic transferential concepts or with transference concepts such as "parent–child tapes," "birth memories," or "wounded inner child"—*seek to frame within the therapeutic relationship the relatedness memories from the past that remain active in the personality.* Transference and resistance memories can be secured for analysis and found to be illusory and delusory in contrast to the realistic possibilities offered in the present by real relationships that the person has the capacity to enjoy.

Winnicott (1974) holds that in more normal development the environment is able to manage infantile frustration and disillusionment through small and tolerable doses, so that the terrifying fear of death and an empty world (and therefore an empty self) may be averted and the breakdown of omnipotence gently helped along rather than traumatically forced and abusively intruded into the child's body and mind. It is now possible to make sense of the strange and compelling nature of recovered memories. Environmental failure in infancy has led to a breakdown of early psychic processes with accompanying terror and the active threat of death (as the infant experiences it). The breakdown experience is blocked by primary repression that says "never go there again." The breakdown fear lives on as the somatic underpinning of all subsequent emotional relatedness but cannot be recalled because (1) no memory of the experience per se is recorded, only a nameless dread of dependence; (2) the memory of the breakdown experience itself is guarded with intense pain, somatic terror, and physical symptoms of all types; and (3) the trauma occurred before it was possible to record pictures, words, or stories, so it cannot be recalled in ordinary ways but only as bodily terrors of approaching death.

THE MYTHIC THEMES OF RECOVERED MEMORIES

The mythic themes of recovered memories (incest, violence, multiple selves, cult abuse, birth trauma, kidnapping, and alien abduction) have been present in all cultures since the beginning of recorded time and can be called upon by the creative human unconscious to allow for a creative narration to be built in psychotherapy that conveys the emotional essence of the infant's traumatic experience. The demand to be believed represents in some way the sense of urgency of the violation of infantile boundaries. The primordial boundary violation is registered and can be interpreted in the countertransference as the therapist feeling violated by the demand to "believe me." The working through of the repeated ruptures of interpersonal contact by flashbacks, sudden physical symptoms, bizarre thoughts, panic attacks, personality switches, and boundary violations can be accomplished through securing the organizing transference and resistance for analysis.[4]

---

4. Two books that detail the problems with these kinds of transference and resistance memories and how to treat organizing issues, whether they are pervasive in the whole personality or only form pockets in the personality (as with most people) are *Working the Organizing Experience* (Hedges 1994c) and *In Search of the Lost Mother of Infancy* (Hedges 1994a). A four-hour videocassette presentation by Hulgus and myself, also titled "Working the Organizing Experience," is available through my office.

THE CONCEPT OF "CUMULATIVE TRAUMA"

Another issue in the problem of recovered memories is the frequent claim by parents, family members, and accused therapists that the adult child now making accusations based on "false memories" has, until stressful problems in living were encountered, always been basically normal and well adjusted. And that family life has always been characterized by basically sound group life and parenting. Masud Khan's (1963) concept of "cumulative trauma" adds a new set of possibilities to those already discussed.

Beginning with Freud's early studies of childhood trauma (1895a,b), psychoanalysis has studied a series of possibilities regarding how the human organism handles overstimulation arising from the environment as well as from within the body. As early as 1920 Freud envisioned the organism turning its receptors toward the environment and gradually developing a "protective shield":

> *Protection against* stimuli is an almost more important function for the living organism than *reception* of stimuli. The protective shield is supplied with its own store of energy and must above all endeavor to preserve the special modes of transformation of energy operating in it against the effects threatened by the enormous energies at work in the external world. [p. 17]

This protective shield later develops into consciousness, but even so remains somewhat ineffective in protecting from stimuli arising from within the body. One way the organism may attempt to protect itself from overwhelming internal stimuli is to project them into the outer environment and treat them as "though they were acting, not from the inside, but from the outside, so that it may be possible to bring the shield against stimuli into operation as a means of defense against them" (p. 17). The false-memory syndrome appears to originate in earliest infancy (pre- or postnatal) when environmental stimuli cannot be effectively screened out, or when strong internal stimuli are projected to the exterior in an effort to screen them out. *In either case, due to the operation of primitive mental processes, the environment may be "blamed" by the infant for causing stimulation that cannot be comfortably processed— though blame may be objectively inappropriate to the circumstances. For* example, one accuser's early problems were traced back to placenta abruptio, a detachment of the placenta from the uterine wall giving rise to at least several prenatal days without nourishment. Often accusations are traceable to shortages of oxygen in utero, to early problems feeding, to infant allergies, to surgeries and medical procedures early in life, to incubators, to severely depressed mothers, to marital distress of the parents, or to an endless array of stressful and unusual early life events that were not deliberately cruel or abusive.

Anna Freud (1951, 1952, 1958) and Winnicott (1952) emphasize the role of maternal care in augmenting the protective shield during the period of early infantile dependency. Khan (1963) has introduced the concept of *cumulative trauma* to take into consideration early psychophysical events that happen between the infant and its mothering partners. Cumulative trauma correlates the effects of early infant caregiving with disturbing personality features that only appear much later in life. Cumulative trauma is the result of the effects of numerous kinds of small breaches in the early stimulus barrier or protective shield that are not experienced as traumatic at the time but create a certain strain that, over time, produces an effect on the personality that can only be appreciated retrospectively when it is experienced as traumatic.

Research on infantile trauma and memory (Greenacre 1958, 1960, Kris 1951, 1956a,b, Milner 1952) demonstrates the specific effects on somatic and psychic structure of cumulative strain trauma. Khan (1974) holds that "'the strain trauma' and the screen memories or precocious early memories that the patients recount are derivatives of the partial breakdown of the protective shield function of the mother and an attempt to symbolize its effects" (cf. Anna Freud 1958, p. 52). Khan further comments:

> Cumulative trauma has its beginnings in the period of development when the infant needs and uses the mother as his protective shield. The inevitable temporary failures of the mother as protective shield are corrected and recovered from the evolving complexity and rhythm of the maturational processes. Where these failures of the mother in her role as protective shield are significantly frequent and lead to impingement on the infant's psyche-soma, impingements which he has no means of eliminating, they set up a nucleus of pathogenic reaction. *These in turn start a process of interplay with the mother which is distinct from her adaptation to the infant's needs.* [p. 53, emphasis added]

According to Khan, the faulty interplay between infant and caregivers that arises as a consequence of strain reactions may lead to (1) premature and selective ego distortion and development, (2) special responsiveness to certain features of the mother's personality such as her moods, (3) dissociation of archaic dependency from precocious and fiercely acted out independency, (4) an attitude of excessive concern for the mother and excessive craving for concern from the mother (codependency), (5) a precocious adaptation to internal and external realities, and (6) specific body-ego organizations that heavily influence later personality organization.

Khan points out that the developing child can and does recover from breaches in the protective shield and can make creative use of them so as to arrive at a fairly healthy and effective normal functioning personality. But the person with vulnerabilities left over from infantile cumulative strain trauma "nevertheless can in later life break down as a result of acute stress and crisis" (p. 56). When there is a later breakdown and earlier cumulative strain trauma can be inferred, Khan is clear that the earlier disturbances of maternal care were neither gross nor acute at the time they occurred. He cites infant research in which careful and detailed notes, recorded by well-trained researchers, failed to observe traumas that only retrospectively could be seen as producing this type of cumulative strain trauma. Anna Freud (1958) has similarly described instances in which, "subtle harm is being inflicted on this child, and . . . the consequences of it will become manifest at some future date" (p. 57).

The implications of this research for the problem of recovered memory are several. There are many kinds of trauma that an infant can silently and invisibly be reacting to that are not the result of gross negligence or poor parenting. In such instances only *retrospectively*, in light of later disturbance or breakdown of personality functioning, can the effect of cumulative strain trauma be inferred. The origin of the difficulty can be traced to the environmental function of the protective shield, to the (m)other's role in providing an effective barrier that protects the child from intense, frequent, and/or prolonged stimuli that produce strain, although there may be no visible signs of trauma at the time.

Early or "recovered" childhood memories representing cumulative trauma are seen by psychoanalysts as screen memories that abstract, condense, displace, symbolize, and represent visually the strain effect. The unconscious of the client creates a compelling picture or narrative that describes in metaphor what the strain trauma looked like in the mind and body of the infant.

Many symptoms and/or breakdowns in later life, occasioned by conditions of acute living stress, have their origins in infancy. The adult experience of vague and undefinable earlier trauma is attributable to the cumulative effects of strain in infancy caused by environmental failure to provide an effective stimulus barrier during the period of infantile dependency. There may have been no way at the time of knowing what kinds of stimuli were causing undue strain on the infant because they were not gross and they were operating silently and invisibly. Or the circumstance may have been beyond the parent's capacity to shield, as in the case of medical problems, constitutional problems, or uncontrollable environmental problems, for example, war, food shortages, concentration camps, family discord, and so on. But the key consideration for our present topic is that when a person in later years, under conditions of living stress, produces memories of the effects of the cumulative strain trauma, what is remembered is abstracted, condensed, displaced, symbolized, and represented visually in screen memories that operate like dreams so that an accurate picture of objective facts is, in principle, forever impossible to obtain from recovered memories.

SOME CONCLUDING THOUGHTS ON RECOVERED MEMORIES

Memories recovered in the course of psychotherapy can be taken seriously if one knows what kinds of early life events are subject to later recall and how the recall can be accomplished through transference and resistance analysis. A review of a century of psychoanalytic observation has demonstrated that the kinds of recovered memories now coming to public attention cannot possibly be veridical memories in the ways and forms that they are being touted. We have long understood the constructed effect of screen and telescoped memories that operate like dreams, as abstracting processes that help to weave together in plausible images and sequences psychic events that might not otherwise belong together, in order to make them seem sane and sensible.

We have studied the way human truth gets projected into creative and expressive narrations and narrative interactions that capture the essence of psychic experience. We know that plausible narration demands such features as a beginning, middle, and an end. Characters must have motives and act in believable ways with purposes and effects. In a plausible narrative various gaps or inconsistencies in the story, the character structure, and the cause and effect of purpose are glossed over, filled in, or seamlessly woven together in ways that are vivid, flow naturally, and are emotionally compelling and logically believable.

We are taken in by the Dr. Jekyll and Mr. Hyde character because we know what it means to experience ourselves in various convincing and contradictory parts. Every time "Sybil" is aired on television or a talk show features satanic ritual abuse, our clinics are flooded with self-referrals. After the atomic bomb we looked to the skies for danger and sure enough our efforts quickly brought us flying saucers. We begin affirming more rights for women and children and our culture began noticing actual abusive incidents as well as many other violent and molest stories that seemed to have other sources. When our culture could no longer believe in conversion hysteria, we saw peptic ulcers, then stress, and now viral contagion. When we could no longer believe in Bridie Murphy's past lives, we turned to multiple selves, alien abductions, and satanic ritual abuse. Our collective imagination continues to generate believable images that can be used in our screen, telescoped, and narrative constructions to clarify what our infancies were like and what the structure of our deepest emotional life looks like. Here are some examples:

> My parents in raising me were more concerned with creeds and ritual than they were with my needs to love and to be loved by them. The reverence they kept was like a cult. My father was the high priest, my mother a priestess who looked on emotionlessly while I was led to the altar and forced to kill a baby (me?) and to drink its blood. Then I was placed on the altar as a sacrifice to the carnal wishes of all of their friends, the other participants that supported their belief system. The most unbearable part of all is that I was forced do the same things they did, to become like them, to sacrifice human life in the same manner they did, in the same cult, at the same altar. As a result, I am a damaged wreck.

> There is a higher intelligence that comes into my sphere, that picks me up, puts me down, and exchanges fluids with me through my umbilicus.

They want my soul, my fertility, and they want to impregnate me with their superior mental structure. I have no control over the coming and going of the higher intelligence that governs my life but I am frightened by it and suddenly swept away. It's like being lost in an endless nightmare that I can't make go away. Like losing yourself in a horrible science fiction movie you just can't shake off. I have no control over these higher intelligences that watch me.

My father loved me too much. I remember when he used to come into my room. I remember my mother was somewhere in the background. My childhood longings were misread by him and he took advantage of me. If she had done her job in keeping him happy like a wife should I would not have been given to him.

My mother ruled my every thought. We were always close; we shared everything. My father was an irrational, alcoholic brute, no one whom I could learn masculinity from. He gave me to her because he didn't want to deal with her dependency and so I had to be parent to her, husband to her—no wonder I am what I am.

In all of these familiar stories we can suppose that what must eventually be expressed or represented in the interactional exchange of the psychoanalytic transference and resistance is the loss of power, the loss of control over oneself, and a personal destiny to continue experiencing emptiness, breakdown, and death as a result of internalized environmental failures. The kinds of stories that must be told and the kinds of painful somatic memories that must be relived will vary according to the nature of the infantile breakdown experience.

Readers may ask, "But isn't this all speculation? How do we know that all these things didn't really happen exactly as they are remembered?" The answer lies in our understanding of the hope that the psychotherapeutic situation holds out for people to be helped in reliving in a dependent state past trauma. And then, of transforming themselves through better relating in the present. The effects of infantile breakdown resulting from misfortune, misunderstanding, neglect, or abuse can only be transformed in our daily lives through reliving in the transference present the traumas of the infantile past. Acting out or displacing the accusation onto the past never helps us transform our inner lives.

A well-meaning accused parent who has been searching his memory for some evidence that he has, in fact, trespassed in the way his adult daughter alleges, may ask, "But Doctor, isn't it possible that if I were so horrified by the deed I had done that I would have repressed it totally?" The answer is unequivocally no. Repression simply doesn't work this way. When we have been traumatized the problem is that we can't forget it. We set it aside, we manage not to think about it for long periods of time, but a sudden noise instantly shuttles us back to the concentration camp, to the trench where our buddy lies bleeding and dead, to the bedroom with the yellow-flowered wallpaper and musty smell where from our perch on the ceiling we look down watching Father take his pleasure with our unfeeling bodies.

Psychological repression happens to a 5-year-old child whose sexual and aggressive impulses press for forbidden expression. Repression as we have studied it for a century only works against stimulation arising from *within* the neuropsychic system, not merely in harmony with abstract moral convictions. Such a notion of repression belongs to Hollywood. "But Doctor, isn't it possible I might begin having flashbacks of my having actually committed the acts my daughter says I did?" Of course, anyone can have "flashbacks" about anything. But flashbacks operate like dreams, not like memories. Flashbacks are unconscious constructions and, as such, have many determinants. If you were working on my couch and started having flashbacks I would encourage careful and systematic attention to them. I would assume they contained the history of *your* infantile past that was now being re-created in dream mode in order for us to study how your relationship with me was pointing toward what had happened in your otherwise unrememberable infancy. If the flashbacks seemed also tied to your daughter and other family members, I would be listening for how the infantile past being revived for us to study in our relationship has also been activated at various moments in transference experiences toward them as well. I would never assume we were looking at facts or memories.

Therapists who, in the course of working with primitive transferences, have lost their professional boundaries momentarily are regularly able to report vivid memories of experiences of dissociation. There is never any question of what they did or did not do—no matter how heinous or how ego dystonic it was. In a given moment they felt the pull of a desperate (asexual, infantile) woman who needed their touch to keep from falling into blackness and death. As they reached out to her they slipped into the place in themselves where long ago they mobilized total reaching, total yearning, and went for the (asexual) breast so powerfully desired and so potently alluring. Retrospectively, they know beyond the shadow of a doubt that they experienced a psychotic moment in themselves while trying to rescue this woman. And while they are duly horrified at what they did, there is no possibility of its ever being truly forgotten. Perpetrators know exactly what they did and did not do, despite however much they squirm to deny, defend, and blame the other. The only exceptions are people who chronically live in psychotic experiences and have never been able to keep very good track of reality. Ordinary people are simply not able to accomplish such "repressions" no matter how much they may wish to.

A century of accumulated psychoanalytic knowledge says that relatedness memory simply does not work the way so many people claim it does, but rather that relatedness memories are manifest in people's daily lives and in transference and resistance memories in psychotherapy. People who have experienced infantile breakdowns attempt to turn passive trauma into active mastery by molesting us with their memories, the demand to be believed, and their insistence on being supported by us in their redress. *As human beings who have been subjected to infantile trauma they deserve so much more from us than simply being believed!*

By believing the traumas and encouraging people to do things in the real world about the horrible memories they recover in psychotherapy, therapists can only be colluding with the forces of resistance as we know them to arise to prevent painful transference reexperiencing. What is being avoided is clearly the breakdown of primitive mental functions that can only be done in the safety and intimacy of a private transference relationship. Not only clients but therapists also dread the intensity and the intimacy of such primitive transference reliving. People who have suffered humiliating and traumatizing childhoods and infancies are yearning for regressive psychotherapy experiences in which disorienting experiences can be subjected to transference, resistance, and countertransference analysis.

Not enough therapists have been prepared by their professional training to delve deeply into the meanings of recovered memories within the context of the therapeutic relationship. And there is great risk to the therapist working with deep personality trauma. There is not only the risk of litigation arising from the wild acting out damage that clients are inflicting on their families as a result of recovered memories. There is the greater risk that the therapist will be successful in mobilizing the early organizing or psychotic transference and will be interpretively successful in not having it deflected toward revenge on the family, but will be caught with the accusations aimed squarely at him or her while the client is in a frame of mind with little reality testing. That is why many therapists are eager to deflect these psychotic anxieties onto personages in the past rather than to attempt to contain them!

As professionals we have not yet begun to assess the grave danger each of us is in as a result of recovered memories emerging in the therapeutic transference relationship. Escalating law suits, increasing disciplinary action by ethics committees and licensing boards, and skyrocketing costs of malpractice insurance make clear that the problem is real and that it is serious. For these and other reasons, I advocate the inclusion of a third party "case monitor" whenever organizing or psychotic transferences are being worked on so that all parties are aware of the work and all parties are protected from accidental derailing of the psychotic process (Hedges 1994c). We know there are abuses and that they must be limited. But the wild, accusatory atmosphere surrounding recovered memories is only the tip of the iceberg of universal psychotic transference feelings.

It is not abusive or neglectful parents and families that are the proper therapeutic target of primitive abusive transference feelings. It is ourselves and the work we do. How are we individually and collectively to protect ourselves from an abusive psychotic monster that an enlightened society with concern for the emotional well-being of everyone has unleashed on us?

IMPLICATIONS FOR SOCIAL AND LEGAL ISSUES

1. *Clinical, theoretical, and experimental research fails to support the popularized "video camera" theory of memory.* The widely held view that externally generated psychic trauma can produce total amnesia for many years and then be subject to perfect total recall of fact is a Hollywood invention that is completely fallacious. As a dramatic device for generating horror and suspense, the

specter of capricious memory loss in response to unwanted experiences has indeed been successful in convincing millions that such things can and do happen—as attested to by an utterly spellbound population at present.

2. *Recovered memories cannot be counted as fact.* Consideration from a psychoanalytic point of view shows there to be too many sources of variance in recovered memories for them to ever be considered reliable sources of factual truth. Memories produced in hypnosis, chemically induced interviews, or psychotherapy are setting, technique, and relationship dependent. The most important recovered memories that attest to a history of trauma originate in the earliest months and years of life. Our knowledge of the way the human mind records experiences during this era makes it impossible for pictorial, verbal, narrational, or even screen images to provide facts from this era that are reliable.

3. *Nor can memories recovered in psychotherapy be counted as merely false confabulations.* We have a series of viable ways to consider the potential truth value of memories recovered within the context of psychotherapy. Much has been said concerning screen memories, telescoped memories, and narrational truth. Little attention has been given in the recovered memory literature to the kinds of transference and resistance memories that can be expected to characterize each developmental epoch of early childhood. The terror that many people experienced in the first months of life due to misfortune, misunderstanding, neglect, and/or abuse is recorded in painful aversions to dependent states that might leave them at risk for psychic breakdown. The effects of cumulative strain trauma in infancy can be devastating in a person's later life, although no trauma was visible and no abuse present at the time. People resist at almost all cost having to re-experience in transference (i.e., to remember) the terrifying and physically painful memories of environmental failure in earliest infancy. But externalizing responsibility for one's unhappiness in life onto people and events of childhood goes fundamentally against the grain of responsible psychotherapy.

4. *A simplified "recovery" approach tends to collude with resistance to the establishment of early transference remembering and, to the degree that it does, it is antipsychotherapeutic.* In acceding to the clients'

demands to be believed, to have their experiences validated, and to receive support for redress of wrongs, "recovery" workers foreclose the possibility of securing for analysis the transference and resistance memories mobilized by the psychotherapeutic relationship. Encouraging the acting out of multidetermined recovered memories in the name of psychotherapy is clearly creating malpractice liabilities for these therapists.

5. *Studies of recovered memories cannot draw responsible conclusions when collapsing over diverse categories of memory, developmental levels, and modes of personality organization. Nor can conclusions uncritically generalize findings from the psychotherapy setting, which is situation and relationship dependent, to other social and legal settings.* Human memory is complex, elusive, and multidimensional, so that all attempts to arrive at simplified or dogmatic conclusions are bound to be faulty. This includes attempts to consider the physiological aspects of memory as well.

6. *Taking recovered memories seriously involves establishing a private and confidential relationship in which all screen, narrational, transference, and resistance memory possibilities can be carefully considered over time and within the ongoing context of the psychotherapeutic relationship.* Therapeutic transformation of internal structures left by childhood oversight, neglect, and abuse necessarily involves mobilizing in the therapeutic relationship a duality in which the real relationship with the therapist can be known in contrast to the remembered relationships from childhood, which are being projected from within the client onto the person of the analyst and into the process of the analysis.

RISKS IN MOBILIZING DEEP TRANSFERENCES

Maintaining Separateness and Safety in the Analytic Encounter

Safeguards against incestual and parricidal involvement are provided by the eye of the third party—traditionally symbolized by the father, now codified in psychotherapy by ethics and law. A mother must be fully and instinctually involved to provide maximal reception for the preoedipal needs of her child. To the degree that a mother's emotional involvement with her young child is limited by personal preoccupations, restrictive notions about childrearing, or rigid internal defenses, what she has to offer as a symbiotic partner is likewise limited. On the other hand, the ancient taboos regarding seduction and violence toward the young teach that under- or overstimulating involvement by caregivers creates trauma and damage in formative minds.

It is the eye of the Other as internalized in the psychic structure of parents and other helping professionals that guards against penetrating and destructive overstimulation of those seeking to expand their psychic development. Without this eye of the Other to monitor and structure intense relationships in such a way that they are nontraumatically stimulating, the person uninitiated into the complexities of human emotional relatedness either (1) slumps for lack of stimulating response, (2) moves into activities designed to avoid the intense stimulation, or (3) receives the stimulation as traumatic intrusion (which may later need to be avenged). These three choices (freeze, flee, and fight) are open to every person in childhood and the way the person solves the problem of intrusive stimulation will also be revived in the analysis as transference and resistance memory.

Because of the characteristic or ritualistic roles of "speaker" and "listener" routinely assumed in the psychoanalytic situation, the sequence of intense transference illuminations will emerge as more obvious, more explicit, and more often clearly spelled out regarding the unconsciously transferred emotional structures of the speaker than of the listener. Traditional psychoanalysis is formulated to imply that there is no emotional involvement on the part of the analyst. And if there is, it is detractive and should be eliminated; it should not be spelled out, and certainly not spoken to the patient. In more contemporary work with preoedipal transferences some reciprocal exchanges around various emotional issues are to be expected. And every analyst knows the internal transformations that occur in the personality of the analyst as a result of each deeply engaging analytic relationship.

Sublimation of Analytically Stimulated Drives

The question of propriety in psychoanalysis and psychotherapy hinges on whether the intensity of the mutually stimulating relationship has been able to evolve to the deeply intimate moment of mutative transference interpretation, with both parties—or at least with the analyst or therapist—being able to sublimate the experience of drive mobilization in such a way that insight and development can spring from this loving involvement, rather than thoughtless emotional penetration and destruction. Our culture vaguely and intuitively understands the power of helping relationships to produce growth as well as damage. The universal existence of rules regarding incest (sexuality) and murder (violence) attests to universally experienced temptations. We certainly don't have laws about things that are not tempting. Recent clarification in ethics codes and laws regarding the essentially parental position assigned by organized society to helping professionals of all types further attests to a cultural commitment to curtailing unsublimated encounters with those individuals who seek guidance and growth from those more initiated in various aspects of human life.

If we did no more than simply consider the psychotherapeutic encounter in this way, we could quickly surmise that the helping partner is always at risk of having his or her own drives mobilized in the process of a significant helping connection and then of somehow getting lost in the process. "Getting lost" might entail a person feeling consciously or unconsciously stimulated by the emotional pull of the intense relatedness experience and then mobilizing rigid defenses or boundaries against personal involvement. But defense and boundary are not sublimation. Defense means erecting an internal barrier to relating spontaneously and instinctively to the other person—a closing off of potential channels for personal affective connection and communication. Likewise establishing a ritualized frame or routine boundaries for oneself represents a cognitive effort to draw limits, which protect oneself by a carte blanche, by a priori refusal to receive and to be affected by the intense stimulation that intimate relating necessarily provides. On the other hand, sublimation entails a (usually more or less conscious) process of experiencing the arousal that naturally arises in consequence of connection. And then utilizing that spontaneous excitement and enthusiasm for the attainment of creative and productive goals in the context of the relationship. The history of our field demonstrates how often analysts have gotten lost in defensive activities when sublimation would have been more useful. In fact, it might even be said that much of the technical lore and dogma of psychoanalysis is aimed at bolstering the analyst's defensiveness and defining ritualized boundaries to ensure nonrelating, rather than encouraging the analyst toward sustaining a posture replete with desire and apprehension.

The current blind and naive morality surrounding so-called dual relationships further encourages therapists to turn away from the essential therapeutic task—that of mobilizing intense emotional constellations (formed in the distant past) in the real here-and-now relationship with the analyst or therapist so that they can be experienced as powerful illusory patterns that govern one's emotional life.

Acting out Transference and Resistance Memories

Many things can crop up to interfere with the unfolding of successive layerings of transference. Resistance to reliving transference memories was first seen by Freud as the patient's will to remain ill. When negative therapeutic reactions threaten to crop up, the finger of accusation is invariably pointed at the analyst in some extra-analytic arena or displaced onto some external person from the present or past. Ideally this finger of accusation is leveled at the analyst as a part of the analysis so that the disturbing affects can be secured as transference or as a resistance to reliving deep transference feelings.

But when, for whatever reason, the resistance to deep experience is great and transference experiences cannot be established with the analyst, the analytic speaker may act out the negative transference in his or her accusations of the therapist. This is not to say that we do not have incompetent, unethical, and unknowledgeable therapists among us who do not want to or who do not know how to manage intense transference and countertransference stimulation. But having consulted on many aborted therapeutic processes, more often than not I find that the therapist has been successful in mobilizing deep transference patterns in the therapeutic relationship. But because we can never know in advance what a given person's deepest patterns of emotional trauma —neglect, seduction, violence—might look like until they are actually mobilized in the analytic transference for study, we cannot know what early (and therefore borderline or psychotic) trauma may be turned toward us without a moment's notice. And since all people have experienced various forms of overt trauma or strain trauma in infancy and early childhood, a therapist is always at risk in that every individual piece of work may dredge up some unexpected piece of psychotic abuse that will suddenly and abortively be aimed at the therapist.

Accusing the therapist (or someone else) instead of analyzing the resistance and transference implicit in the patient's traumatized position only serves to wreak further havoc on the now self-defined and self-maintaining victim. After the fact, and without benefit of many working-through memories, the third-party eye of the Other (the social justice system) is then engaged for the purpose of avenging experienced abuses. But no working through, no healing, no deep contact with one's invisible personality structures ever occurred to a person who is standing in front of a judge, a jury, a licensing board, or an ethics committee. While there may be times in life that an adversarial situation is necessary or even desirable, searching for one's soul is certainly not one of them. In situations where an analytic speaker questions the propriety of the analytic situation, I advise extensive third-party consultation and in extreme instances a change of therapists. Filing a complaint serves to polarize positions and solidify the victim sense in one's mind prematurely—before adequate working through has occurred. If there is a valid need to file a complaint, that can always be done at a later time. The stakes on working through are usually much higher. Considering the purpose of psychotherapy—that is, to revive past emotional patterns in direct relationship to the person of the therapist so that they can be expressed, experienced, and examined by the client and therapist, and so that resistance and emotional transfer can be established and worked through—it should not surprise us if a primitive impulse derails the process, leaving a displaced accusation aimed inappropriately, and only too realistically, at the therapist.[5]

In considering these issues I am reminded of the recent absurdities that have arisen with the advent of Prozac, a drug prescribed for profound depression. We have a whole population of severe depressives whose life and aggressive energies are so stifled they are seen to be in chronic danger of suicide or homicide. Clinical lore even tells us that these people do not generally have the energy to aim their full aggression at themselves or at others, but warns of potential danger when the

---

5. Further ways of safeguarding the therapeutic process during the working through of psychotic transference, such as the utilization of a third-party case monitor, are discussed in Hedges (1994a,c).

depression begins to lift. These people are then given the new drug that is miraculously successful in raising their spirits. The occasional subsequent suicide or homicide is then attributed to some unknown chemical side effect of the drug! Psychoanalysts and psychotherapists deliberately arrange a setting in which primordial abuse patterns can be remembered by the client's feeling them repeated in the vicissitudes of the here and now transference relationship. The therapeutic regression is begun and fostered by the therapist. When the abusive pattern is resurrected in relation to the analyst, and the expected resistance to transference does not yield to analysis for whatever reason, the therapeutic process is aborted with the accusatory finger pointing at the therapist. Those many naive watchdogs who serve as the eye of the Other conclude that the Prozac caused the suicide, forgetting entirely that the treatment has addressed the issues successfully, but that not all aspects of the hidden unconscious can be fully anticipated in advance and controlled.

A psychoanalyst or a psychotherapist does not have the power to transform anyone. He or she can only provide a setting in which invisible dimensions of the person's character can come to light. The analyst cannot fully anticipate or control how the person in analysis chooses to experience the transference or what the analytic speaker may do with the transference memories once revived in present experience. Stimulating the transference to be active and present is the analyst's task. But the analyst cannot prevent the acting out of the impulses mobilized by the transference. The analyst cannot prevent the acting out of the resistance to change—especially when the primitive and intrusive psychotic content of traumatic stimulation from childhood becomes attached to the person of the analyst, or when the resistance to the transference analysis is acted out in the form of accusations against the analyst or outside others. The treatment process has succeeded in unmasking the hidden abusiveness and the identification with the aggressor defense. But the person in analysis is unable or unwilling to allow the primordial defensive rage to melt into ordinary human fear, frailty, and helplessness. The fault for this, if any, cannot lie with the analyst, for this deep transformative melting is not under his or her control. Transformation can only be attained by the courage and persistence of the person in analysis. Clearly the greatest risk of a psychoanalyst or psychotherapist is allowing him- or herself to be fully emotionally present, to risk living in an analytic relationship perennially enlivened by desire and fear.

CASE CONSULTATIONS INVOLVING
RISKY RELATIONSHIPS

What follows are a few examples that have come to my attention that illustrate the helplessness of the analyst to effect change and how he or she has then suffered as a result of a negative therapeutic process that turned into an accusatory process.

Consultation One: Marge

(This case is presented by a male therapist with fourteen years of experience.)

"I saw Marge for two and a half years. She came to me after her children were grown and left home. She was a chronically depressed housewife in danger of alcoholism. A psychiatrist prescribed medication for her but she kept going downhill. Nothing I could do or say seemed to help. She didn't want to go to work or school to bolster her skills. She belonged to a church, which was enough group for her. She worried about whether her husband was having affairs on his sometimes week-long business trips. She mostly stayed home, watched television, ate, and slept.

"On the day that later came into question Marge was more depressed and despairing than I had ever seen her. Many times she had spoken of having nothing to live for, and of being despairing because no one cared about her and life was meaningless. The few friends she had she couldn't talk with. Marge said she was ready to end it all. Inside myself during the entire session I had to continually assess the seriousness of the suicide threat. It seemed serious. I could see that today I was going to have to obtain a contract for her to call me before she did anything to hurt herself. But could I trust her even that far? Was I going to have to call the paramedics or police before I let her leave? I tried everything I could think of but could achieve no connection.

"Marge had sat on the end of the couch further away from me than usual today. With ten minutes left I asked her if I could sit on the couch with her for a few minutes, thinking that perhaps that might help. She assented with some faint signs of life. A few minutes later, in desperation, I asked if it would help if I put my hand on her shoulder (in a reassuring way). She thought she might like that and shortly perked up enough for me to let her leave safely. I have four children. I know what a father's reassuring arm can mean and what it feels like—and I swear to God that's the way it was. I also believe that was the way she received it at the time because we seemed to connect and she took heart. We continued therapy some months and Marge began to get better, to relate to people more, and to take night classes.

"To make a long story short, her husband lost his job, her insurance ran out, and I drastically cut my fee so we could continue meeting. After some months the financial situation was getting even worse so she decided to stop seeing me, but the door was left open for her to continue her therapy at a subsequent date. Several years later I closed my practice entirely and left the clinic where I had been seeing Marge to take a full-time job for a managed-care company. She wanted to be seen again and she contacted me. I explained to Marge over the phone the reasons why I could not continue working with her—at that point I had no office, no malpractice insurance, no setup in which I could see her. She was enraged. I had always promised to love her and to see her no matter what, she claimed. She wrote a threatening letter to the director of the clinic where I had worked. He asked if we three could meet together. She was insinuating I had behaved inappropriately with her, had hugged and kissed her and made all manner of promises to her—none of which was true. All of it was apparently fabricated from that one incident and my lengthy commitment while working with her. This meeting with the clinic director settled her down a bit and she recanted the things she had said in the letter. He tried to arrange for her to see another therapist, which she refused to do. Shortly thereafter she caught her husband in what she was sure was a lie about some woman he was involved with at work. Again she demanded to see me. I spoke with her on the phone, and tried to assuage her rage that I would not see her. She was in a tirade of how I was abusing her. By this time she had been in an incest survivor's group for a while and she had gained plenty of validations for her rage at her parents and so was much freer to rage at me. I gave her appropriate referrals.

"The next thing I know an armed investigator from the state licensing board shows up at my work with an attache case and a lot of questions. Marge had written a letter alleging sexual misconduct. I was not allowed to see the letter. You know we have no civil rights in administrative proceedings. We are presumed guilty until proven innocent. But I did discover that she accused me of making love to her on my couch for a whole hour, promising her unending love and devotion, and then made her promise not to tell. The "promise not to tell" part clearly linked her current accusation or delusion to her childhood molestation.

"Whatever she told the licensing board, my attorney tells me I am in deep trouble because I'll never be able to prove it didn't happen. I have some notes but ten years ago we didn't keep many notes, so I don't know what good they will do. And anyway I don't keep notes on things that don't happen: I'm told I may lose my license to practice psychotherapy. And if she wins at this level there's a million dollars in malpractice settlement money waiting for her to go after. I'm really worried. I have a good job and a family to support. If charges of sexual misconduct are made I could lose my job and everything I have in trying to defend myself.

"We were doing good work and we both knew it. We got to many of the really terrible things that happened to her in childhood. I had her on her feet and moving in the world again and I think I could have gotten her out of her deep and life-long depression and low self-esteem if the insurance money hadn't run out. But now this.

"I came to see you, Dr. Hedges, because when I read your paper, "In Praise of the Dual Relationship," and I got to the part about the psychotic transference I suddenly saw what had happened. You said something to the effect that the tragedy is that the therapy has succeeded in mobilizing deep psychotic anxieties in the transference. But then reality testing becomes lost and the therapist is confused in transference with the perpetrator of the past. That really happened. We were never taught about such things in school. Do you have any ideas about how I can get out of this jam?"

Commentary

The most dangerous thing a therapist can do when working with an organizing transference is to successfully connect to the person without adequate working through of the resistance to emotional connection. Yes, this man saved the day and didn't have to hospitalize his patient. He succeeded in pulling her "back from the brink." But he is deluded in thinking that connection is experienced as good by people living out primitive states. I think she never forgave him for approaching and connecting when she wanted distance. And that he then became fused into her psychotic fantasies as yet another perpetrator. Her distress that she cannot have him further fuses him to the image of the perpetrator. Also, physical touching for the purpose of providing comfort or reassurance is never a good practice, because if it's not misunderstood as a seductive invitation it will surely be seen as a replication of an abusive penetration. I do see one certain, carefully defined potential use for interpretive touching in work with organizing or psychotic transferences. But interpretive touch is a carefully calculated concretized communication given at a critical and anticipated point in time when the person is having a hard time sustaining a connection and clearly understands the communication (Hedges 1994c). The error that the licensing board will have no way of understanding is that the therapy was going well until outside forces interrupted, plunging Marge into despair that her therapist successfully connected with. The psychotic transference then operated to fuse his contact with that of childhood abuse.

Consultation Two: Louanne

(This case is presented by a male therapist with twenty years of experience.)

"This middle-aged, childless professional woman came to me twice weekly for about six months. She had been to dozens of therapists all of her life and had taken various psychotropic medications for years. She had a psychiatrist who was giving her antidepressants at the time. She had a well-developed mimical self so she could talk well about all kinds of things at work and home. I began to sense that she had come to me because her husband of ten years was emotionally pulling out of the relationship. He had said noth-ing directly to that effect nor had she. They were constantly fight-ing but that was the way it had always been between them. And that was the way all relationships were for her. In a variety of ways I gingerly began to ask if maybe he was distancing from her, but she couldn't tolerate any such suggestion. Meanwhile she was getting more frantic at work. She was in trouble with her supervi-sor for inefficiency and chronic severe tardiness. She couldn't get out of bed in the morning. She spent hours in bed masturbating and was horrified that the fantasy that sexually satisfied her was nursing on a woman's breast. She was terrified this might mean she was a lesbian, another totally intolerable idea. She demanded reassurance from me that she was not. I spoke of how despairing she was about her husband's lack of responsiveness, about the in-creased fragmentation she was experiencing at home and on the job.

"She frequently indicated that there was only one way out but had no plan, no fantasy, only a wish to escape from pain or to hurt her husband. The idea of a hospital stay appealed as a place to be taken care of, but she adamantly refused it because that would be the last straw and her husband might divorce her.

"Louanne enjoyed seeing me for the most part and I attempted some interpretation of the nursing fantasies as pictures of the kind of care and nurturance she wished for from her husband and from me. Her medication had to be increased. But she began spending whole days in bed after her husband started talking about getting an apartment. She hired a detective to be sure he wasn't seeing anyone. He was out of patience—ten years of nothing but anger and depression with no relationship and no sex. Although he claimed he loved her he was fed up with her manipulations. He had had it with her.

"She began talking about her mother's physical abuse of her throughout her childhood. And on one fragmented occasion remembered with horror how her father and both brothers had molested her repeatedly throughout her growing-up years. She said she had never told anyone this before. She was so damaged I had no special reason not to take her memories at face value, except that the memories appeared during a period of severe fragmentation and at a time when she was experiencing harsh rejection from her husband. She begged and pleaded for him not to leave, but he had by now found an apartment and would be moving out in six weeks.

"On the evening that later came into question she had a session with me in which she was no more depressed or obsessed than usual. In fact she seemed a little more intact and oriented than she had been for some weeks. She left my office, swallowed a bottle of her husband's sleeping pills in the car on the way home, and collapsed in her husband's arms. The gesture was clearly a last ditch manipulation to get him to say he loved her (which he did) and that he would never leave her. He knew it was a manipulation and was so angry he later confessed to me that he seriously considered letting her die. She came to one last session the following week. Now that she was getting divorced she said that she couldn't afford to see me (which wasn't true—they were quite wealthy).

"All efforts then and in follow-up calls and letters to persuade her to resume her therapy fell on deaf ears. It seemed clear that I had failed to help her save the one relationship in her life that had been nourishing—and it had been. He was a good man and despite her illness and manipulations he did care about her and had stood by her through a series of crises.

"A year later both I and her psychiatrist were sued for failure to hospitalize. She had a long list of damages that she had suffered because we had failed to provide proper care and holding while the world at work and home battered her. We both had adequate records. Expert witnesses reviewed the case and rendered testimony that validated that we had upheld a proper standard of care, and that there were no immediate indicators for hospitalization. Even her husband testified that we had responded well but happened to be 'in the wrong place at the wrong time.'

"Now the attorney for the malpractice company has proposed a hefty settlement. Depositions have taken two years and I have spent a considerable sum consulting with experts and with my own attorney. He says I could refuse to settle so as not to have the settlement on my record, but the estimates of cost in terms of the time and money involved are staggering. The same insurance company canceled the coverage of a friend of mine shortly after a settlement for far less than the sum they are offering her. I tell you it's all insane. If insurance companies keep settling for large amounts every time a person with a psychotic transference sues, we soon won't be able to afford the premiums. Besides, everyone involved in this case knows it's wrong. I'm convinced even she knows it's wrong. But she knows she can get away with it, and she needs the money now since she was fired from her job. I feel morally obligated to stand up and fight it. But I also have a life to lead and a family to care for. It would take every penny of what my wife and I have saved for years to keep this wrong thing from happening. And the insurance company doesn't care. They want to avoid the high costs of deposing dozens of therapists she has seen over the year, having to fly them all here from Miami.

"There may not be much you can help me with at this point except not to feel guilty for throwing in the towel. But how does one avoid such circumstances in the future? Shall we stop seeing borderline psychotics altogether in order to be safe?"

Commentary

When dozens of others have failed before you, do not assume it's because they were incompetent and you will be the first therapist to really help her. People with psychotic or organizing transferences have, at some point in their infancy, had the experience of having to fight to stay alive. Despite their frequent suicidal threats they are, in fact, survivors who have had to work harder than most of us just to "pass" as normal in a social world full of relatedness complexities they have no way of understanding. Survival and desperation they do understand, and consideration of others has no importance when psychic death threatens. Yes, there are many people with primitive anxieties we should not be seeing in our private practices—or at least not without an involved case monitor (Hedges 1994c). Such people can be referred to public nonprofit clinics where the liabilities to the therapist are not so great.

Consultation Three: Edward

(This case is presented by a female therapist with fifteen years of experience.)

"My client, or I should say ex-client, grew up in poverty, never being cared for or having anything. His earliest memories are starving in a crib with no one to feed or change him. He remembers scavenging in garbage cans and begging for food in the slum of a large eastern city. By age 6 he was selling newspapers on the street. Soon he was a newspaper distributor, then he got his own newsstand, and onward and upward defying every obstacle all the way to the top of a major international corporation, finally becoming a wealthy man. But, of course, he was only 4 months old inside. He could mimic but he had no idea how to emotionally relate to himself or anyone else. He could put on elegant appearances and had made it through college, so he sounded quite good. But it was the infant that showed up in my office.

"I won't go into details of the treatment. Suffice it to say that I saw him as often as possible, sometimes several hours a day trying to contain him before some big meeting or business confrontation. He pleaded with me on several occasions to meet him for sessions in distant cities so he could be with me in advance of important deals. The therapy was going well. It all centered around supplies, never having enough, being afraid of dying of starvation, and a veritable frenzy of concern and grasping at everything in sight—all of this clearly wounds from a neglectfully abusive infancy.

"His concerns sooner or later came up in terms of preoccupations with body parts. He had dozens of doctors and literally hundreds of medications of all sorts. After I became more secure in my position I got him to a good doctor who could follow him regularly and arranged to have all of his pills taken away except those this doctor prescribed. He had a psychiatric consult with a top psychiatrist whom I thought might try an antipsychotic or lithium, but instead started him on Xanax, to which he later became addicted. There were, of course, his many beautiful and grasping women, deceitful business colleagues, and greedy family members, all of whom wanted a piece of him. But he slowly learned to limit the demands and at times even to say no to outlandish requests. I became his sounding board, his source of reality testing, and practically a business and relationship consultant.

"It was difficult trying to give him as much time and support as he wanted. And it was tricky trying to stay in the role of therapist because he was so emotionally needy. It was clear he had never had a single human being in his life who cared for him and who wasn't out to exploit him. But the long and short of it is that there was a financial disaster in the corporation with everyone blaming everyone. There were lawsuits, scandals, the whole bit, and he was effectively financially wiped out. I couldn't hold onto him. I called for another psychiatric evaluation, which he refused. I spoke of possible hospitalization to get some rest time, but he refused. He was fragmenting severely from the stress, the worst I ever saw him in.

"Then he disappeared completely. He locked himself up in a hotel room without coming out until he was found a week later. He had starved himself. It was a luxury hotel with all kinds of ser-vices but he holed himself up, a fragmenting mess totally isolated from humanity popping pills and drinking. He was finally located when a concerned housekeeper alerted her supervisor who con-sulted the manager. He was found in terrible condition. He had turned away from everyone and everything—even me. He would not respond even to my paging him with our secret code. I left messages everywhere. I searched everywhere, had the police out and everything. He had become a basket case—paranoid and suicidal.

"When the authorities found him and hospitalized him another psychiatrist got hold of him. He was diagnosed as bipolar and put on lithium. He had a loyal manager who had held onto as much as he could and salvaged something—enough for him to still be well to do. But by now he had experienced starvation and I was his neglectful mother. There was nothing I could do. For months I left phone messages, sent cards and letters, and even some flowers to cheer him up.

"Some time later I heard from his lawyer. By the time the case shaped up with his crooked attorneys and psychiatrists he wants millions in damage because I diagnosed him as lower borderline, hypomanic, and prescribed psychotherapy, soaking him with excessive expensive treatment when I should have seen that he had a bipolar biological disturbance and should have put him on lithium from the beginning. Of course, his former doctor and psy-chiatrist are named, too. But aside from the scam involved from a financially desperate man seeking to rebuild an empire, he said some really horrible things to me in our last phone call. He was dazed and confused and his basic message was that I wasn't there when he needed me. That I never helped him, never gave him anything. That I forced him into a fraudulent position by not giving him enough, by not containing him sufficiently.

"I gave that man everything I had to give—and I'm a pretty good nurturer too, you know. But an external disaster intervened before we got over the hump where he could trust. Maybe he is incapable of trusting. He certainly was never to be trusted in his business dealings. I was frequently revolted by the ruthless things he did to people. But I understood that he had no capacity for empathy. All of my expenses, which were many, are being investigated. He was so demanding that of course he paid for a considerable amount of my time. I kept hoping, truly hoping he would someday be able to emotionally connect. We were close but it never happened. So his new empire will have a shot in the arm with a sizable settlement—his attorneys will stop at nothing. Their Mafia-connection reputation has the insurance company intimidated.

"This man so needed to be regarded as a person, to feel like a human being. He was kind of a Howard Hughes type, and just as pathetic and as exploited. I did my best, but now I'm seen as one of the many exploiters. They are even claiming that my bills for services are fraudulent, that he was charged for services never rendered—it's all so bizarre and untrue. How will I ever recover from reaching out so far to this pathetic human being and in the end having a starving mad viper hissing and snapping at me.

"I know you speak about psychotic transference and I understand it intellectually. I could even understand how it operated when I would be five minutes late with a phone call and he would fly off the handle. But I could always somehow soothe him. We could talk about what it meant, about how the infant inside simply can't tolerate delay and how sorry I was to cause him such pain. All of that was okay, was manageable. But when the fragmentation leads to rage and realistic destruction of these proportions . . . How will I ever feel safe with a fragmenting patient again? I repeatedly went beyond the call of duty in every possible way to accommodate this man. He has left me severely damaged, disillusioned with the human race, despairing about treatment, and questioning if it can ever really work. When I feel discouraged I even question my competence as a therapist."

Commentary

Giving more doesn't cure psychosis. When you begin thinking that you are the only human this person has ever been able to deeply address, and you are the only person so dearly needed by this client to overcome horrible deprivation and/or abuse in childhood, then perhaps you need to back off and examine the psychodynamic basis of your altruism. This is not the only case where a fluke in reality turned an otherwise good psychotherapy sour. This client is a life-long expert at grasping and clawing when the odds are against him. Most therapists are naive amateurs in survival skills, and have no way to anticipate what such desperation might look like.

Consultation Four: Horace

(This case is presented by a male therapist with twelve years of experience.)

"We finally reached the psychotic transference. I had been trying for months to bring some deep abuse into focus, but unsuccessfully. But he had a business presentation to make the next day and he was terrified of the challenge. It would be a reach for him and he might be questioned on some difficult issues. He didn't know if he could maintain. He was afraid. He went numb on the couch— had actual body paralysis for fifteen or twenty minutes. Had this not been a gradual descent into the psychotic pocket I had been hoping to explore, I might have been alarmed for medical reasons. In fact I did check with him to be sure he thought everything was okay. While he was in the trance he experienced severe blows to his face and head accompanied by loud, startling, and frightening yelling. They came suddenly out of nowhere. He had never been able to cry, never been able to raise his voice in pain. Now he knew why. It seemed certain that his father had abused him as an infant for being a needy baby, for whimpering and crying. He was feeling whimpery and needy that night with me because of the presentation the next day that I had been encouraging him about. In trans-ference he experienced me abusing him for being needy.

"He now suddenly knew where his own sense of violence came from. He had always known that his taciturn father was a harsh man, but by the time he was old enough to remember in pictures, his father had withdrawn from emotional relationships in the family in order to contain his rage. This paralyzing insight into himself, his infantile rage, and the abusive humiliation he had suffered as an infant for feeling needy explained how he had come to believe himself defective and incapable and had forced him to 'fake' his way through most of life. He was terrified to have to feel the full impact of his psychotic core in this dramatic total body paralysis. He was deeply shaken and traumatized by having touched this primitive transference.

"That night his therapy basically ended. He ran a fast retreat from that frightening place that he never wanted to be in again. He had been running from this terrifying body memory and the total agony it represented to him. Retrospectively, I see that his 'setting me up' began at that point. He began needing a great many concessions and unusual arrangements in our work, which I did my best to accommodate. These seemed interpretable in a variety of ways within the context of his life history. But it turns out he was working behind the scenes collecting a list of variations in his professional relationship with me that could later be distorted in court to look as though they were inappropriate.

"He terminated his work with me without ever successfully bringing the primitive transference into the analysis. When a sub-poena for my records arrived I was in a state of total shock. His manner of turning against me when I was least expecting it—harsh blows coming out of nowhere—replicated what I had seen him experience on the couch. He never wanted to go there again and shockingly arranged to turn the tables so that it was I who felt like a fool for trusting."

Commentary

Never trust that someone in depth therapy will not attack you ragefully and mercilessly when the psychotic transference has been mo-bilized. Primitive transferences know no limit. Trusting that this person would never sue you is to be a fool about the very thing your therapy seeks to bring out—madness, desperation, and sociopathic manipulations.

Consultation Five: Jeffrey

(This case is presented by a female therapist with twelve years of experience.)

"I see this young man four hours a week and we are in our fifth year. Because he had a mild learning disorder he early on fell into bad company and spent most of his youth as a tough guy. His mother is seductive and intrusive, and I was slowly able to move him away from the overindulgent relationship he had with her. His father continues to bail him out of all kinds of trouble and to sponsor him financially so he never has incentive to achieve for himself. In the course of time I have been able to get him largely to back away from accepting so much from his father and to begin modest achievement on his own. We get along very well.

"I want to talk to you about Jeffrey because I have read your work on countertransference and I have recently had a strong erotic countertransference reaction to him. I am a happily married woman and I have good boundaries, so I'm not worried anything would ever happen between us. After I helped him see how psychotic his last girlfriend was so that he finally got rid of her, he began making it better on his own doing some casual dating. He was planning to spend some time with this older woman over the weekend. On that weekend I became sexually preoccupied thinking about him—I don't know exactly what I was thinking and I don't remember my fantasies, but I know my husband enjoyed how sexual I was. The following week he didn't mention his date until the third hour. He said he did not want to upset me by talking about sex. He had a wildly erotic story, however, about which he spared no details. I wasn't sure if he was trying to excite me or to make me jealous. But his conscious accent was on trying to make me proud of him for having picked someone to spend time with who had some substance and sanity for a change. I don't know where all of that's going, but we have a good relationship so whatever happens I'm sure we can talk it out.

"But there's this other thing that started happening. He would begin to fall asleep in sessions. I spoke with several consultants who interpreted it as his feeling safe enough to trust himself with me. Or that he experienced the interpersonal stimulation as so strong that he needed to pull away at times. But Jeffrey would awake from these naps with dreams that we could then use to help us understand where he was with me and in our work together. In fact some of the best material we have ever had to work with has come from these dreams. So much so that about six months ago he asked about hypnosis. What it was and would I hypnotize him so we could find out what is really going on down there that he avoids by sleeping, but then has access to in his dreams. I have never been trained in hypnosis but I said I would do this for him. So I have since taken a number of workshops in hypnosis and have a consultant I expect to use when we finally do try it. It was around the time I was beginning to think about starting some hypnosis with him when I felt the erotic countertransference. But trying to deal with the erotic element slowed me down."

Commentary

When you find yourself wanting to do special things to accommodate your patient, be suspicious that there are some invisible dimensions operating. Here the mutual sexual excitement reaches a weekend peak when you are considering what it may mean to penetrate his consciousness with hypnosis. Recall this man had both a mother and a father who intruded with good things so extensively that he failed to thrive academically and socially. Of course he yearns for helping support from his therapist; but the direction you are going runs the danger of replicating the destructive intrusiveness of well-intentioned parents. It further suggests that well-intended but destructive intrusion may be an erotic scenario, which matches his history of sadomasochistic love relationships.

Whenever we pride ourselves on being someone special for our clients a red flag should go up. What kinds of psychic representations might appear to signal an infantile molest that is being psychotically fused with the benevolent intrusiveness of the therapist? Erotic transference and countertransference certainly occur and can be useful informers about the therapeutic process. But when they are simply taken in stride, especially after just getting rid of a psychotic girlfriend and just when hypnosis is about to begin, they seem like warning signs to be reckoned with.

Consultation Six: Matthew

(This case is presented by a female therapist with twenty years of experience.)

"I know you basically know it all by now, you have heard it from my patient when he came to you for consultation. I sent him to you because I knew you could help him through it without encouraging anything destructive. I should have come to you myself months ago, and it's stupid that I didn't. In a way I saw it coming. And in a way I didn't. But if I'd talked about it, a lot of grief could have been avoided. It's stupid that I didn't open up to some of the people in my office. They've known me for years, they love me, they would have understood. I knew you wouldn't judge me. I knew they wouldn't judge me. But it was a stupid mistake and I'm out of it by the skin of my teeth—at least I hope I'm out of it. The therapy was going well. Matthew was very intense from the beginning and soon begin feeling emotions for the first time in his life. He had never emotionally connected with anyone before. He's very bright, witty, and he always showed a great deal of concern about how I was doing with the things he had to tell me.

"Meanwhile I was in this really awful place with my husband that I won't even talk about now. It was a really horrible break up. I was fragmented and lonely. I called my client on impulse to have a drink. And that was really all that happened. But you know, sometimes a drink isn't just a drink. I could imagine situations where a chance encounter with a client or ex-client might spontaneously lead to a brief friendly exchange and a drink together. Not that I would recommend it to anyone. But I could imagine circumstances where it might be okay. Well, this wasn't okay and I knew it. I was clearly needy and turning to him for some consolation. I knew it was wrong and I even felt it coming up in all of my distress. If I had just said something to Becky or Bob, my office partners. They would have understood. They would have talked some sense into me. They would have pulled me back from the brink. But it was a fatal attraction. And this is a powerfully seductive man as you know.

"I really wanted to tell you about this. Because do you know what the worst part of this is? It's the stupid shame. Shame that I would be attracted to a client. Shame that I would want to be seen and liked by him. Shame that I didn't rely on my friends when I felt this happening to me. Shame that I did not call you and ask for help. It's true he loved my personal involvement and couldn't understand why I felt I had violated his trust and couldn't continue seeing him professionally. To him, I was the first person in his life who had ever seen him, who saw how wonderful he was, who knew how he felt. Our sessions were magical—I'm sure he told you. It was like we were right together all the time. He loved it and he loved that I really cared for him. And I did. That part can't be wrong. It's not wrong to care for a client, even to love a client. That's happened many times in twenty years of practice and it's been beautiful and enhancing to the work.

"But here I don't know what happened. Except that I really liked him and I was really feeling needy and vulnerable. You know, this is not the sort of thing you imagine happening to yourself. And, in fact, nothing really happened. It's not like we even kissed or held hands, we didn't. It was simply two people meeting for a drink, but a man's therapy was ruined.

"Please tell people that you teach. Please write about it in your books. No one should be allowed to say, 'It can't happen to me.' You now tell me that when you saw him you saw a psychotic core, a manic frenzy to seduce the nurturing mother so he wouldn't die. And I fell right into that! If I hadn't been such a mess at the time, would I have been so enthralled by him, so pulled in by him? I honestly don't know. But its a lesson in humility. And a lesson in false pride—as though I'm too good to make a mistake, too good to be tempted, too sane to get my thoughts all fucked up. I can't believe I'm even saying all of this. I hope others can learn from my mistake. I lost a good client. And now you even suggest that I'm a fool to think I am protected from his taking legal action because he's not 'litigious.' And because he has caring feelings for me. I guess I don't know enough about the power or unpredictability of the psychotic transference. Even though I've seen some pretty horrible things in other situations, I got to believing I knew what I was doing and it would all be okay. Is mania contagious?!"

Commentary

It's not discrete behaviors, what we do or don't do, that counts in protecting the therapy situation from overstimulation. But it's the spirit of the relatedness involved that defines the personal boundaries. Furthermore, we are always in trouble when we think we know for sure what we are doing. Especially if we think we are safe from the unpredictability of the psychotic transference or from our own psychotic anxieties. We have to be free to turn to colleagues when we feel shaky. If we don't seek consultation in time, the power of the hidden psychosis can overtake us. She's right—it's false pride that makes fools of us all.

Consultation Seven: Trula

(This case is presented by a male therapist with twenty-two years of experience.)

"I know I did wrong and the worst part is that I knew it was wrong while I was doing it. It was uncanny, it was like a part of me was up on the ceiling looking down watching and knowing what I was doing was wrong.

"We had worked well together for three years but the challenge of a major promotion at work that was just beyond her grasp set off a major regression with fragmentation and depression. She became increasingly desperate and wanted to stop coming to see me. Finances were an issue. I insisted we couldn't stop this way. I lowered my fee and after some weeks of watching her desperately floundering just beyond my reach, I couldn't stand it any more. I moved toward her, I embraced her to protect and reassure her.

"A part of me for a long time hoped she would sue me. Being punished would have been sweet relief. Instead, I had to experience the most agonizing regression imaginable in my own therapy.

"My own mother was gravely disabled and couldn't care for me when I was born. I grew up in foster care and remember endless painful Saturdays waiting on the porch steps for her to come. Sometimes she would, sometimes she wouldn't, but I waited all day anyway, hoping. Even as an infant I must have somehow known she was fragmented, hurting, desperately needing help and reassurance. When my client entered this same despairing, unreachable place I could not bear it. I moved to rescue her, to try to give her the love, the containing, the touch she so desperately needed. And my client did respond favorably at the time. She pulled herself together and made a great success of her promotion. But when a devastating personal tragedy later hit her I succumbed to blackmail to avoid public embarrassment."

Commentary

The psychotic transference always hooks us deeply. As the analytic speaker continues to pull away we are in danger of reliving our own infantile, organizing period and feel the desperation that we may die if we cannot find mother, and it is always the breast we are inclined to reach toward. It is the successful connection with the organizing transference that produces terror—replicating the original terror that the infant somehow experienced that foreclosed the possibility of an emotional bonding experience.

There is one last aspect to this problem of people reaching out to find one another that I would like to illustrate. A surprising feature of the analytic speaker's reaching often makes the psychotic transference difficult to detect, much less to respond to creatively and safely, as the next encounter demonstrates.

Lunacy At The Sushi Bar: Morgan

Not long ago I was working late on a rainy night and stopped at a sushi bar on the way home. I chanced to sit next to a pleasant looking young fellow with dark hair, glistening eyes, a close trimmed mustache, and tight fitting Western clothes and boots. While I was scanning the menu selections, his tuna rolls arrived and he offered me one while calling for a second sake cup for me. We quickly lapsed into a fascinating conversation that lasted until the bar closed.

Morgan was a friendly and good-natured fellow. But as soon as he began to talk I could see he was a strange-enough person that most people would have quickly and politely moved away. Whether it was because I was tired and needed to unwind, or because he was plainly inviting, or because the sake went to work so quickly—I found myself interested and engaged. We talked about the weather, the recent disastrous fires, the unfortunate people spending this rainy night in tents after the devastating earthquake, and the many among us dead or suffering from the AIDS epidemic. Morgan's eyes filled with tears as he told me about his lover who had passed away almost a year ago—a loving man who had taken him under his wing and cared for him for many years. We linked arms in traditional Japanese fashion and lifted our sake cups in memory of Peter.

Then came crab, swordfish, shark, California rolls, and more sake. We talked about the colleges we had gone to, the fraternities we had belonged to, and what we were doing now. When Morgan discovered I was a therapist, he explained he had seen many counselors through the years since he was 12. He liked these counselors and wondered if I knew this one or that one. Then began a sequence that kept me spellbound for over an hour, partly because Morgan was so sincere, so innocent, and so intense, partly because I was genuinely enjoying him, and partly because I was seeing in pure culture a spontaneous, unadulterated version of an instantly formed organizing or psychotic transference operating freely before my very eyes. I couldn't help but play into it.

Morgan leaned forward in an intimate fashion. Though quite masculine, he seemed like a soft and affectionate teddy bear who could easily melt into a gentle cuddle. In contrast to this bodily yearning and reaching out for contact, for human warmth and affection, as he addressed me Morgan's eyes opened widely and dilated as though he were startled or terrified. "I could really tell you some things you wouldn't believe," he challenged. I took the bait. The sequence started off with mildly unbelievable, "new age" styled quasi-mystical events. Without flinching I nodded in assent to his "amazing and unbelievable" experiences, expressing surprise that he did not expect me to believe him. I spoke in favor of trusting our own experiences, even if others might not be able to follow them. There surely are uncanny happenings in the universe that many people would find difficult to believe. The illusions, delusions, and hallucinatory stories then began escalating with Morgan continuing to lean forward affectionately with those same widely terrified eyes—a posture simultaneously begging for connection and challenging me to reject him by disbelief. Not to be easily thrown over, I firmly maintained my position that while many might indeed doubt what he had seen or heard, I saw no reason for him to doubt his own experiences.

The sushi, the sake, the recounting of psychic events, and the challenging engagement drew Morgan's bar stool closer to mine. I could clearly see something through Morgan that I had long intuited from experiences in the consulting room. But it was so much clearer, so much more vivid and real in this setting. I was witnessing a life long investment in seeing to it that no interpersonal connection could possibly be made. That is, he was certain that it would only be a matter of time before I began to question, to doubt, to turn away, to see him as crazy, and to shrink away from him in fear or disdain. But in me Morgan had met his match! There was nothing he could say that could possibly make me turn from his penetrating terrified gaze, from his soft affectionate approach, from the stories he told with hallucinatory vividness.

The climax finally came—of course in a story about his mother, Laverne. One night some years ago, shortly after his father died, he was at Laverne's house having a smoke on the patio. At the time she lived on the outskirts of a small town in Arizona. The desert behind the house stretched miles into the night to the high mountains barely illuminated by the summer skies. Suddenly the heavens begin to fill with an intense iridescent blue light. Spellbound, Morgan watched a giant craft silently and gently descend to the floor of the desert and small aliens appear, scouting the surrounding territory. Morgan wondered who they were, where they came from, and what they were here for. He felt afraid. Perhaps they wanted him. He ran to get his mother. He wanted to show her the great blue light and the strange night visitors. Laverne was irritated at having her television program interrupted, but reluctantly she followed him out onto the patio. Would you believe she could see nothing? No blue light, no aliens? She said he was crazy, that he was seeing things. But they were there. He was sure of it. He didn't know why Laverne couldn't see them. Morgan was leaning forward on his bar stool clutching my arm, terrified eyes searching my face. I was sure to doubt, sure to raise questions, sure to pose alternative explanations—sure to somehow challenge his sense of what was real, to echo Laverne's pronouncement that he was crazy. I would certainly not be able to believe what he had seen when even his own mother didn't believe him when the evidence was plainly before her eyes!

Not to be undone at such a critical moment, I asked Morgan why it even mattered to him what his mother thought. It was silly to worry about what other people believed, I said. He saw what he saw, experienced what he experienced—and if she couldn't deal with it, that was her problem not his. Morgan turned into a statue before my very eyes, frozen in fright that I had heard him, had connected to him. He looked as though he anticipated my suddenly hitting him. Mind you, good reader, it was the sake that made me do this! Morgan was thrown into a state of total terror and confusion by our connection. He had spent a lifetime developing a technique to ensure that his desperate need for warmth, for loving reception, would be thwarted by the other's turning away in fear, horror, or disdain. *The internalized break in contact was skillfully incorporated into Morgan's way of reaching toward me, into his very way of being in the world. The internalized breach of connection with the other was already woven into, already implicit in, already ensured by the very way he approached me.*

I suddenly realized how many people live this way. The infantile trauma they have suffered, and their primordial way of limiting the overstimulation, has become internalized in such a way that the very manner of approach for contact itself forms a social demand that assures that the other will reject connection by shrinking away in horror, impatience, anger, fear, or disbelief.

I also understood in a flash that had I simply reached out towards him by naively "validating" the truth of his experience,

Morgan would have known that he had found a kindred soul—someone else who was also terrified of connections and who managed in the world by issuing interpersonal invitations to have my deep yearnings responded to.

But Morgan was foiled in his encounter with me. For some reason I liked him very much. I enjoyed his manly softness, and his desperate search for nourishing touch. I felt compassion for his terror and I connected deeply with his pathos. In me he momentarily touched the mother he longed for; and she had tenderly touched him back—throwing him into a state of terrible confusion and sudden fear of some sort of abuse. External reality was not matching internal reality for a horrible moment that must have seemed like an eternity to Morgan. We sat together for a while in silence.

The sushi bar was closing. Morgan and I passed through the lobby, past cherry blossoms and a great golden dragon breathing fire, through the red lacquered doors, and into the crisp air of this strange California night. The rain had stopped and the skies had cleared. Before we headed our separate ways, Morgan and I shook hands. Then we embraced   two strangers having achieved a rare moment of intimacy laced with fear. The full moon rose above the temple gate of The Mikado.

THE DANGER OF THE ORGANIZING OR PSYCHOTIC TRANSFERENCE

The emergence of organizing or psychotic transference momentarily places the crucible of a person's life in a delicate balance. The traumatic reality of the primordial past is emotionally and powerfully pitted against the reality of the intimacy of the present relationship. Ten thousand years of human experience says the deck is stacked against us—that craziness is intractable and untreatable, that in time we can expect the power of the infantile past will inevitably reassert itself in a delusional way, that we can expect the potentially curative present moment of relatedness will be forsaken or renounced in such a way that the therapist will be held responsible for the deep sense of trauma. At this critical moment of transference experience the affective past is fused with the present and the power of the infantile trauma totally eclipses the transformative possibilities inherent in the present intimate relationship. The peril inherent in the psychotherapeutic relationship is not caused by the recent widely publicized recovered memories controversy. The problem of transference psychosis has always been with us. It is real. It is dangerous. It is universal. And it isn't going away. Our task is to find creative ways of meeting, managing, and working through the organizing experience. In chapter 6 I will present a lengthy case study illustrating the development of a transference psychosis, the accompanying countertransference dilemmas, and the working through process.

3

The Perils of the Intimacy
of the Therapeutic Relationship

Robert Hilton

Therapists are aware of the risks clients take in being vulnerable and trusting us in the intimacy of the therapeutic relationship. The last time they trusted someone with their deepest thoughts and feelings, they were betrayed, ignored, shamed, or abused, and they fear that the same thing will happen again. They fear retraumatization at our hands.

The perils of the intimacy that are created in the therapeutic relationship for the client are obvious, and working with them is an essential part of the therapeutic relationship and process. But what about the peril that is present for the therapist in being part of this intimate relationship? One of my clients is a new mother. She began seeing me when her child was 2 months old. She brings the baby with her to the sessions where we spend a great deal of time talking about her child's needs and how she responds to them. It is easy to see and empathize with the vulnerability of the baby and the real peril he faces at the possibility of losing her or being traumatized by her neglect. Yet the mother also faces a peril. In opening her heart to the needs of her child she is also opening up her own defenses against the pain of intimacy. She too has been hurt or neglected. She too does not trust the environment to support her in her needs and yet she must risk reopening her own woundedness in order to provide for her child's needs. She does this consciously knowing full well that he is not there to meet her needs but actually must eventually reject her for his own self-realization and independence. While she is opening to her child and acknowledging her own needs, I must help her accept the pain and sorrow of her own unmet infant needs that should have been fulfilled by her own mother. If she unconsciously expects the child to meet these needs and he disappoints her, which is inevitable if the child is given the freedom of self-expression, she will then be in the position of acting out upon the child the anger and hurt she felt at the hand of her own mother. The child is in peril and so is the parent.

So likewise is the therapist and client. While the therapist is helping the client deal with his fears of intimacy, he also must deal with his own. However, there is an additional twist here for the therapist. When the therapist fails as a good therapist, which he must do so that the client can have his own self expression and identity, he not only faces his own childhood pain but in addition faces the consequences of the loss of his role as "therapist," which has become part of his self organization. The unconscious motivation for the therapist to do this kind of work has been to overcome his deep feelings of inadequacy and pain brought about by his own inadequate parenting. So when the patient does not respond to his efforts to help him, he is in effect denying the therapist some of the important self-nurturing supplies that his role as therapist is intended to provide and upon which he has unconsciously learned to depend.

Bacal and Thompson (1993), two self psychologists, state:

> When the analyst has what we call a countertransference reaction, the analyst's self-object needs, that are ordinarily being met by the patient during their interaction, are now being frustrated and his sense of self is concomitantly threatened, or shaken, or worse. This self-object disruption in the analyst will affect the analyst's capacity to attune and to respond optimally to the patient. . . .

They also state that therapists' enhanced awareness of how their psychological needs and vulnerabilities have become organized into their professional working persona will enable them to become clearer about the limits to their capacity for optimal responsiveness to any particular patient [pp. 7–8].

As a young therapist thirty years ago, I had no idea that my psychological needs and vulnerabilities had become organized into a professional working persona. I was totally unaware that my role as psychotherapist functioned as a form of self organization and that in this role I was attempting unconsciously to overcome the impotence I felt as a child to organize the chaos around me and to get my needs met. But I was soon to learn this lesson in a very dramatic way.

During the early 1960s I had gone to Esalen Institute in Big Sur, California. Esalen represented the cutting edge of humanistic psychology and exploration of alternative lifestyles and methods of healing. At this time I was on my way to Oakland to be the principal speaker at a religious conference. I was a new Ph.D. and teaching counseling in a theological seminary. I met a young woman there and proceeded to impress her with my newfound status. When she asked me if I knew much about LSD, I found myself not wanting to appear naive and ignorant so I told her I had heard Timothy Leary and Richard Alport speak. But I did not acknowledge that I really knew nothing about drugs personally or theoretically. She then asked me if I would stay with her while she "dropped some acid." Caught between my naïveté and my need to appear cool and knowledgeable I could not ask her what this would actually mean. So I agreed. My fantasy was that I would sit and read a book while she took this drug and that in a couple of hours it would be all over and we would talk about it.

About an hour after she took the LSD, she came out of what appeared to be a sleep state and was experiencing a full-blown psychotic attack. She turned to me and screamed, "I am going crazy! This is for real! This is for real! It is happening right now and you have to help me! You said you would help me! You have got to tell me what to do! I am really going crazy! I am going away and I will never come back!" I panicked. I had no idea what to do. I thought, My God, out of my naïveté and illusion of omnipotence I have given this woman the false belief that I could be with her and now that she needs me I am terrified and helpless. I ran down to the dining room and recognized a psychiatrist whom I had seen earlier and told him my terrible plight. I pleaded with him to come with me to see her. He was not interested.

He told me that he has to deal with situations like this all the time and had come to Esalen for the weekend to get away from work. However, I was able to convince him to come with me. He walked into the room, looked at her, and said, "Why are you doing this?" She muttered something incoherent in reply. He then turned to me and in a rational, objective manner said, "She'll be okay in ten to twelve hours or so. What you have to do is stay with her." I told him that was impossible and I went into the bathroom and threw up. He left, and I in my desperate state finally found an old hippie who lived in the woods nearby and had been on a hundred of these trips. I persuaded him to see her. He took one look at her and said, "Hey, what's happenin' here? Wow! Having a bad trip, huh? What's it like anyway?" As soon as I saw he was there with her, I ran back to my room. I was in a desperate state of anxiety. I couldn't eat or sleep. Finally, the next morning, having not slept all night, I went back to her cabin and looked in the window to see that she was all right. She was sleeping soundly. I took off as fast as I could. When I reached the city of Oakland, another panic attack came and I had to stop the car, get out, and lie on the grass at a park. I tried to grip the ground in an unconscious attempt to ground myself to keep from falling apart. I felt as if I were having a psychotic break. I felt as if I were losing myself, as if I were becoming disorganized.

I realized much later that my role of psychotherapist was part of my self organization. It functioned unconsciously as a way of containing my primitive anxiety and helping me to organize myself in such a way as to avoid the panic of this undifferentiated and unintegrated state. In this role I remained naive toward the depth of my own and others' primitive states, and, in addition, held on to the infantile illusion that I could help anyone without recognizing the serious limits to my abilities. What had happened in effect was that my role, based on these false assumptions, was exposed for what it was, and I panicked.

I mentioned that this role of psychotherapist was based on *naïveté*. I use this word rather than *innocence*. Naïveté comes from a shattered innocence. When a child's innocence is shattered, such as with physical abuse or sexual seduction by a parent, it is unbelievable to the child. She cannot process the depth of this kind of pain. She therefore is unable to allow it to penetrate her awareness. If she did so she would be completely devastated or driven mad. She therefore denies to herself that it is really happening. Or that it is so bad and assumes somehow she is responsible. She psychically and physically armors herself against the awareness of a tragedy that would destroy any hope of psychic survival. People and nations during World War II acted naively around the Nazi persecution of the Jews. Such atrocities are not possible to the rational mind. The abused child grows up to choose an abusing spouse because he cannot allow the original pain to be processed. Likewise, my naïveté as a therapist came out of the denial of my own abuse. I find this true for all of the therapists with whom I have worked. I realized also that my role of psychotherapist was based on an unconscious belief of infantile omnipotence. I had to feel as if I could help anyone. I could not acknowledge to myself or others the true limits of my knowledge and expertise. I did not realize that I was holding on to the irrational belief that if I could not help someone else, I could not help myself and if I could not help myself I was lost. This belief, of course, came out of my childhood where I felt totally helpless and terrified.

My defense against this unlivable state of helplessness and terror was to develop the illusion that I could help someone outside myself, namely, my mother. In this way I had a task that saved me from the feelings of impotence. When my mother and I colluded together that I should save her from her pain, I had laid the foundation for my role as a psychotherapist. I believe, along with Alice Miller that everyone who chooses this form of work, does so out of an unconscious need to protect himself from his own state of panic and disorganization and is therefore constantly in peril of returning to this state of being. Client and therapist are both forced to face these perils in the intimacy of the therapeutic relationship. To the degree this joint effort is successful, healing takes place; to the degree it is not, retraumatization may occur for both.

What must we as psychotherapists understand and experience in order to make the intimacy of the therapeutic relationship less perilous for ourselves and for our clients? The first thing is to understand the function of our role as therapist. Most of the therapists I have worked with over the past thirty years have come out of a background not dissimilar to that of a child in an alcoholic family. The child faces the chaos of his surroundings—the inconsistency, drunkenness, lack of personal contact—and experiences a basic terror of being alone and uncared for. She soon develops a form of psychic survival and self-affirmation by becoming attentive to her parents. She is still a child, but when they are drinking she becomes the little adult. This is the way she handles her primal terror of isolation. She finds a way to connect to the disorganized state of her parents in order not to experience the unbearable state of her own disorganization. This was my story with my mother.

In this way the child remains naive, which is a denial of fear, and holds on to the illusion of omnipotence, which is the denial of power-lessness. Beneath these illusions lie feelings of shame and self-punitive helplessness. Even these feelings are better than the alternative, which Winnicott called "unlivable states," where the person experiences the disintegration of the self. These constitute an extreme state of panic so severe that even psychosis is a way of living with the unlivable. We as therapists, no less than clients, enter into the cauldron of intimacy from which we had previously extracted ourselves with the unconscious commitment never to go there again and with the conviction that if in fact we were to fall into the cauldron again, we could not survive. Yet, because of the naïveté of our defenses, we are constantly exposing ourselves to this potential form of retraumatization with the illusion that we can handle it. We unconsciously invite back into our lives a relationship that is potentially harmful. The function of this is twofold: (1) to prove we can take it and not be broken, in other words, that our defenses work; and (2) to hope that this time we will be broken again, only to find another way to survive other than the way we were forced to find as a child, a way that we fight to hold onto our self expression but that in fact greatly limits it. Both therapist and client come to the intimacy of the therapeutic relationship with this unconscious agenda. To minimize the risks to both parties, the therapist is responsible for understanding the nature of his role and how it functions in his self system and for mustering resources both without and within to cope with the clients' challenges to that role. However, most therapists, like myself thirty years ago at Esalen, have not taken the time to understand the nature of the role they play and have not developed these resources for coping. So, when this role is challenged by the client—and challenged it must be—the therapist responds defensively and both thera-pist and client experience retraumatization.

Five years after my Esalen experience, I experienced a personal retraumatization with a client.

A couple was referred to me for marriage counseling. The referring psychologist said that the husband had a tendency toward violence. And in fact, while I was working with them, she had to call the police on at least one occasion because of his threats. I also knew that when this man had been fired from a job, he followed the boss around in his car and tried to force him off of the freeway. I also knew that his personal history included being tied to a post and beaten by his father. In the therapy sessions I confronted his anger and fear but never allowed myself to feel or own my own fear of his aggression.

When a therapist approaches such a client from the position of naïveté and omnipotence—from a denial of powerlessness and fear—he does not allow his own fear to penetrate his defenses. If he were to acknowledge his fear in regard to the client he would experience his own terror at the hands of his own parents and this would threaten his sense of self. Or, the fear he felt with the client might activate a defensive rage against the fear of annihilation and cause the therapist to be out of control in his countertransference reaction. It is just such denial of one's fear with the client that causes a therapist to risk physical harm. The paranoid and powerless client will have to impress the therapist with his presence even if it means physical violence.

Being unable to acknowledge to myself my fear or anger with this client made our relationship unreal. When I felt threatened by his actions, I would accommodate him rather than confront him. Soon he took advantage of this unreality and began to run up a bill. When I confronted him, he always had an excuse as to why he could not pay. At last, after he had been out of therapy for several months and still had not paid his bill, he decided he was not going to pay at all. Suddenly I was overcome with the feeling that he had taken something from me that was mine, that he owed me. It was now no longer just a bill to be paid but a deep personal loss. I became vulnerable and the facade of my denial of feeling was shattered. My own shame, anger, and fear surfaced. In essence I was talking to my mother and saying, "You owe me." Of course I could not win with her when I made a direct request. Now, I was in jeopardy. I had tried not to be, but my defenses led me back to my own beginning again.

I consulted a colleague who unwisely advised me to send the

bill to collection. Regrettably, I took his advice. The day the collection agency contacted my client, he called me and said, "You had better call off the collection agency or I will sue you. "

"*You* would sue *me?*"

"Yes."

"On what grounds?" I asked.

"Oh, I'll make something up. I'll say you made a pass at my wife. Believe me, it won't be worth your time and effort to collect this bill."

Now the tables had turned; I found myself in the role *he* had assumed as a child. Now *I* was needy, *I* was helpless, *I* was being threatened. But, we had now moved outside of the therapeutic context and into the legal system in order to face this core issue that I was unable to confront adequately in the therapy. I knew that this man was not to be taken lightly. Fortunately my survival fear emerged and I called the collection agency. They said they would withdraw their claim but that I would have to pay them a minimum fee for their efforts. Now my rage became full-blown. Not only was I humiliated. Not only had he won. But now I had to pay to call off the collectors. For the two or three years that followed, the feelings of rage, shame, and humiliation would flood through me at the very idea of facing this man again.

By being unable to acknowledge my fear and powerlessness, I had convinced myself that I could handle the issues that reminded me of my own abuse background. I thereby set up a trap that was sure to knock me out of my role as a therapist and throw me back into a state of panic. The first time this happened at Esalen, I ran with fear. The second time, with this violent client, I experienced a tremendous visceral rage that I had never before experienced and wanted to attack. Now, years later, I know that it was very important for me to feel that helpless rage because that is what he felt as a child and was unconsciously trying to resolve. But, by the time I got to feeling it, the therapy was totally out of hand and there was no way to work with it with him.

I have said that the therapist needs to understand the function of his role as therapist and how this is part of his self organization. I have also illustrated what happens when this role is challenged and the therapist faces the panic that is covered up by the role. To demonstrate how this role is created, I would like to direct your attention to Figure 3–1.

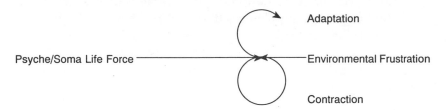

Figure 3–1. The role of the therapist.

The straight line in Figure 3–1 represents the life force of a person, in this case the therapist. When this life force, which represents the physical and psychological needs of the person, meets the environment and the environment is responsive enough, the person maintains a sense of integration and well being. An energetic equilibrium is maintained in the person and a unified sense of self emerges. When the environment is too frustrating, so that the natural expression of the person's needs is constantly denied, the person begins unconsciously to contract from extending himself further into the pain created by the frustration. This is like the pseudopods of an amoeba that extend from the nuclei and then are pricked by a pin. The pseudopod contracts and extends again. If the pricking continues long enough the pseudopods contract permanently and ossify so that the amoeba dies. When the human being reaches out and his basic needs constantly meet the pin pricks of the environment, a contraction takes place psychologically and physically, but then a unique accommodation begins to be made to live with, to absorb, or to overcome the pain of the rejection. This unique accommodation becomes an adaptive self.

Behind the contraction lies the cauldron of feelings associated with the shame, pain, helplessness, and despair that accompany not being able to find a way of self-expression in the world. Just as the child in the alcoholic family finds a way to survive by suppressing her own needs to meet the needs of others, so the adaptive self develops a "role" that others will respond to but that is really a defense against the panic and pain of her own unmet needs.

The client comes to see us because he is discovering that the adaptive role he once developed for survival is no longer rewarding. The price of survival over pleasure and self-expression has now become too great and yet he does not know another way. He is usually depressed but also anxious about any changes that might take place. At first the therapist and client are able to meet each other's narcissistic needs. The client learns what kind of responses the therapist needs and the therapist learns how to become attuned to the client. The two adaptive selves slowly develop an alliance.

However, a good therapist realizes that the adaptive role of the client is limiting the client's self expression and protecting him from the cauldron of emotions and unmet needs that lie beneath the surface of his adaptation. Slowly, using whatever approach is familiar to the therapist, he begins to help the client explore the function of the adaptive role and to investigate what lies beneath it. He invites the repressed feelings to emerge and be brought forth into the transference relationship established in the therapy. As these feelings emerge they are directed toward the adaptive role of the therapist and the therapist is now in jeopardy. After all, the therapist's role is there to protect the therapist from being overwhelmed by his own repressed feelings.

The response of the therapist to the challenge of his own adaptive self seems to follow the patterns set down by Karen Horney (1950) in her book, *Neurosis and Human Growth*. She described three neurotic patterns of relationships, namely, moving away, moving against, and moving toward the other person. The first time my adaptive role was challenged at Esalen I panicked and moved away. The second time, I became furious and wanted to move against and to destroy. But there is a third response, namely moving toward, which seems to apply to a great number of therapists with whom I work. I would like to describe this third way.

About ten years ago a therapist came to see me because he was suicidally depressed. He told me the story of having seen a woman client for eight sessions when he realized he had become too emotionally involved to continue to be her therapist. He said that during those few sessions, partly because of her and partly because of where he was in his life, he had touched the depth of the longing and loneliness that was beneath his facade as a therapist. This same loneliness and abandonment-depression was in the client, although the client was not aware of its depth. When his client touched these feelings in herself, she looked at him with eyes of idealization, much as a child would look at a parent. He knew this look was not for him as a person, since she really did not know him. But rather it was the look he knew was repressed in himself. Her eyes said to him, "You are loved and wanted and the answer to my abandonment." The therapist reported that he experienced the same abandonment feelings as she, but when she looked at him it was as if he felt the two of them could fuse together and neither one of them would have to experience the terror and grief around their loss. He said he knew it was not an adult relationship, that it was transference. But part of him wanted to believe her feelings were for him and he could somehow save them both.

He was in charge enough to know that he could not help her as her therapist while being so emotionally involved. He asked a colleague for a consultation. The result of the consultation made it clear that he should refer her to another therapist. But since this was the early 1970s, and since she was single and so was he, the advice was that he should go ahead and date her. Therapists now generally have an ethical guideline that says a therapist cannot see an ex-client for at least two years following termination. From my experience with this therapist and with others, my personal opinion is that it is a very wise rule.

So, he referred her and began dating her. During the first date he reported that he continued to relate to her as a therapist. Then on the second date he dropped his role and the deep longing that had been stimulated during the sessions emerged and he asked her to marry him. It was as if the two abandoned, lonely children in each other had found a way to merge. They were married, had two children, and divorced seven years later. During that time he discovered that she was an alcoholic. All of the unresolved rage that lay behind her abandonment-depression came out at him. He realized that he had married his alcoholic mother and was supposed to take care of her. He became more and more depressed until she left and he faced his suicidal feelings. These feelings came about because of his own unmet needs, but also because he knew he had betrayed her and her needs. In this way he felt as if he had acted toward her the way his mother had acted toward him.

We have illustrated three ways a therapist can respond to having his role challenged; moving away, moving against, and moving toward the client. The point is that beneath the adaptive role of the therapist lie all of her own unmet needs with all the emotions that were attached to them. Entering into the intimacy of the therapeutic relationship puts her in peril of having these needs emerge when her role is challenged. She must understand the function of her role and how it functions as a means of self organization. We now need to understand the function of having the role of the therapist challenged both from the point of view of the client and the therapist.

I would now like to discuss why the client has to challenge the role of the therapist, and why the therapist needs to have it challenged. Why does the client have to confront the role of the therapist? Why can't the therapist and client just have a nice time and agree to mutually support each other's narcissistic needs? I believe the first unconscious need the client has in challenging the therapist's role is to find out if it is *safe* to live and to experience the state of being the therapist is encouraging him to risk. The therapist is asking the client to live in a world where her narcissistic needs are not always going to be met. And some of her needs for merger will not be met at all. In this world she will feel helpless and unable to control the environment. This is a world that is frightening and unpredictable. The last time the client was in this world she was overcome with anxiety. This is the real world, and the client, in confronting the protective "role" of therapist, needs to know if the therapist can survive in it. In essence she is saying to the therapist, "You first. Let me see how you exist in this room with me without being in control of the relationship; where I am not rewarding you in your role in the manner to which you have become accustomed. How do you live with your vulnerability with me? How do you live with your narcissistic emptiness and rage at me when I withdraw from you or no longer follow your rules? Can you exist and function where you are asking me to go? Can you continue to make contact with me when you no longer have your 'role' to rely on, when you are as unmasked as I am?"

To test this question, the client must do to us what was done to him as a child. He must act out his own parents' judgment on us and see if we can survive and how we survive in order to make it safe for him to risk being in the real world again. If we fail by moving away, against, or toward him, then he feels there is no hope for him and the therapy ends by bogging down or in acting out behavior, suicidal depression, or recriminations leading to law suits. However, if the therapist is able to go where he has been helping the client to go, and from that place invites the client to join him, the client must now face the terror of risking a real relationship in a real world. Often the client does not know which is worse, to have the therapist fail, so that while he is disappointed, he is relieved and now has an excuse not to risk. Or, to have the therapist come through this trial by fire and be present for him so that he has no excuse for not risking and reaching for what he has been asking. The role of the therapist must be challenged so the client can feel safe to risk experiencing his terror and helplessness again and this time, with the therapist's help, since he has been there, to recover a part of the self that had been lost.

The second reason for clients to challenge the role of the therapist is to find out if they are really chosen. It is one thing to relate to clients when they are being responsive to our empathic listening. But what happens, they want to know, when they are difficult and are no longer rewarding us the way they did their parents in order to be liked? They are consciously or unconsciously asking, "Will you still want to be with me when I am difficult?" And, every person I have ever worked with fears of course you won't. They further fear that the therapist is going to be disgusted with them, but will never tell them. That the two of them will live a lie just as they both did in their original families. That in some way the true negativity and resentments that are created in the relationship will not be explored so that the client will not feel chosen for being who she is. That the therapist will hide behind his therapeutic mask of professionalism and the client will never experience true acceptance, just empathic reflection.

I recall a lecturer on self psychology who said that the therapist should slightly idealize the patient, that is, to convey to the patient her right to have the therapist be available for her in the manner in which she needs. When I heard this, I started to laugh because I thought of one of my therapists in the past slightly idealizing me in this way and I could not imagine it. He was so caught up in idealizing himself that there was no room for me. Then I began to feel sad. I thought about what it would have been like for him to say to me, "You know, Bob, you are trying to communicate something to me and I am just not getting it. I really want you to have the experience of being understood and I am failing. I need your help. You are not bad for needing what I cannot give, it is I who must look at myself and discover what I need to face in order to hear you." And, even though I cannot imagine this kind of response, I know if it were to happen, even today, years later, I would begin to cry and feel as if in fact I were being seen and chosen for me, not for the good client I was. Fortunately, I eventually did have a woman therapist who was able to convey to me this kind of acceptance. I needed to know that I made a difference to her; that she would miss me if I were depressed and withdrew. The client needs to challenge the role of the therapist in order to feel chosen for herself, warts and all.

The third reason the client needs to challenge the role of the therapist is to recover the feeling of omnipotence. This is not the illusion of omnipotence of which I spoke at the beginning of this chapter. That illusion is actually a defense against feeling the loss of power in a self-object relationship. When the therapist chooses the client for himself, and acknowledges that the difficulty in the therapeutic alliance is due to his own inability to attune properly to the needs of the client, then the client recovers what Winnicott feels is the essential ingredient in the development and recovery of a self, namely omnipotence within the therapeutic relationship. Winnicott says that the client needs the experience of being able to tolerate empathic failures in the therapeutic relationship by seeing them as failures on the therapist's part. This leaves him with the essential ingredient for self development that was missing as a child. When the client was a child, he was made to feel inadequate for needing what could not be provided. Now, instead of blaming himself, he can acknowledge the limits to finding his needs being met in the countertransference of the therapist.

This kind of relationship, which reinforces the feelings of omnipotence, functions to help the client accept reality and the limits of the environment to meet his needs without feelings of shame and blame. When this does not happen developmentally, the child holds on to the *illusion* of omnipotence in his adult life. When a child feels toward a parent, "You really *have* to love me, don't you? You really don't have a choice, do you?" he experiences the "power" of the bonding experience and can let go of the illusion of power and control because he feels safe. The commitment of the parent gives the child the freedom to feel omnipotent at a crucial time in his self development. This power can later be surrendered to reality. If the child never experienced the power of feeling safe *with* the love object, he maintains the illusion of power *over* the object to protect himself from the fears of abandonment and annihilation. This experience of omnipotence must be regained and surrendered in the therapeutic relationship. This can only be done through challenging the adaptive role of the therapist and thereby discovering the true nature of the relationship and the commitment of the therapist to the client and to the relationship.

I have been considering the function for the client of challenging the role of the therapist. What is the function of this challenge for the therapist? That is, why does the therapist need her role challenged? The first reason is that the therapist needs her role challenged in order for her to recover her true self. Her authentic self expression and self realization was sacrificed as a child for the role of therapist. This role provided certain narcissistic supplies that we have already discussed, but it also becomes a prison from which the therapist, at least unconsciously, wishes to be released. We cannot release ourselves, but perhaps a client will see the phoniness in this role, the inauthenticity. Or perhaps the client will take us seriously enough to demand more than we can give. At this time our underlying needs emerge and we have a chance to recover our true self within this relationship. So, like the country and western song that says, "If you won't leave me, I'll find somebody who will," we as therapists unconsciously say, if you won't confront me and this adaptive role I have taken, I will find someone who will. I need to recover my self authenticity.

Second, just as the client challenges the role of the therapist in order to discover if in fact she is really chosen, so the therapist likewise needs the experience of feeling that her authentic self is chosen by the client. In other words the therapist needs to have a validation of her person that affirms her self-esteem. The therapist's true self-esteem was diminished in her own childhood and replaced by her role. She now needs to have this sense of personal value reaffirmed. Just as the client feels that if she did not give the therapist the responses she needs and wants she will not be chosen, the therapist likewise feels that without her role she has nothing to offer and no one would want to see her or find it meaningful to relate to her, much less to pay her. A client once said to me, "You have given me a lot of help over the years. And the therapy has worked, in spite of what you have said." The healing in any therapy does not take place until after the client is disappointed and the therapist feels she has nothing to offer. At last they come together to discover each other without the adaptive selves interfering. It is very difficult for a therapist to truly believe that just her accepting presence with the client is a healing force. The therapist needs her role challenged in order to recover her lost self-esteem and to feel valued for her presence as a person. This is a lesson that must be learned over and over again.

The third important reason why the therapist needs his role challenged is to have the experience of living through being the bad parent and being forgiven. As therapists, we begin our journey thinking we will be to others the good parent that we never had. What happens eventually is that we respond to a client in the same way our parents responded to us. When this happens our illusions about ourselves are challenged and we feel exposed.

I had a client that I worked with for several years. We came to a place in our therapy where she felt she wanted to stop. We seemed to be at an impasse. She needed something that I could not give and we both felt frustrated. I knew the therapy was unfinished, but there was some relief in her decision. She came back about three years later and we began our sessions again. At one point, shortly after we had begun the second time, she painfully said to me, "You let me go." What she meant was that I had not tried to stop her when she previously wanted to leave. That in some way she had become too much for me and I did not fight for our relationship. I simply let her go. I knew exactly what she meant. Fortunately, I was able to stay with myself and say to her, "You're right. I did." She then broke into an overwhelming abandonment cry. At that moment when she said, "You let me go," and I said, "Yes, I did," I was owning to the client what my mother could never own to me. I wanted to say to my mother, "You didn't really want me. I was a bother to you and you let me go. You were not bonded to me. You didn't make an effort to stay with me." Now *I* was the bad mother. The one who let her go, who did not make the effort to stay connected to her and as I listened to her cry I knew it was also mine. I had to sit there without excuse and wait to see if she could forgive me and we could connect again.

This experience was particularly powerful for me. I was once asked what my mother could do to make up to me for having left me. I replied without hesitation that the only thing she could do was commit suicide and leave a note acknowledging what a terrible thing she had done in having me and not being able to bond with me. I was now faced with the tragic awareness of having done to the child in the client what had been done to me. But I also knew I cared about her and wanted to be able if possible to reconnect and to continue on in the therapy. I also knew it was up to her. She cried her cry and mine and our reconnection was a healing force for both of us. I did not have to kill myself and she did not have to stay locked in her anger and grief. In accepting the client's forgiveness and my reality of being an imperfect parent, I took another giant step toward my own healing. The therapist role needs to be challenged so the therapist can accept his human limitations and find forgiveness.

In summary, effective psychotherapy involves an intimate relationship in which both client and therapist are in peril. The peril is in being open authentically to each other to the degree that each faces potential retraumatization at the other's hands. The client must challenge the "role" of the therapist in order to feel safe, chosen, and back in control of his life. The therapist needs his role challenged in order to recover his true self, to affirm his self-esteem as a person, and to accept his limits as a good parent. This is not an easy task, and often the therapist, while unconsciously wanting and needing the confrontation when it comes, responds defensively by moving away, against, or toward the client. The "role" of the therapist functions as a form of self organization and beneath this role lie all of the unmet needs and emotions of a frightened and disorganized child. Yet the therapist is responsible for having worked enough with these unmet needs to be able to invite the client where he needs to go. But what kinds of experiences must a therapist have in order to recover sufficiently from his own woundedness to be available for the pain of the client? What is the healing process for the therapist? This is the topic of chapter seven.

4

The Seduction of the Innocent Therapist

O. Brandt Caudill, Jr.

RECENT TRENDS IN THERAPIST LIABILITY LITIGATION

Repressed memories are a surprisingly recent focus of litigation against therapists. I have been defending therapists for fourteen years, but the first repressed memory case was two and a half years ago. There were virtually no suits against therapists until after the *Tarasoff* decision in 1976. That was the case that woke the plaintiff's bar to the potential for suing therapists.

While I was in law school in 1976, I wrote a paper on sex with patients. At that time there were only six cases reported nationwide. Since then, I personally have handled over seventy cases claiming sexual misconduct in the last ten years. That works out to about seven a year, just for me. The 1980s was the period of sexual malpractice litigation at all levels—ethics committees, civil suits, and administrative law. Malpractice attorneys anticipated that litigation during the 1990s would deal primarily with dual-relationship suits. Nobody anticipated repressed memory litigation, but it has so far dwarfed dual-relationship lawsuits. The figures put out by the American Professional Agency (the broker for American Home Assurance Company, a major insurer of therapists) show that 19 percent of the lawsuits they received as of 1994 were sexual malpractice lawsuits, which accounted for 48.8 percent of settlement dollars. In the year 1993–94 16 percent of the new claims received by the American Professional Agency were repressed-memory claims. We now expect that during the 1990s repressed memory will come to account for about 15 percent of the cases, and 40 percent of settlement dollars. The amount of money involved will probably exceed $250 million over the next ten years. This area is clearly going to dominate professional practice in the 1990s, and the pace is picking up. I spoke with one plaintiff's attorney recently who asserted he has forty active lawsuits against therapists in California that are repressed-memory lawsuits.

I was fortunate enough to be present for two days of testimony of the Ramona trial. I listened to Gary Ramona's testimony, and I listened to the testimony of one of the experts. There are two issues in that case that have nationwide implications. The first is, did the defendants owe any duty to Gary Ramona? The traditional theory has been that therapists only owe a duty to patients, unless the patient actually threatens somebody and then they have a duty to warn that person. The duty to warn exception was announced in the *Tarasoff* case and codified in civil code 43.92. In *Swartz v. the Regents of the University of California*, a therapist was sued because the man's wife abducted their child, who was in therapy with the psychologist. He sued the psychologist, accusing the psychologist of conspiring with his wife to abduct their child. The Court of Appeals concluded the father was not the patient, even though he was paying for the therapy. The Ramona case and the other repressed-memory cases are contending that *there is a duty to third parties if they are likely to be identified as targets of abuse allegations*. Out-of-state cases finding such a duty to third parties include *Sullivan v. Cheshier* and *Montoya v. Bebensee*.

The problem for therapists is how to define the scope of those involved in each patient's case. Is it all family members? What if the person that allegedly was the abuser is not a family member but a neighbor? Does the therapist also owe a duty to that person? There is, at present, no definition of the scope of the duty, but there is an active attempt to find precedents. There have been two such decisions to date: *Sullivan v. Cheshier* and *Montoya v. Bebensee*. Further, some people are promoting a law that would create a specific duty to third parties and would specifically allow third parties to sue therapists. In addition, the new statute would provide criminal penalties if a therapist implanted memories of abuse. Moreover, the new statute would outlaw specific therapy techniques and dictate how therapy is conducted.

The second issue in the Ramona case that is of importance here is the contention that there is a nationwide standard of care in how therapy is rendered. That is not, and has never been, the law in California, nor do I believe it is elsewhere. California law says you are only required to comply with the standard of practice in your local community—whatever that may be. An expert in the Ramona case testified to a national standard of care. It may not be a coincidence that the expert was not licensed in California and could not testify to what the local standard of care was because he never practiced there. Plaintiffs want a nationwide standard of care so that anybody around the country can testify to it.

The False Memory Syndrome Foundation has announced that there are up to 15,000 families that may pursue litigation although there has been no corroboration of this number. One of the facts that gets glossed over is that a number of mental health professionals who are affiliated with the False Memory Syndrome Foundation will end up being experts in these lawsuits and stand to benefit from hundreds of thousands of dollars in expert fees. Thus, the issue of economic bias on the part of the experts must be explored.

There is clearly a very active repressed-memory publishing industry and a very active repressed-memory talk show circuit. In 1993 our computer database had 99 newspaper and magazine articles on the false memory syndrome since 1991. On March 21, 1995 there were 593 articles.

I have analogized this to a civil war. It is in fact a very uncivil war. The impact of the repressed memory war is much greater because it is a war within families, a war that is on the evening news, a war that is fought in the minds of the participants. There is a sensationalism factor here that I have not seen with any other issue within my professional practice. Sex with patients was never as sensationalized as this, although individual cases might have had scandalous overtones or bizarre details. However, there was never a serious professional controversy about whether or not sex with patients was unethical. So we have to ask, "What is really going on here?" There is no clear and immediate answer, but targeting therapists seems to be a strategy that originated with the McMartin preschool case. That was the first well-known case to focus on attacking therapists, and specifically on how therapists ask questions of child patients.

One problem with repressed-memory cases is that there is a large-scale theoretical dispute over whether the phenomenon exists. One school of thought asserts that repressed memory is always valid, and the false memory syndrome school asserts that there is no such thing as repressed memory. Most professionals, in my experience, fall in the middle of the dispute. They believe repressed memory can happen in some cases, and that implantation can also happen. However, most professionals want to know the facts of the particular case, including the techniques used, before drawing a conclusion. This is a battle that is carried on with almost religious fervor. The False Memory Syndrome Foundation's members deny that any type of repressed memory is scientifically verifiable. For example, Dr. Richard Ofshe, professor of sociology at the University of California, Berkeley, has taken the position that what he calls "robust repression" does not occur (Ofshe and Watters 1994). The other end of the spectrum is represented by therapists who routinely treat incest and incest survivors. They believe that any attempt to question the validity of any repressed memory impugns victims and perpetrates additional abuse.

My law office has seen several kinds of repressed-memory lawsuits. We have seen the standard Ramona approach, which is where the person accused sues the therapist. We call those "alleged abuser suits." Then we see "retractor suits," where the patient originally believes he or she suffered from repressed memories, then takes the opposite position, denies being abused, and sues the therapist for implanting the memories that were believed at one point.

A third category that is currently emerging is where the patient goes to a therapist for therapy that eventually terminates, and then goes to a second therapist and in that therapy recovers memories of abuse by the preceding therapist. In other words, instead of repressing child sexual abuse, the patient is claiming to have repressed what happened in prior therapy as an adult. These cases are among the most questionable repressed-memory cases. Our office has seen five such cases to date.

ESTABLISHING A STANDARD OF CARE

The therapist must be aware of both sides of the story. The therapist must read professional articles on both sides of the dispute, no matter what his or her personal view is. Because there is a dispute among professionals, the individual therapist cannot decide for him- or herself which side is right. The therapist must be educated on both sides and must be prepared to educate patients as to both sides. If the therapist chooses to give patients literature, it must be balanced literature, or the therapist may be accused of pushing one side or the other.

Dr. Elizabeth Loftus's (1993) article, "The Reality of Repressed Memories," was the first definitive statement that supports the False Memory Syndrome Foundation's viewpoint. On the other side is an issue of the *Journal of Psychology and Theology* edited by Martha Rogers (1992) that puts forth a spectrum of viewpoints about this issue. It presents people who very strenuously believe in repressed memory and satanic abuse. A more balanced psychodynamic account of repressed memory is Hedges's (1994) *Remembering, Repeating, and Working Through Childhood Trauma.* Other books on the subject are Dr. Lenore Terr's (1994) *Unchained Memories,* Dr. Michael Yapko's (1994) *Suggestions of Abuse,* Lawrence Wright's (1994) *Remembering Satan,* Dr. Elizabeth Loftus and Katherine Ketcham's (1994) *The Myth of Repressed Memory,* Margaret Smith's (1993) *Ritual Abuse,* Dr. Judith Herman's (1981) *Father–Daughter Incest,* and Renee Fredrickson's (1992) *Repressed Memories.*

Because issues involving recovered memories and satanic ritual abuse are often mixed together, the therapist needs to be conscious of the dispute about satanic abuse as well. The problem is not the existence of satanists, because the existence of satanists is readily verifiable. We have accounts by Richard Ramirez, "The Night-Stalker" and Anton LeVey, author of *The Satanic Bible* and a leader of the Church of Satan. There was an incident in Matamoros, Mexico a few years ago in which some Mexicans who were in a cult were kidnapping and killing Texas tourists. There has been no substantial proof of cults engaging in child sexual abuse or child dismemberment that has been verified by any reported appellate decision.

A key article in the area of satanic abuse is "Investigator's Guide to Allegations of 'Ritual' Child Abuse," by Ken Lanning (1992), who has been with the F.B.I. investigating reports of cult abuse for more than 25 years. His job is to be a resource person for law enforcement throughout the country. His view is that it is possible that there are satanic child abuse rings on a limited scale, but he has never seen one in the thousands of reported cases. Does that mean it never happens? No, it does not. But the therapist must be cognizant of Lanning's view when approaching these cases, particularly if the therapist comes from a background of abuse and may be biased. An interesting counterpoint to Lanning's article is a series of articles by psychotherapists attesting to their belief in cult abuse in a special issue of *The Journal of Psychohistory* (Spring 1994) entitled, "Cult Abuse of Children: Witch Hunt or Reality?"

The therapist who believes that he or she may have been a victim of ritual satanic abuse needs to give serious thought as to how wise it is to treat somebody complaining of similar abuse, because in any litigation the therapist's background and potential biases will be an issue. Historically, the therapist's own therapy has not been discoverable in litigation. In Texas the *Cheatham v. Rogers* decision held that somebody who is accused of child abuse can obtain the therapist's personal therapy records. That decision is contrary to the law in most jurisdictions, including California, but it is part of a general trend as plaintiffs are targeting the therapist.

Another set of issues in the standard of care is how a therapist diagnoses psychological problems. In defending therapists, I periodically see some unusually quick diagnoses. For example, a patient may say, "I have a phobia of cigarettes," and the therapist may say, "You must have been orally sexually abused." Clearly such a diagnosis would be questionable without other information indicating sexual abuse. If the therapist uses accepted methods of arriving at conclusions, an incorrect conclusion is not necessarily negligent. The standard of care focuses on the thought process and the method involved in arriving at conclusions, not necessarily on the results. To put it another way, because no one is perfect, the standard of care does not and cannot require perfection. It allows mistakes in judgment, if you use an accepted process to collect data and arrive at conclusions. The standard of care is a "C" student standard based on the average professional and does not require the therapist to be brilliant. What is important is *how* the therapist arrives at his or her decisions. Leaping precipitously to a decision can be negligent, but forming the same conclusion after reviewing the literature, observing the patient's symptoms, obtaining peer consults, and performing the appropriate steps to arrive at a diagnosis is not.

It is essential that therapists in all therapy, but especially regarding repressed memories, make a concerted effort to take notes. This has been an area of conflict between therapists and the lawyers defending them for years. I hope it has been put to rest by the American Psychological Association's recent policy statement specifically requiring note taking, which has established a national standard of care that all therapists should be aware of. As a practical matter, there are two reasons for note taking in repressed-memory cases: first, for the therapist's own protection, which I, as a defense lawyer, am always biased in favor of; and second, because when the repressed-memory allegations are asserted against a third party, the therapist's records are going to be scrutinized intently, specifically to be sure (a) that they show the progress of therapy, (b) that they were prepared contemporaneously and not at a later time, and (c) that there is some correlation between the notes and the billing records. In many of the cases I see in my office there is only a minimal correlation between the date services are billed and the date of notes in the file. A plaintiff's attorney will take the billing records, compare them with the notes, find the discrepancies, and ask the therapist why the notes don't correlate with the bill. The usual answer, and I have no reason to doubt it is true, is that the therapist doesn't do the billing. Accurate notes are essential when the therapist enters a litigous area such as repressed-memory therapy.

In a case I was recently defending the plaintiff testified that she had been a victim of childhood sexual abuse by her father, who had raped her, buried her alive in a box, and done all kinds of other truly heinous things to her. We learned that the father had a letter from his daughter from years before where she said that when she was a teenager he had accidentally bumped her breast and it triggered in her sexual fantasies about him. The fact he had the letter was critical in showing that the accusations of abuse were distorted.

Hedges (1994b) argues that in many, if not most, instances of memories recovered in psychotherapy, people are taking as literally true matters that are best viewed as psychological metaphors for otherwise unrememberable traumas. People whose memories are inaccurate are not lying in the usual sense of the word. What they believe is a psychological construction or metaphor for something else, some other trauma that indeed happened but cannot be remembered accurately. However, no one ever gets sued in a complaint that says, "Oh, and metaphorically, you're accused of . . ." One is either accused of negligence or one is not. It is important to understand that a metaphor can lead people to a false conclusion.

COMMON RISKS FOR THERAPISTS

The single biggest risk occurs when a therapist goes from being a therapist to being an investigator. I see this happening in a lot of repressed-memory and satanic-abuse cases. Therapists lose their objectivity and begin going with the patient to graveyards to check on where bodies are buried. They go to old homes to see if it is physically possible for abuse to have occurred there. Other kinds of investigative activities occur that are geared to determining when, where, and what type of abuse did or did not occur. A recent California case held that while therapists may have protection under the standard of care for therapy, they don't have protection for action as investigators (*James W. v. Superior Court*). Every case I have seen where investigation comes in, it creates serious problems for the therapist. When therapists lose sight of their professional role, their liability increases.

The second risk involves hypnosis. Therapists must be extraordinarily cautious in the use of hypnosis because of its suggestive power and its potential for impairing a patient's ability to be a witness. When a patient is likely to be in litigation, and the therapist uses hypnosis incompetently, it may preclude the patient from being a witness in a viable and legitimate criminal prosecution. Therapists using hypnosis need to be familiar with judicial decisions and the Evidence Code in their jurisdiction regarding how to keep the patient's testimony from being thrown out of court. This usually means having a taped record of their prehypnosis memory, written notes before the session, a tape, preferably video, of the actual session, and follow-up notes.

Another area of risk is the use of experimental or unusual treatment techniques, such as use of crystals, use of spirit guides, and energy balancing. It is very difficult to explain to judges and jurors how techniques such as shamanistic journeys, astrological consultations, body techniques, and spiritual healing fit within the standard of care. A technique can be used if it is practiced by a significant minority of therapists, but a therapist must carefully explain the technique and obtain a clear, informed consent for its use (see *Mathews v. Morrissey*).

Another sign of risky therapist overinvolvement is the therapist's belief that because the cult is out to get the patient, the cult is also out to get the therapist. At that point the therapist needs consultation and needs to give serious thought to getting out of the case because he or she has likely personalized it to the point that objectivity is effectively lost.

Patients may say, "I don't want you to keep notes because the cult is going to break into your office and steal them." The only proper therapist response is, "No. I am legally required to keep notes." The therapist cannot predict whether this patient is going to recant two years later and turn around and sue the therapist for implanting the memories. If there is an implantation suit, the first issue that is going to be considered is who raised the question of abuse first. If the patient raised it before therapy began, the therapist is more likely to be found not negligent. If the issue came up for the first time in therapy, then the question becomes, Who raised it first in therapy, and how? If therapists don't have a documented way of answering that question it can be very difficult to get out of that litigation.

Another risk area involves professional boundaries. Repressed-memory/cult-type cases call for extraordinary time and availability. This may lead to what becomes perceived as boundary violations. It almost always leads to what I call the "feet of clay" syndrome, which is where the therapist initially takes such heroic, extraordinary measures that the patient idealizes him or her. However, the therapist can't maintain that level of involvement and the patient then feels abandoned and neglected. These patients often want the therapist to drop everything and run over to their house at all hours of the day and night because some new memory has come out that is particularly terrifying. Despite the compelling nature of the plea, it is important that the therapist draw the line and say something to the effect of: "I know it is terrible, but you must find a way to bring it up in a therapy hour. We can schedule more therapy time if you need it, but I can't come to your house." Those limits are extremely important because many of the cases we see end up with those kind of boundaries being violated. When a patient is reporting a horrific event the therapist's natural reaction is to somehow rescue him or her. By doing so the therapist can create problems for both parties: there is a heightening of the patient's expectation that the therapist will be available in extraordinary and boundaryless ways, and the therapist's objectivity is lost and boundaries are violated.

Another risk is that these cases can become utterly fascinating to the therapist. The therapist starts reading literature the patient brings in. I suggest the therapist read *everything*, not just what the patient provides. Therapists may go to meetings and conferences with patients to learn more about satanic abuse, multiple personality disorder, or related issues.

Therapists must also be aware of the power for certain people in being victims. It is a way for them to excuse anything and everything. Victimization, whether real or perceived, can create a bond of sisterhood or brotherhood with other people who have similar problems in various lay support groups. When a person is labeled as a certain kind of victim, he or she can get tremendous emotional support they wouldn't otherwise have as just an ordinary neurotic. Every time I've seen a really questionable case of any type, the plaintiff patient has been in some type of lay support group. Often the groups encourage the patient to file a lawsuit against an alleged abuser. Patients can get fired up by group support and they go charging off often without an appreciation of the emotional impact of litigation on them and others. Another phenomenon that occurs is the patient goes to a group and absorbs elements of other group members' stories into his or her story. It then becomes extremely difficult to determine which parts of the story are the patient's. This kind of contamination exacerbates treatment and creates difficulties in determining what the patient actually experienced.

THE SEDUCTION OF THE INNOCENT THERAPIST

In the area of sexual relationships between therapists and present or former patients, someone is always asking about the "true-love exception." A therapist says, "But it wasn't really a violation because it was true love." There is no exception in the statute for "true love." In a 1991 American Psychiatric Association survey of psychiatrists, approximately 30 percent said it was acceptable to terminate and start a relationship if it was true love (Herman, Gartrell, Olarte, et al. 1987). There is an amazing power in this concept of true love—that one's missing half is somehow suddenly found and serves to justify the two lovers together defying fate. Call me skeptical, but most times these sudden passionate attractions don't last more than six months, so it seems to me that this kind of true love has a short half-life. However, the therapist's career that used to have a life of twenty or more years is now down to about two and a half. It is very important for therapists to understand that no matter how strong the feeling, there is an immediate need to talk to a peer or get some type of consultative feedback. An interesting article on post-termination sexual relationships is the 1991 one by Paul Applebaum, M.D. and Linda Jorgensen. In this regard an excellent book to help understand these feelings is *Sexual Feelings in Psychotherapy* (Pope et al. 1993). Based on my experience, I can report that too often what we are talking about is the seduction of the innocent therapist, not a predatory sexual involvement by a therapist.

Most of the cases that we see involve a situation of a good therapist in a bad circumstance: somebody who is generally competent and ethical, who may be in a life crisis, and who encounters a particularly seductive or manipulative patient. Sometimes the seductive or manipulative patient is also a therapist, who knows all the ethical rules, and who knows how a therapist can be set up. In my personal experience, there are few predatory therapists and most of them have been removed from the profession. The vast majority of sexual misconduct cases today involve the seduction of the innocent therapist.

FALSE ACCUSATIONS AGAINST THERAPISTS

There are two types of false accusations. There is the deliberately false accusation, which is, in one sense, easy to defend because the person who is lying knows he or she is lying. It is just a question of proving the patient wrong. We prove it through minutiae. The patient says something happened on the fourth of July, at a certain location, and we check everything that happened that day at that location.

The difficult situation is the second type of false accusation where the patient reports a sexual experience with a therapist that is not true, but which the patient believes wholeheartedly. I have seen many of these cases. One woman said she had sex with my client in Los Angeles, California, on a certain date. Her account was detailed, passionate, and compelling. In deposition I asked if she was positive it was that date. She was firm that it could be no other date. My client was in London that week, the week before, the week after. We had his wife as a witness. We had his passport. We had the London hotel receipt. However, if I had just listened to her, I would have believed her, because she wasn't lying, she believed it was true.

Another woman alleged that her therapist engaged in sexual misconduct with her. In taking her deposition I asked what he did. She replied that she was having a hard time expressing her anger, so he had her get down on her knees. I asked her what happened next? She said, "Well, he told me to push against his hands." I asked, "Were you both fully clothed?" She said, "Yes, we were both fully clothed." "What happened next?" She said, "It was the most overwhelming sexual experience of my life." I thought I must have missed something. I said, "You were both fully clothed?" "Yes, we were both fully clothed." "The only body parts that touched were the hands?" "Yes." In her view, that was the most powerful sexual experience of her life. It seems to me that we may have a major problem exposed by this single situation. Many people are so overwhelmed by the intensity and intimacy of the therapeutic relationship that they experience an otherwise inconsequential gesture or statement as a full-fledged romance or romantic intrusion. Obviously their current life context as well as their relational history are involved in how they perceive such events.

No matter what a therapist thinks, there is no reasonable likelihood that a sexual liaison with a patient will be legal or turn into a long-term relationship. The therapist may think there are some exceptions to that rule, but the enormous risks are simply not worth it. It can lead to loss of the therapist's license to practice, criminal charges, and civil suits, not to mention destruction of the therapist's reputation, marriage, and livelihood.

5

The Therapist's Response to Accusation: How to Avoid Complaints and Suits[1]

Virginia Wink Hilton

It is my observation that, more often than not, a client's intention to sue or file a complaint does not begin with the experience of an ethical violation; it begins after the client has confronted the therapist about the violation and has found the response unsatisfying. I am therefore tempted to go so far as to say that suits and complaints are more related to the way the therapist responds to accusations than to the violation itself.

I have noticed that when therapists are confronted by wounded clients their response seems to fit a certain pattern that is almost predictable. It has three parts.

The first response to an accusation is often *denial*: "I didn't do it." "It couldn't have happened that way." Or "I don't remember." The accused often seems quite genuinely shocked. Why does this happen?

---

1. This chapter was published under the title "When We Are Accused," in the *Journal of Bioenergenic Analysis* Vol. 5 No. 2, 1993.

The accusation, after all, comes from the perspective of the client's experience. The therapist's experience of the event may indeed have been very different. The incident may have carried far less significance or had a different meaning to the therapist. And when this is so it probably indicates some degree of an empathic disjunction or failure.

Second, the therapist becomes *defensive*: "That was twenty years ago!" "I didn't know any better." "Everyone was doing it." "I did the best I knew how." Or "That wasn't a part of my training." It seems it is almost impossible for the therapist not to defend or explain his or her actions.

Third, the response includes *blame*: "She was seductive." "He came on strong." Or "She knew what she was doing."

Denial, defensiveness, and blame. It has been amazing to me to notice just how frequently these three feeling-responses are evoked when a therapist is accused of some manner of abuse, misconduct, or incompetence. Most therapists are sincerely dedicated to the task of being good-enough professionals or parent figures, and any accusation that one has fallen short, let alone perpetrated an abuse, cuts right through to the personal as well as the professional quick.

As I became aware of the frequency of this response pattern—denial, defensiveness, and blame—in response to *serious* accusations, I began to watch for its appearance in lesser confrontations. When a client—or for that matter a spouse or a child—would say to me, in effect, "You did something wrong," or "You didn't give me what I needed," I observed that the same three feelings were evoked: "It didn't happen that way." "I did everything I possibly could." Or "You didn't ask for what you wanted." The very first knee-jerk response was some degree of denial, inevitably followed by an almost irrepressible defense of my behavior, and finally at least the impulse to blame, even if subtly or indirectly. So I am pointing to a response pattern that I believe to be quite common to all human relationships when confrontation takes place.

What is the effect upon the wounded client of this almost inevitable pattern? First and foremost, when the response is denial, defensiveness, and blame, *he or she feels unheard.* Often the client will verbalize it this way: "My therapist just didn't get it." And when the issue is an ethical violation and the client feels the therapist doesn't "get it," doesn't understand, doesn't comprehend what is being communicated, then the wounding is compounded. And often it is at *this* point that what might possibly have been a continuation of the healing process gets derailed, and the confrontation escalates to become a complaint or a suit.

What does the client want from the therapist? What most wounded clients want is two things: First, *they want to know that the therapist knows and understands how deeply they were wounded.* Frequently the wounding is a replication of an early, primary wound, and the re-wounding is not only devastating but may affect many aspects of their life—their ability to trust, their self-esteem, their marriage, their friendships, their work. Second, *they want to feel assured that the same thing won't happen again to them or to someone else.*

I have heard injured clients say something like this, following a confrontation with the therapist: "He said all the right words but I still feel he's defending himself. I'm not convinced he really gets it." Saying all the right words is definitely not enough. Why is it so hard for us therapists to "get it"?

Because of the litigious environment these days, we are all edgy in the face of accusations. But it's also quite difficult not to feel defensive, particularly when the accusation comes as a surprise, or from a client with whom we have struggled and worked and given of our energy and our insight. Not infrequently it comes from a person whose issues are complex, who has demanded a lot of time and attention, and about whom we have agonized and struggled. We may have felt we have done the best we knew how. Under these circumstances it is extremely painful and difficult to have that person telling us that we have been a bad parent. It is not hard to understand how any one of us could fall into denying, defending, and even blaming.

But there is also a much deeper explanation. When faced with a charge of abuse, chances are the confrontation puts the therapist in touch with his/her own core wound. By "core wound" I am referring to those deep and early traumas around which we have had to construct elaborate and effective defenses in order to assure emotional safety or psychological survival. Much of our behavior is an unconscious attempt to heal those wounds. And very likely the therapist was attempting to do just that by engaging in the very behavior that was experienced as abusive by the client. Peter Rutter (1989) suggests that the therapist who has sex with a client is unconsciously trying to heal his or her own sexual wound. Another example: The therapist who crosses boundaries and touches a client excessively or inappropriately may be acting out his or her own deep unconscious need for nurturance.

When a therapist's personal wound is touched through an accusation, the person's character(istic) defense will be activated. For example, when the client says to the therapist, "The way you touched me didn't feel appropriate," the therapist will instinctively respond the way he has always defended against his nurturing needs: "I don't need you; I'll never let myself need anyone." Then the jaw tightens, and the person becomes cool and distant.

In a group setting a woman accuses a former teacher of wounding her by inviting her into an intimate relationship. He responds with the "facts": "I wasn't your teacher at the time. It was only a brief encounter. You were fully aware of the nature of the situation." The woman is unrelenting in her accusation, the man is cold, unyielding, and quietly angry. He feels victimized. The two remain locked in their positions with no resolution seemingly possible. After lengthy work the man finally is able to acknowledge that the character defense that has been elicited is, "I'll never let you win." To acknowledge her feelings, and thus to acknowledge an error on his part is to let her "win," which would leave him feeling totally vulnerable and weak and castrated. It has summoned up a deep injury and the only way he can respond is in defense of that injury. There is no way he can attend to her pain.

The therapist in this situation has to take the risk of letting go of this deepest core defense. Then he can feel his own vulnerability and the pain beneath it. Only then is he in a position to really "get it."

I feel this approach is essential for us all in any situation where we find ourselves being confronted or accused. As difficult as it is, we need to allow the defensive reaction to lead us right back to our own wound, and then to experience and to accept the pain and vulnerability around it. I don't know of any other way we can be open enough to truly hear and to understand when a person tells us we have wounded him or her. How do we do this?

I suggest that, whenever we're confronted by a client, the first thing to do is to find a therapist, consultant, or a supportive colleague who can facilitate for us a healing process. The most crucial step in the process is to fully express one's own negativity toward the client: "How dare she say that I'm insensitive after all I've done for her!" "I've taken phone calls from that ungrateful so-and-so over and over and never charged him and now he's angry with me because I'm not there enough!" "I really cared about her, I did everything I knew how to help her. And now she's angry and threatening me. I could kill her!"

We have to express fully the anger, the resentment, and the outrage we feel. I don't mean just talking about it in a nice, controlled, rational way. That won't help. I mean we need to *release the full force* of the nonrational feelings. Otherwise our negativity will get acted out in some indirect way. Or suppressing it will constrict us and prohibit us from responding empathically.

When the expression of negativity is complete, the pain that lies beneath it can emerge. And it is the experiencing of the pain that is the next step in the process. If we can allow ourselves to acknowledge the pain, then we can follow it right back to our own personal wound. Only then can we experience our own vulnerability around it.

Let me illustrate this: During a session a client's anger toward his therapist comes to the surface. In effect he is saying that she has failed. That she is an inadequate mother. That she has not understood or responded to his needs. With what feels to her like sadistic delight he launches into a diatribe that hits all the weak spots. He cites several instances when her responses to him proved that she had no real understanding of him, that she was obviously inadequately trained and defective as a person. She was stunned. Inwardly she goes through all the stages: "I couldn't possibly have responded the way he said I did. That didn't even sound like me! He's distorting the whole thing. It's clearly about his anger toward his mother. . . . My God, I wonder if he'll find some way to sue me!" Outwardly she is calm and says the right things. But there is a slight crispness, a matter-of-factness in her voice. She can feel herself withdrawing. The defense that has been activated is: "If you don't love me, then who needs you!"

Later, when the stun wears off the therapist realizes how angry she is. She seeks out a consultant who helps her to release it. After she has expressed her rage at being attacked and devalued, she breaks into tears. Now she feels the pain. As she expresses the hurt she recognizes the source: "I could never do it right for Dad. No matter how hard I tried, my best was never good enough. I could never secure his approval and therefore his love."

Having touched her own deep hurt, which was the source of her feeling reaction, she doesn't have to defend anymore. She can feel her vulnerability. And the vulnerability—or nondefensiveness—allows for openness to return. Now the therapist is prepared to relate to her client in a very different way.

Whenever we are confronted or accused by a client, we need to find someone to support us through this process: expressing the full range of negativity, experiencing the pain, locating our own wound, acknowledging the vulnerability. This can leave us with an openness not only toward the client, but also to further and deeper work on ourselves. For I believe we can view any accusation or confrontation as a wake-up call to alert us that there is some unresolved issue in us that is affecting our work and that must be explored and understood. The effect on the client of that unresolved issue may be to create occasional empathic dysjunctions, or it may be that we are unable to take clients to the places they need to go. And it may be that serious harm could be done.

So once we've made the crucial change from defensiveness to openness, how then does the therapist deal with the accusation of the client? I have said that what the client wants is two things, and the first is to be heard. So the first and most important thing, I believe, is to *acknowledge* the validity of the client's feelings.

> Recently a woman came into my office quite distraught over a "blow up" that had happened between her and her husband the weekend before. The husband had become enraged over something she had done. Being herself a therapist, she had responded to his charges with, "I understand why you're so angry, Dear, but . . ." and then she went on to explain her behavior very carefully and rationally. Her explanations would simply hit a blank wall, and the arguments escalated throughout the weekend. Finally, she simply stopped before the "but." "I do understand why you are so angry." Period. Her husband then replied with enormous relief, "Now I finally feel that you've heard me."

What happened to my client here, and what often happens to us all in such situations, is that we get caught in feeling we must rush to our own defense, particularly when we feel we have been unjustly accused, or that we have been the object of a projection or a negative transference "dump." We have to prove we are right, or at least that we have done nothing wrong. It is hard to feel that we do not have to first be right to hear the other person's feelings. In fact, the important thing here—and the hardest thing to remember under such stress—is that primarily *it isn't about who's right and who's wrong.* It's about feelings, and feelings are not right or wrong. The wounded person needs to have the feelings—let's say, of betrayal—validated, and needs to know that the therapist is affected by his/her feeling experience. It makes little difference that there was no intention to betray, or even that betrayal was not an objective fact. We know very well that in therapy when a client speaks about the unloving or hateful or abusing parent, the objective reality of the parent's behavior is beside the point. The client's *feeling* is real, and that is the reality that we validate and work with.

When the client confronts us, we have to accept the reality of her feelings. She will never *feel* her feelings validated as long as the therapist is explaining, justifying, or contradicting in an attempt to prove himself or herself not guilty.

In the example above my client saw that empathically acknowledging and accepting the reality of her husband's feelings was not the same as an admission of her guilt. And her acknowledgment and acceptance of his feelings brought the end of destructive escalation and allowed the process to continue toward the resolution of their problem.

The second thing that seems necessary to do when confronted or accused is *to allow and to encourage the full expression of the client's negativity and pain*. We are not likely to allow this if we're stuck in a defensive mode. None of us would have trouble conjuring up the dangers to a marriage relationship, let's say, of glossing over, short-circuiting, or inadvertently suppressing anger and hurt in all its intensity and energy. In the therapeutic relationship when we are the target we need to have the courage to reach into all the dark corners and invite out all the negativity, as uncomfortable as it may be for us and for the other person.

Third, the therapist needs *to take responsibility for his/her part*. Crucial to the healing process of any wounded person is for the other person to acknowledge what he/she has done.

A few years ago, an acquaintance of mine sued her former therapist for malpractice. According to her, the therapist had been guilty of unethical behavior that included sexual misconduct. As a result she experienced depression, dysfunction, suicidal ideation, deep disruption in her marital and family functioning, and other symptoms. When she first confronted him about the pain she was in, he did not deny the behavior. He said the right words, but, as she put it, "He didn't get it." She did not believe that he really could feel what had happened to her.

Nor could she sense that he really had any understanding of what it was in him that led him to cross the boundaries or that he was doing something about it so that he would never do it to someone else. She then decided to take him to court. No doubt the therapist felt betrayed and feared for his professional life. In the long drawn out legal process he denied everything, and made her out to be an unstable, hysterical fabricator. When it was all over and a settlement was reached in her favor, the woman felt that she had not gotten what she had really wanted all along: for her former therapist to truly own his part and to be able to say, "I'm sorry."

The first "Home Alone" movie was an entertaining story about an 8-year-old boy who was the identified family "goof-up." I recently read an article wherein the screenwriter was quoted as saying that the movie was so enormously successful because it hit a nerve: it was about abandonment. The boy's parents and siblings went off to Paris for Christmas vacation and accidentally left him behind. His abandonment became the ultimate latency adventure fantasy of a boy who never could do it right. With great ingenuity and creative genius he outwitted the two robbers who came to carry away all the family belongings. Because the would-be thieves had cut the telephone lines, his panic-stricken and guilty parents were unable to communicate with him when they arrived in Paris, so the mother got on the next plane back.

The mother spends miserable, anxious, guilt-ridden hours on her journey home, not knowing whether her son was okay, no doubt every minute struggling to justify how this unthinkable thing could have happened. What could she say to him? In the scene of the reunion between guilty Mom and abandoned son, the screenwriter did it right.

When she finally arrives home, the mother rushes in, searches for her son. When she finds him she looks at him with feelings of relief, love, guilt. The words she manages awkwardly are, "Merry Christmas, Sweetheart." The boy stands back silently, looks at her with reproach and hurt. The unspoken words in the silence are, "Mom, how could you ever have done this to me?" The mother says simply, softly, "Oh, Kevin . . . I'm so sorry!" It's all he needs. He breaks into a grin and runs into his mother's arms. And everyone in the audience feels enormously relieved!

Sometimes—many times—a heartfelt "I'm sorry" is all that is needed. However, there are also many times and situations when "I'm sorry" is the right beginning, but it is not enough. A part of taking responsibility is asking the wounded person, What can I do to aid in the healing of this wound? It may require a lot of courage on our part to ask such a question. We certainly cannot ask it unless we have gone through the prior steps as we have discussed. How the question gets answered depends of course upon the nature and seriousness of the wound, and upon many other things. But in so enlisting, the therapist is communicating the desire to do what is in the best interest of the client right through to a resolution.

Finally, I think it is important to observe that when we as therapists confronted by a wounded client can take these steps—when we can acknowledge the person's feelings, encourage the full expression of his/her negativity, and when we can take responsibility for our part—then we have not only facilitated the healing of the client's wound, but some part of our own wound may be healed in the process. For the client's wound is also somehow our own. We may well have wounded the client in the very way our parents wounded us. Now finally we are in a position to respond to the client and to ourselves in the very way that our parents were unable to respond to us.

6

Surviving the Transference Psychosis[1]

Lawrence E. Hedges

A 31-year-old woman who for a number of years always had a great deal to tell me—many stories, many interesting vignettes— arrived one day full of stories she was eager to relate. In the waiting room, she suddenly began to feel something else—an intense desire to be very emotionally present this hour. She somehow understood at that moment that the stories she had wanted to tell me would be her way of not allowing herself to be psychically present in the room. She keenly felt the disappointment of letting go of the exciting stories she wanted to tell. She slowly began to sink into a very quiet, frightened place. She had been working for some time on trying to allow herself to be more emotionally present —to be fully alive in the room. She wanted to feel herself and to feel my presence, but she had so many things to talk about this was

1. Portions of this chapter were previously published in *Remembering, Repeating, and Working Through Childhood Trauma* (Hedges 1994b). I wish to gratefully acknowledge Robert Hilton as my consultant in this work.

generally difficult for her to accomplish emotionally. On a few occasions she had had a glimmer of it.

On this particular day as she settled down on the couch, she reported starting to feel chaos. With the internal chaos came tears of fright. I stayed with her fears and was able to support her experiencing the chaos of wanting to remain emotionally present but not knowing how. She was able to clearly differentiate this fear from other kinds of fear she's had before. When I indicated that this frightened, chaotic place was a place that she had been working for a long time to allow herself to experience, the tears came profusely. With relief she said, "You mean it's okay that I'm in this frightened place?" She had interpreted my comments as reassuring her that no matter how frightened and confused she felt at the moment, this was an okay place to be. I pointed out that it wasn't simply a matter of being okay; the chaos and fear she was feeling was very real at this moment, which she reaffirmed. It held a sense of present reality that was very different from what she would have experienced if she had gone ahead and told the stories she had intended to tell.

For about ten minutes she stayed in a quiet state of fear, making occasional quiet comments about physical sensations and her awareness of troubled breathing. Occasionally I checked in with her to see how she was doing, with her reporting that she was still present but frightened. She contrasted this more quiet, tearful, chaotic fear with a number of previous "regressive" experiences that she has had in which she has felt wildly out of control, terrified, sinking, and falling—in much more urgent and frantic forms. She could see now how those were ways of defending against this place of quiet terror of allowing herself to be emotionally present with another person. At one point when I checked in with her, she said, "I feel like I'm slipping away." Whereupon I extended my hand and said, "Can you stay? Can you stay here now?" She reached her hand toward mine and for a brief moment the two of us felt that we had retained our emotional connection with one another. Her comments were to the effect that this was the first time in her life anyone had ever invited her to stay with them or ever asked her to remain present.

She then began to close in a little more tightly on my hand. She turned on her side, facing more toward me and, with her other hand, grasped my hand. I had the distinct sense that something had changed from the experience of simply being together from the first moment our hands had met. Gradually it became clear that her presence was leaving the room. Upon inquiry she replied, "I'm slipping away, I can't stop it. Something's happening to remove me from you." She began talking about the stories, the unrealness, and how the way we spent our time today had been more real. But once her emotional presence had started to slip away it was beyond her power to keep herself present in the room anymore. The emotional contact, which was real, chaotic, and frightening, gradually melted into a sense of being together and calm. But that sense in turn set off a retreat. The onset of the retreat was marked by her reaching, grasping, and clinging to me, *as if* for reassurance. But the very contact itself and the grasping set off a sense of uncontrollable slipping away.

At this point, I had an opportunity to point out the similarity between the way she was now grasping my hand with both of hers, and how sometimes she clings to me physically in a hug toward the end of sessions. I said, "This clinging, attaching sense is very different from real chaos and then the ensuing fulfilling moment of contact we had before you began to slip away, when you were able stay for a few more intense connected moments when I asked you to."

I likened this clinging, grasping, attaching physical contact, which is reassuring, to the stories that she so often excitedly tells, which are also reassuring to her. But both the stories and the clinging contact have a certain unreal sense in that they do not contain the real terrifying emotions of being with another person in the present nor do they contain safety and calm. Rather, they seem to mask or foreclose the true terror and difficulty of being together, as well as the comfort that can also be real. Her comment was, "Then those reassuring feelings are not quite real." I agreed that they were a way of not allowing the more real feelings of fear as well as comfort to be experienced. She immediately said, "I now feel ashamed of the way I have been using physical contact because it seems so phony." I asked, "Whose mother is speaking now?" She responded that it was the mother who frightened her, who broke contact with her, who accused her of being somehow bad. I commented that she had been abusively shamed for many things, for being "dramatic," "phony," and "manipulative." But that is not the case. The fears she felt at being alive, vulnerable, and present today had not been received by her mother. Her real presence, with her genuine needs for love and connection, had been deflected by her early mother, causing her to withdraw and/or to assert herself more frantically (as in clinging or storytelling) in an effort to be received and to feel loved, comforted, and safe.

At the end of the hour she was tempted to reach for the customary good-bye hug. Yet she felt awkward about it, realizing that the hug would never quite be the same again. The reassurance it had held for her was in some sense a false reassurance, in comparison to the moments of presence and contact that were terrifyingly real—and so reassuring in a very different sense.

Several months later, as the approach to understanding the organizing transference began to occur, there was a great deal of panic and confusion. For the organizing transference to become more visible, seven-day-a-week contact had been maintained for three weeks. The contact included four days of regular sessions and three days of scheduled brief telephone contacts or office appointments. After working through some of the difficulties in maintaining contact there had been a week of fairly good contact. By "contact" it is meant not merely the loving attachment that she had been able to feel for some time, but an emotionally interactive engagement. She had been pleased that the week had gone well and that she had felt emotionally in contact with me around many important issues. The two days of phone contact came, which happened to be Friday and Saturday, and then a special session was scheduled for Sunday. The contact that had been sustained throughout the week had undergone some shakiness during the two days with only telephone contact. During the Sunday session there was initially some limited but good emotional contact. After a period of time she began to be aware of pulling away, of trying to be close again, and then of pulling away again.

During this delicate period I found myself watching very closely for the exact moment at which she might begin a full-fledged withdrawal. At the moment I began to feel her presence leaving, I reached out my hand and asked, "Could we hold onto each other this way?" At first, she was reluctant because it seemed that she was needing to withdraw. But after a little urging she made hand contact. For a few moments there was a real sense of being together and sharing an experience. I remarked on how difficult it was for two people to be together and to sustain an emotional experience with one another. She shortly reported that she was slowly and silently receding, that she was "withdrawing inside." There was nothing she seemed to be able to do about it. She was pulling away. She was frightened and panicked, but clearly withdrawing. Soon the hands that were held together seemed meaningless and she left the session discouraged, feeling that the weekend disruption had made it impossible for her to sustain the sense of connection, that she was physically constricting and closing off. She stated, "Sometimes I can feel much closer to you when I'm not here. Sharing closeness together is hard to do."

I had the impression that my being present only for phone calls on the weekend days reminded her of the countless times her parents, particularly her early mother, had withdrawn from contact, setting up an intense need to clamor too for what she needed. But the clamor was objected to by the parents and she was viewed as spoiled, overly needy, phony, or manipulative. The cycle that had become slowly represented in the analysis began when the child's needs were not responded to. This, in turn, led to increased intensity of demand, which the parents had found disgusting or intrusive. Finally it seems she would retreat into autistic isolation. In many overt ways her parents could be there for her and were able to provide basic physical care. But it seemed they never could enjoy being with her and harshly responded to her frantic expressions of chaos and fear that their flawed parenting set up in her. It was as if their emotional deprivations had set up an intense fear of breakdown, emptiness, and death. Their promise of availability coupled with their emotional unavailability was a betrayal of the child's emotional needs.

By the following day she came in practically bent over double with severe pains in her neck and lower back. She had already been to two doctors that day and received several tentative and potentially dire diagnoses, from possible meningitis, to a severe virus, to a chronic chiropractic condition. For the next three days she was under medical care and stayed at home taking pain pills and other medications. Sessions were held by the telephone with the main discussion centering on the intense pain and the withdrawal. While medical possibilities must be ruled out, we both shared the conviction that the severe pains and somatic constrictions somehow reflected the movement of the analytic work. She was inclined to see the disruption (abandonment) of the weekend as causal. I raised the possibility that the week of good contact followed by the brief Sunday revival of connection seemed causal. That is, *contact itself is the feared element because it brings a promise of love, safety, and comfort that cannot ultimately be fulfilled and that reminds her of the abrupt breaches of infancy.*

The following weekend phone contact was maintained. Some domestic difficulties arose between her and the long-term boyfriend she lived with. Monday, Tuesday, and Wednesday she made it to her sessions and was very glad to be back. She talked a great deal about what was going on. There was some residual weakness left from the illness the week before, but mostly the focus was on "How on earth am I going to be able to continue to stay in the relationship with Marc!" By Wednesday she had been looking at apartments and was on the verge of moving out. Throughout the relationship this had been a pattern. At various times when there would be difficulties in their relationship, it would seem necessary for her to leave. The fantasy was to go somewhere where she could simply be alone, pull away into herself, and feel closed off, comfortable, and safe.

By the end of the Wednesday hour, while there had been obsessive concerns about her relationship with Marc and about whether to move out or not, there was a certain sense of closure. She said, "I think I'm just not fit to live with anyone because I can't get along with anyone. It's like I just can't relate, I can't stay connected, and when I do, it goes badly. I finally have to withdraw into a safe place where I can feel whole and alive by myself."

That night a horrible nightmare was reported. She got up in the middle of the night and typed up the dream as follows:

"This dream was totally vivid and real. It was happening in the here and now, in the very apartment I live in on this day's date. I couldn't really tell the difference between what was going on in the dream and what was going on in my life. Marc and I are fighting or I'm fighting with him and it's the very fight that we're in right now. I'm in the kitchen trying to talk to him. I'm trying to explain and I'm getting more and more hysterical. I look at him. He has short hair so that he looks quite different. He walks calmly away from me and into the living room. I am hysterical. He is calm. I say, "Do you need me to go to your company picnic with you?" I know that he does. He looks at me calmly and says, "No." He has decided that I shouldn't go with him, that he doesn't need me to go. He's totally calm. His neck in the dream is very different from his neck in real life. I know he doesn't look like that with his hair short. I start going after him, all the while aware that I'm being hysterical. He's still totally calm. He begins walking up the stairs. I go after him, grabbing onto his leg. He proceeds upward, ignoring it. Totally calm. He goes to the study. Then I retreat to my room looking out, aware that there are other people in the house. Everyone in the house is calm except me. I'm crying and hysterical.

"All through that last part of the dream there's an overlay of children's 'Golden Books.' I don't know where or how they are there. It's more of an image. When I wake up hysterical I feel the Golden Books symbolic of lifelong struggle. I wake up crying and silently screaming and flailing my arms and my legs and kicking. I am aware in the aftermath of the indignity of the whole scene. For whatever reason, whether or not it's my fault, I am the one who is raging and hysterical, with Marc being totally calm. It feels like it is symbolic of my whole life's struggle, and that loving has something to do with it. That it is because I love him that I am locked into this. I love him and I want to make the connection with him desperately and no matter what I do it fails. The little voices in my head, both in the dream and now, are saying, 'Yes, but it's because you are so infantile and hysterical and don't know how to connect that you have created this situation.' But the stronger knowledge, both within and during the aftermath of the dream, was that this relationship is set up to perpetuate the indignity, the hysteria, and the frustration of my early life. I make constant and futile attempts to connect, while he remains interested but dispassionate with the rest of the family in the background listening to my hysteria.

"I also wonder whether the short hair and the fact that he looks very different in reality than in the dream is symbolic of the fact that his true self and thoughts are different than I would like to believe they are. That unmasked, he is not who I think he is. It feels like he puts out a lot and is resentful that he doesn't get it back in kind. I don't get or give emotional relatedness on a mature level. The relationship remains in an infantile state emotionally, with me raging and hysterical. The indignity of it all is what seems so powerful in the dream. This seems like a replica of my childhood where all of the necessities were more or less taken care of. There was only a moderate amount of mistreatment and even some semblance of love. But there was an overall emptiness and neglect that was abusive. I am done in by my love, because I do love him as I did love my family. The image of the man with his hair short being so different from my image of him haunts me."

During the remainder of the session the interaction was marked alternately with periods of understanding between us, and moments during which she, in confusion, would say, "You know I don't understand all of this. You know I'm not getting it." At some level things were being processed. But at the level of deeply understanding the dream discussion she did not feel that she really did.

After the dream was associated to in various ways the concern from the previous day reemerged as to whether or not she should get an apartment so as to find a retreat where she could be safe and comfortable. I asked if it would be possible for her to apply the dream to understanding the therapeutic relationship. That is, if the dream were representing a transference situation, what would that look like? She thought for awhile but was not able to connect the dream to the analytic relationship, although as my interpretation unfolded, she understood it. I suggested that I was represented in the dream as her boyfriend. She immediately said, "Yes. It seems like it was your neck and short hair in the dream that I was seeing, not his." I interpreted the dream as a picture of the childhood situation that was being transferred not only into the relationship with her boyfriend but also into the analysis. I thought that this dream presented a version of her living disconnection. I recounted the week of connection, the disruption of that connection through the Friday and Saturday phone calls, and how difficult it was to regain the connection on the Sunday. I reminded her that even the Sunday connection was nip and tuck until I had reached out and asked her to try to stay present and connected. I recalled that she had in fact been able to sustain it. But that in less than ten minutes she had felt herself inexorably being drawn away. She had felt her entire body constricting and herself withdrawing, so that even though hands were in contact, her soul had withdrawn from the interaction. I interpreted that the dream picture represented what was going on in those moments of withdrawal, that "from an objective standpoint you and I may be able to agree that we were in connection and that then you slowly broke the connection. But the dream picture tells us what your subjective internal process was like. That is, you experienced my not needing you, not enjoying you, and then pulling away from you in much the same way that your parents did. And in the dream as your boyfriend did. I calmly left you and went off to study for the weekend, oblivious to your needs." The nightmare gives a picture of how the withdrawal happens after contact is achieved.

At this point she remarked that her boyfriend often complained that even when they did have moments of closeness and intimacy, immediately afterward she would start some kind of a fight. I commented that the fights were a cover-up or a defense against this more terrifying, painful, and dangerous contact situation, remembered from earliest childhood. "The Golden Book overlay of the dream suggests that this is the story of your childhood. Golden Books tell the way life is supposed to be. Your Golden Book tells you the way life was and somehow is still 'supposed to' be. There were people in your environment, your mother, your father and your family, who had a great deal they could give you, and they did give you basic care. But when it came time for emotional interactions they turned their backs leaving you grasping at straws in a wild hysteria and finally withdrawing to your closet for safety. You were always made to believe that problems in relationships were your fault."

It horrified her to think that her withdrawal is the reaction to *the connection* rather than her reaction to the other turning away. That is, she has consciously perceived her becoming hysterical because the other person wasn't connecting. But the dream, viewed as a transference representation, suggests what happens when, in fact, she does connect. There had been a week of good connection followed by a slight disruption, a strong reconnection, and a pulling away. Within 24 hours she was in excruciating physical pain and agony and remained so for several days, being physically traumatized by having made the connection that was then experienced as traumatizing.

She replied, "Then you really don't think I should get that apartment?" By this time, I was quite clear about the meaning of the moving-out fantasy. I pointed out how in the past, as in the present, the moving-out fantasy has served as an autistic retreat for achieving a means of surviving and gaining a sense of comfort when she cannot safely connect to a person whom she needs.

I had been considering Tustin's (1981, 1986) formulations in attempting to understand her. Tustin thinks that the infant and mother are in a sensuous relationship during pregnancy. During the earliest extrauterine months the physical sensuous relationship optimally continues comfortably until psychological bridges begin to be made between the mother's mind and the child's mind. If the mother cannot maintain the sensuous relationship with the child, or abruptly ruptures it, the child begins engaging in withdrawing autosensuous behaviors. These ideas were presented informally. She interrupted, "You mean the spacing out and withdrawing I do at times?" "Yes, when sensuous connection to your mother was needed but she did not provide it, you retreated to the safety and comfort of self-stimulation." She in fact had physically withdrawn in childhood to her closet and in adulthood to separate apartment-type settings to escape several relationships, feeling—at least briefly—soothed by the aloneness.

This vignette spans perhaps six weeks of intensive contact. The actual time it took to produce the dream picture of the withdrawal was about twelve days. The intervening time was spent in intense physical agony, frenzy, and daily contact. During this period there was no interpersonal emotional connection with me. The contacts were of a frenzied "attachment" kind. She is correct when she speaks of her love for others, but she was also becoming aware that there is an "attachment kind of love" and a "connection kind of love" in which there is an emotional engagement. She is readily able to experience desperate, clinging attachment love, but is limited in being able to experience or to sustain the mutually emotional engagement kind of love. When she experiences others as not needing her, not enjoying her, abandoning her to their own preoccupations, she becomes desperate and clinging. The dream portrays her experience of the other coldly turning his back, unconcerned about her desperation and the autistic retreat that follows. The entire cycle is internalized and endlessly repeated.

In the discussion following the dream, the focus was on whether or not her boyfriend would someday be able to interact with her. At this point in time, that could not be predicted. I maintained, "You chose him because he was sufficiently emotionally withdrawn so that you could maintain an attachment with him over a long period of time without this threatening transference from your childhood cropping up to destroy the relationship. As you begin to find a way to be more present and to ask for more emotional connection and emotional interaction, the question remains whether he will be able to evolve with you and develop increasing connectedness as well. At the present you simply don't know the answer, because you've not been able to stay present long enough to allow him to struggle with what he needs to struggle with in the relationship in order to remain fully present."

Following an extended summer vacation break there was much news and settling down for three weeks, with the earlier working through of connection experiences seeming to her to be a long way in the past. After having worked for some months on a creative and complex marketing strategy, she had presented her proposals to colleagues and company officials late one Thursday afternoon. She received an overwhelmingly positive and enthusiastic response. People were interested and asking complicated questions she had had good answers for. People really connected to her in a favorable way. She enjoyed it and took pride in her work. A group took her out for celebration drinks afterward and she felt surrounded by a warm glow.

Within hours doubts and fear began and throughout Friday and Saturday a downward spiral of self-criticism, hopelessness, and despair evolved until she went into a panic and called me at home on Saturday night. We spoke for about forty minutes. The panic gradually subsided and the main connecting issues from before the vacation break were brought back into focus. The details of the marketing meeting were reviewed. The admiration, respect, and warm personal connectedness she experienced by her colleagues and her superiors were interpreted by me as causal in the down-ward spiral. She was reminded that connection and self-value are forbidden and dangerous. We felt deeply connected and I alerted her to the danger of a reaction to the good connection she was now achieving with me. I agreed to call her Sunday morning.

During the brief Sunday call several reactions emerged. She was in a mild state of confusion and perplexity. Not wanting to lose the good connection she had experienced the night before, she had pulled out some newspaper articles on childhood devel-opment I had written and spent time reading and trying to stay in touch with the good experience of our connection. But confusion started as she read, because many of the ideas on the written page seemed to be her own ideas. Had I taken her words and made them into my own without asking permission to do so? Or had the ideas been mine, but with so much interaction, had she taken them in and felt them to be her own? She cited several examples, wanting to know whose words they were. I discussed the issues with her, on the one hand showing that some of the ideas came from others who were quoted that both of us had taken in. Other ideas had clearly been picked up from me, but possibly there *were* some that came originally from her, although examples were not available at the moment. I encouraged a search, indicating that I always wished to obtain permission or to credit whenever possible and appropriate.

Privately, I thought that the content seemed to express the organizing level uncertainty of "Whose body is this? Whose breast is this?" and heralded disillusionment with the infantile omnipo-tent wish that usually precedes a breakdown experience (Winnicott 1974). That is, my mind (words) should belong to her, but after the good connection it appeared that I was running away, stealing my (nurturing) self from her and she became confused and fright-ened. The working-through experience was being resumed after the vacation break but with some new themes: being affirmed sets off a downward spiral and the confusion of the source of nurturance.

She then presents a "screen memory" that had arrived earlier in the morning. "I was back at my parent's home. You know how I used to have my closet set up with a small desk and things for me to read and do—my retreat? Well, I had something really important to say and came out of my closet and went to tell my father. Whatever it was, he immediately put it down and humiliated me in the process so I went running back to hide in my closet." The interpretation offered was that the night before she had come out of the safety of the vacation break and permitted a regression precipitated by the gratifying marketing meeting. She had then made successful contact with me Saturday night. But while reading my articles she became agitated and confused about whose words these were. The feeling of being devalued by my differentness or "word theft" was viewed as a transference feeling demanding that she flee from the frightening and humiliating contact back into her closet. The screen memory suggested that the infantile omnipotent possession of the maternal body was abruptly and unempathically broken by mother's narcissistic preoccupation with her own concerns, causing an autistic retreat. What she thought belonged to her was claimed by her mother, leaving her suddenly in frightened and uncontrollable confusion and a retreat into herself. More adverse reactions were anticipated, I warned, as contact was being needed and being found.

By Monday evening she arrived in my office dragging, looking terrible, and barely able to speak. She had been in excruciating pain all day, experiencing problems with breathing and talking. She felt she was extremely ill and disoriented. Did I think she should go to a doctor to see? I encouraged medical coverage and also reviewed the events, saying that it has been a strain getting up the courage to begin the deep analytic work again but that on last Saturday night it had begun. The total aching body, the gasping for breath, the chest pain, and the near laryngitis all seemed like reactions to the contact—her body was protesting the forbidden pleasures of relating that had been enjoyed.[2] We were touching that terrifying wall of relating that went back to the original

---

2. The bioenergetic interpretation of such pains is that they are body memories of early constrictions in the throat and bronchial area. The constrictions, begun in infancy, represent a bodily reaction to deprivation of food and/or air and simultaneously an effort by the life force to assert in the musculature a desire to live. As this desire to be alive in human relationships is revived in the real world and in the analytic transference, the early and painful body memories assert themselves.

wish to be biologically safe and in control of vitally needed sub-
stances. What became somatically internalized was expressed in
the screen memory of an abusive rebuff at the hands of a narcissistic father (or crazy mother).

On Tuesday she reported that she had been to see a doctor
who thought she had pneumonia. Every bone ached and she could
barely talk or make it to session. There were deep heaving sighs
on the couch as she expressed the fear that she was dying. She was
anticipating being so bad tomorrow she would not be able to come
to session. She asked if she should try to make it if at all possible.
I affirmed the need to take care of herself and respect her illness
and the effects of the antibiotics. I also affirmed the importance of
coming to her analytic session if possible.

I pointed out again how the sequence seen before the summer break had been revived. There was the Thursday triumph, the
downward spiral, and the Saturday analytic contact, followed by
the losing of the contact with the confusion of whose thoughts were
whose, and the screen memory involving total body agony, humiliation, and running terrorized in pain back to her closet after a
devaluating contact with the narcissistic father.

Wednesday arrived with great pain and distress, much talk
about the physical symptoms, problems sleeping, and the agonies
of the week. I attempted, as on Monday and Tuesday, to contex-
tualize the agony as the body's retreat from fulfilling contact. Agony
and retreat were body memories that arose in relation to the analytic contact. But in her illness today, more than in the previous
two days, she seemed totally inaccessible in any way to my words.
While she listened to attempted interpretations, she could only
nod her head. But nothing could be discussed or processed. She
reported "slipping into a black void and nothing can stop it."

On Thursday she arrived with a pained facial expression, an
antibiotic in hand, and a request for water to take it with. She continued talking in the same vein as the previous days for about ten
minutes. Suddenly she asked, "Why are you being so silent?" I responded, "Because I hadn't thought of anything to say yet." This
enraged her and the remainder of the hour was spent railing at me
for being emotionally absent, for being narcissistically preoccupied,
and for not empathically "coming after me to rescue me." My instinc-

tive response was to be somewhat defensive to the barrage of accusations. "This always happens. It has happened every time I have really needed you—when I am slipping into the black void, when I have no way of staying alive, you back away emotionally. You just vanish when I get dependent and regressed and need you. You would let me die." The anger mounted until she bolted out of the room seven minutes early, slamming the door saying she didn't know how she could stay alive (it was not a suicidal threat the way it was said).

I had been struggling not to be defensive, to understand the mounting despair and rage. This type of tirade had been present before but the context had never been so clear as now. But with the hour cut short I didn't get the opportunity to point out that these kinds of rages in the past had tended to be either when she longed for reassuring mergers or on Thursdays before the weekend break. I did not get to say that we could certainly schedule phone contact over the weekend if that would help. Although once or twice I attempted to relate the present rage reaction to events of last weekend, the reaction and the violent accusation of coldness, distance, and narcissistic preoccupation made all possibility of interpersonal contact impossible.

I found myself quite upset by the raging intensity of the hour and the rageful exit, but had experienced a similar intensity on prior similar working-through occasions with her so decided to wait out the reaction rather than to cut it short by intervening with a call. She knew my home number and that I would be at home for the three days. So if connection was needed it would be readily available.[3]

Monday session was missed. Again, I believed that contact was possible if needed and so decided to wait. The rageful exit and missed session had a dramatic, manipulative flavor, making the evolving situation all that much more interesting for understanding the unfolding transference sequence. In past understandings

---

3. In a subsequent consultation I questioned the possible meaning of my seemingly not very helpful or outgoing role in this difficult situation. It seemed to me upon reflection that, as uncontained as the situation might appear on the surface, the context and previous experience suggested that the ego function of body memory recall was in operation and needed to be heard out.

of the infantile situation, what I had experienced as the woman's pressured manipulations had been discussed at length as an internalized residue of an infant whose needs were ignored to the point of terror and a fear of dying. They had been seen as the historically meaningful manifestation of an infant fearing imminent death through neglect or abandonment and learning to do everything in its power to force people in the environment to respond to its needs, to rescue it from aloneness and psychic death. The muscular constrictions in the chest and throat were further indications of how deeply embedded the desperation was. Although a manipulative flavor was present, what seemed more important on this occasion was the clearly articulated desperation, the despair, the fear of dying, the rage at my perceived emotional abandonment, the wish to be rescued, the fury at my spoken "helplessness," which was seen as "narcissistic preoccupation," and the "bailing out when true need is present." Because the sequence had been somewhat experienced previously, because it was being articulated so clearly and forcefully with meaningful transference accusations and body memory, and because I would be readily available should she attempt contact, it again seemed best to wait this out rather than to intervene in the unfolding elaboration of the primitive transference sequence.

Tuesday was spent in anger, silence, and despair. "Why didn't you save me last Thursday? I was dying. You just let me fall off the face of the earth. Why didn't you call Thursday afternoon or over the weekend? When I wasn't here yesterday weren't you worried about me? You knew I was in bad shape. Why didn't you call?" My calls in the past were always by appointment so there was no historical precedent for her expecting a call in response to analytic distress. I tried to remain as present at the feeling level as possible, so as not to become defensive in the face of the barrage of accusation. The session teetered on some empathic engagement around the despair and rupture because of my "narcissistic" inability to stay with her "true need." In one moment of rage near the end of the hour she slipped and called me by her boyfriend's name. She was horrified and redoubled her anger saying that now I would capitalize on the slip and use it against her.

Wednesday she sat up to confront me on the series of breeches, my brutal and insensitive personality, how I could have handled each event, and how my failings were cold and cruel.

All this occurred as is to be expected in the development and working through of the transference psychosis. The experience of the diabolized parent is strongly authentic, the analyst *becomes* the hated object of infancy (the "psychotic mother") and no capacity for a split-off observing ego or reality testing ego is present at the moment of the experience. As on the previous two days I attempted empathic attunement with the despair and anger, but also continued to bring forth the overarching context of all the events. She insisted the breach was on the previous Thursday when she needed me to be empathically attuned to her despair. I believed that the breach was internal and related to the Saturday night of the previous week when, following a long break, deep contact had been made that was immediately broken by the confusion of words, the screen memory of father devaluing and humiliating her, and the ensuing painful body memories. The entire round of rageful accusation and painful physical symptoms was seen by me as the reemergence of an internalized primitive reaction to the treacherousness of interpersonal contact.

Unlike the previous session, small parts of my argument gradually did seem to be reluctantly taken in; but only after my patience had worn thin and I was clearly on the verge of anger myself. The countertransference feeling was clearly, "God damn it! I'm here, I'm holding on to you in this regression the best I know how. Why are you accusing me so fiercely—where is your rationality, your sense of human decency? Why do you treat me so badly?" This was, of course, not spoken at the moment because the present priority was clearly with the emergence of the organizing transference. She stated, "I always have to give in, to do it your way. I can never win. It's always been that way. With my parents they were right, I was wrong. They were okay, something was wrong with me. My only choice is to sell out and be false." I did get a chance to point out that despite how badly injured and angry she felt, "We are not in adversarial roles like you were with your parents. We might be in a tough spot at the moment, but winning and losing are not what we are about. We are working together to allow patterns and memories of past sequences of agony to appear so that we can study how your mind operates. The last thing I would want you to do is to sell out, to give in. You've got to hold firm while we get all of this sorted out." We were slightly calmer at the end of the session.

On Thursday she resumed the couch and for half an hour a conversation with more understanding of each other's views was possible. I commented to the effect that I am who I am and that I misbehaved according to my personality was one matter. But her *reaction* to shortcomings of my nature provided an opportunity to see the whole sequence as a part of her mental structure. This did not mean that my behavior was being justified or that I, as the analyst, was "right" and she was "wrong." But rather that I had my personal way of responding that sets off primordial rage in her because my personality limitations are reminiscent of those of her parents. This was repeated and then somewhat reluctantly taken in.

I pointed out that the other person's self-preoccupation is always our enemy and has to be dealt with. In every relationship it would be only a matter of time before she found the other person's narcissistic preoccupations that would remind her of traumatic infantile encounters with her parents. Our investigation was into her reactions when she did encounter the other's narcissistic limits. What we have been seeing these two weeks in the unfolding of a mental sequence is *her*, her own personal reactions to others' narcissistic limitations.

She then reported a dream from the night before in which she discovered someone putting her boyfriend's clothes in her closet, where, she protested, they didn't belong. She saw the dream as condensing the childhood retreat from unempathic invasions into the safety of her closet, the transference humiliation and fury she so often experienced with her boyfriend, and the current transference situation with the analyst in which she felt my identity (clothes) an intrusion into her autistically safe place.

On the telephone the next morning she confided, "I'm afraid to tell you this. You know one of the injunctions of my growing up years was 'never tell anyone anything.' I'm afraid I'll lose this if I tell you. That you will somehow interpretively blow it so I don't want you to say anything about it." She explained, "By the time I left here on Tuesday I realized that I cannot relate to anyone, that I've never been able to, and that there is no hope. Since I don't know how to relate to people I have to relate to something or die. I thought I might start relating to my body, just trying to be in tune with it and I did. When reaching you is beyond possibility, I can be with myself and, even though it is painful, I can be okay." Respecting her wishes, I only echoed what was said at the time and agreed that staying with her body was of paramount importance. The overall context of the sequence was spoken again and arrangements were made for phone contact the following evening.

After two full days of heavy social demands the next call was again filled with agony, which did not surprise me given the inevitable strain of the anticipated social events. She wanted to run, withdraw, pick a fight but could remember there was some reason she was not going to do this. She couldn't remember the reason but she hoped she could stay with it. I chose to remind her that she had been able to stay present Tuesday night because she had chosen to stay connected to a sense of herself, to her body, no matter how painful that might be. The intense social interactions were upsetting enough that she was wishing to retreat to her closet and to soothe herself. Perhaps she could stay. Staying with the painful reactions she was having in her body at present seemed more important than leaving them. Why not curl up in bed for a while? That way she would be by herself, could reduce incoming stimuli, and focus on the physical pains caused by attempting to relate to people. It sounded like a possibility.

The next day the retreat to bed was reported as successful in that by focusing on herself she was able to feel her labored breathing and chest pains slowly diminish into physical calm, thus reconstituting a satisfactory self state. She asked, "Do you think that maybe the breach, instead of that Thursday marketing meeting, was around my reading your newspaper articles and becoming confused Saturday night?" I said, "No, that was when you began feeling the fragmentation, the slipping into traumatic confusion as a result of our connecting on the phone. Connection serves to remind you of when you were once satisfyingly connected to mother's body and then abruptly lost it. It happened on Thursday at your marketing meeting and set off the downward spiral until you called me and connected again to me on Saturday night. It is the connection that is feared because it was always somehow destroyed by your parents' narcissistic preoccupations. At present it is impossible to feel interpersonal connection without immediately expecting the traumatic and abusive turning away of your parents."

AN ASIDE ON PSYCHOANALYTIC EMPATHY

This vignette further raises an interesting and difficult issue regarding empathy. Kohut and the self psychologists have stressed the importance of selfother attunement—the analyst remaining tuned in to the subjective concerns of the person in analysis. Kernberg and others have sharply criticized this approach (see Hedges 1983, pp. 269–270), saying that it is relatively easy to formulate an interpretation that agrees with the subjective state of the client. It is more difficult to provide psychoanalytic interpretations that empathize with the broader personality picture, but may be subjectively unpalatable or unpleasant at the moment.

When working the organizing experience this problem often becomes acute, as illustrated in this vignette. One could argue that I was unempathic when I did not respond in a rescuing mode to this woman's despair. When I attempted to stay with what I saw as the broader personality issues, I was accused of being narcissistically preoccupied, out of tune, and wrong. There is always a delicate balance when responding empathically under conditions of accusation. On the one hand the subjective experience of the client has a certain priority or urgency in the immediate setting. But simply going along with the client's subjective demands may mean colluding with the resistance to establishing the painful, helpless, humiliating, rageful infantile transference. Here to have simply rescued the client from reexperiencing the contact rupturing organizing transference would have been to collude in acting out the resistance. But to hold too firmly to this broader perspective runs the risk of a damaging clash of subjective worlds, which could precipitate a negative therapeutic reaction (Freud 1918, 1923, 1933). The problem of intersubjectivity as seen here involves walking a tightrope between receiving the despairing, manipulative, rageful accusations as the transference object and avoiding defending oneself from the accusations—*usually ones that are going to strike home deeply somehow.*

V. Hilton (Chapter 5) points out that when we are accused there is a three-part response that arises almost instinctively from most of us: (1) Denial—"I didn't do it," (2) Defense—"I did the best I could," and (3) Blame—"She knows better than this, this accusation is pathological." The real problem, says Hilton, is that an accusation often is aimed, somewhat successfully, at a core wound, at a blind spot, or Achilles' heel. Until the accused is able to work through the core wound as it is active in the present relationship, it is unlikely that he will be able to give a satisfying response to the accuser who "knows" she is somehow right.

The problem of the core wound of the analyst, at which the accusation is aimed, becomes complex when considering the nature of the organizing experience. With developmentally more advanced symbiotic or borderline experience the fear of the client is abandonment, and an accusation of empathic failure means, "you abandoned me." But with organizing experience the transference is paradoxically comprised of structured terror around the issue of connecting or sustaining an interpersonal connection. That is, it is deeply empathic *not* to connect. Accusations focusing on the analyst's somehow letting the person down, of empathically failing, arise from the organizing level resistance to experiencing the transference, not from the transference per se. Not until the person in analysis can somehow let go of the accusation or demand, and then permit a lapse into deep yearning, helplessness and terror, not until the utter sense of breakdown, emptiness, and death can be fully experienced in the here and now relationship, can the infantile transference be secured for analysis. Rescue by means of subjective "empathic" agreement in this situation would have been antitherapeutic.

Thus in an accusation situation involving organizing level issues, the broadest psychoanalytic empathy would entail being able to navigate between the Scylla of colluding with subjectively valid resistance and the Charybdis of unwelcome, unpleasant, "unempathic" transference interpretation. Hilton charts our course: (1) Avoid denial, defensiveness, and blame. (2) Use consultation to work through the core wound the accusation touches in oneself. (3) Show the person that you know how deeply he or she has been wounded by you or by the position you have taken. And (4) provide some reassurance that this particular kind of injury can somehow be averted or softened in the future, that "this won't happen again to you or to someone else." This reassurance may take the form of the analyst's recognizing that there was a technical or empathic misunderstanding or mishandling of the situation by him (the usual Kohutian response). Or in the sort of dilemma presented in this vignette, the interpretation needs to include some reference to the ongoing, overall transference circumstance. Unfortunately, at the moment of organizing transference experiencing the person is living in a concrete, nonsymbolic world of infantile trauma without his or her usual reality testing capabilities or ordinary access to symbolic logic so that sensible and meaningful discussion is virtually impossible. In the example, the dilemma revolves around the problem that, "narcissism in others is always a danger. But by our coming to understand your *reaction* to my narcissistic preoccupations as a part of your mental structure, as a sequence of your ongoing mental life, we have a way of working together more effectively to understand how the pattern repeatedly shows up in your life." Her response was, "Oh, what this all is is a piece of how my mind works? I think maybe I can get hold of that."

Readers ask, "But doesn't healing result from the client's feeling the old pain in a new situation in which he or she can be satisfactorily met in a different and more satisfying way in the present? Can't the person feel their raw experience contained in an empathic way so that the experience can be reorganized into a cohesive and meaningful self-structure? If we develop forms that are larger and more containing, doesn't the healing that is required occur? Now the person is able to be in another place, a place of greater self-containment. Doesn't the analyst's overall containment provide the environment for the development of new personality tools?" The answer is yes and no. Yes, in that the new and broader canopy of interpersonal containment is needed for more complex representational relating to develop. But merely positively reliving traumatic situations in a more satisfying environment is not enough. In infancy, the first time around, love and containment might have been enough. But after organizing-level extensions have been made and found unsuccessful or painful, a psychological structure is built up that must be dismantled, analyzed, or broken down. A delusion has been created that henceforth makes relating dangerous and terrifying. In analysis the transference can come to include organizing or psychotic elements that revive the early memories of trauma in the form of transference and resistance to the experiencing of transference. In these vignettes we slowly see the transference developing. The analyst is begged to participate in the resistance to remembering the horrors of being rebuffed, humiliated, and sent back into an autistic closet.

"KILL THE BABY": A COUNTERTRANSFERENCE REGRESSION

(What follows is a first-person narrative of the countertransference experience that emerged at this point in the ongoing vignette.)

The earliest instance of the theme which stimulated my countertransference regression occurred several years ago. I recall a vivid fantasy of this woman about ten feet away facing me in a small subdued crowd, jumping up and down enthusiastically smiling and waving, trying to attract my attention. I reported my fantasy to her at the time. It was discussed in terms of how she had never felt seen by her parents. In fact, she never felt that she belonged to them, or to anyone else for that matter. She had always felt somehow different, set apart, isolated and separated from others, not really a part of any group or relationship. As a result of our analytic work she now feels that sometimes she "belongs" to Marc, her long-term boyfriend, and at times to me.

Sometime later the theme emerged of her interpersonal "intensity." In agonizing over a series of relationships in which for some mysterious reason she felt that people seemed somehow to shun her, to silently ridicule her, to turn their backs quietly on her, to fail to reciprocate her friendly overtures, she worried if she were too intense. *Intense* was a word that seemed to summarize a set of qualities that she felt were perceived by others as intrusive, aggressive, demanding, challenging, complaining, insisting, being pushy, and so forth.

On the one hand she was proud of her assertiveness as a woman and pleased at her ability to make things happen, to express concern for others, to stand up for what is right, and to not be pushed around. But she feared that her intensity drove people away, caused people to be afraid of her, or not to like her. She is a bright woman with keen insight into people and it seemed that perhaps she saw too much, that she knew too much about what motivated people for her own good. It seems she reads people deeply in ways that make them uncomfortable or perhaps provoke them in ways. But despite these intense, somewhat abrasive qualities she has many friends, is well liked, and is respected for her integrity, vision, and insight.

In the context of an ongoing dialogue about her intensity I had occasion to remark on several occasions how, when she first saw me in the waiting room and sometimes on leaving the office as well, she seemed to take me in, to scrutinize me deeply to the point that I sometimes found it uncomfortable. I have cultivated a habit in this business of avoiding heavy eye contact, of often averting my eyes so as not to make people feel watched. Limited eye contact with clients now feels natural and comfortable to me, especially analytic clients who use the couch. But often she would pull for eye contact by staring and then follow up her gaze or scrutiny with questions about how I was, was I okay today, what was I thinking. I found all of this mildly invasive and uncomfortable.

On several occasions she intuited that I was having an "off" day and commented to that effect. Although I had not perceived any mood irregularities in myself, on two or three occasions when she was upset by what she perceived as my mental state I was able to report back to her that later in the day others had noticed my being somewhat bland or unresponsive as well. I reported this to her in the spirit of validating her perceptions of my unconscious moods. I questioned the possible meanings of her extreme sensitivity. The main conclusion we drew was that as a child she was so traumatized by her parents' unavailable or destructive moods that she routinely surveyed people for "where they might be coming from" at the moment. It seemed some basic survival mechanism was being noted. She needed to know if I was okay, how I was feeling, was I going to be emotionally available to her, was she going to be safe with me today, or were there hidden emotional agendas or dangers?

In time, the question of her interpersonal intensity that seemed to create some discomfort in others was linked to her need "to read unconscious moods and motivations." I volunteered how uncomfortable I felt being scrutinized visually and emotionally, but understood her need to check me out each day, although the need was clearly greater on some occasions.

Early in the analysis she began to ask for hugs at the end of sessions. These good-bye hugs began in the context of regressive moments when she felt desperate and wasn't sure how she could leave or make it to the next day or through the weekend. Afterward on several occasions, I explained my discomfort with the hugs. She assured me that hugs were human and expressed connection. I explained that while I wasn't committed to total abstinence of touching, like most traditional analysts, I always felt physical contact of any sort needed to be understood, and I was always uncomfortable with physical contact that had not yet been understood.

She thought analysts were phobic of physical contact and had a problem themselves, no doubt fearing overstimulation themselves or sexualization of contact by the client. Hugs at the end of sessions had nothing to do with that, she asserted. They were an ordinary part of human warmth and understanding. During periods in which she felt stronger, hugs at the end of the session could be omitted.

She did, however, experience a series of powerful sessions in which, when she was emotionally pulling away, I extended my hand and held on to her while struggling to maintain emotional contact with her as well. I later explained what I believed to be a critical and concrete aspect of touch on such occasions, as it served to help keep us together when she was losing her sense of me at the moment. In time I came to sense her desire for hugs and responded accordingly and spontaneously.

Slowly the organizing transference began to be traced or defined in how she was more or less "present," in the room, more or less "available for contact." At first she believed she was present and in contact most of the time. But slowly she realized that she was almost never present in an interpersonally emotionally engaging way. And that she often had not the slightest idea of who I was. She said on several occasions, "I can feel so much closer to you when I'm not with you." This was interpreted as how difficult it was to actually establish a sense of deep and meaningful interaction with me in which she could actually feel my presence as a real person separate and different from herself. She had developed a fantasy of me, of who I was, and could carry on a reassuring dialogue with me in my absence. But when it came to knowing who I was, in the sense of being able in the here and now to interact with me, she often felt lost. She felt discouraged by this and gravely disabled.

I was able in time to draw a distinction between her feeling "attached" to me in a safe way and her being "connected" to me— able to feel open and active channels for communication and connection between two real, live, interacting beings. She was at first upset when I applied the attachment-connection distinction to hugs at the end of the hour. She did not like the idea that her reaching out for physical contact stemmed more from an attaching, clinging impulse or need for physical reassurance rather than from a communicating, connecting interaction. But on several occasions she clearly felt the distinction and then began to limit the hugs to more special occasions, although she did not like my interpreting them as attaching without connecting.

A series of breaches occurred over time in which she felt emotionally unresponded to by me. Her view was that just when she really needed me to be emotionally present I would somehow withdraw. She believed that I couldn't tolerate neediness or dependency and so would withdraw or disconnect and go to a cold, critical, imperious place. I could indeed feel the abrupt disconnections, her despair, her agony, and her rage at how I wasn't there for her. But I could not see or experience the pattern she believed to be present. To me it seemed her agonies and disconnections came upon the heels of some connection that she had established with me, and I attempted to point this out to her.

After several breaches I learned to note that at the first inklings of rage or of an intense, invasive, or accusatory demeanor on her part I tended to become more silent because I would be puzzled, attentive, and thoughtful—not having any idea where she was coming from, or not understanding the nature or meaning of her manner. My caution and increased alertness would then be felt by her as cold withdrawal.

Afterward I would be told by her what I should have done or said in these moments that would have been more empathic. However, the empathic response I "should have" given did not occur to me because at that moment I had gone into a more abstract tracking mode trying to figure out what was happening. That is, when I sensed sourness, intensity, or invasiveness I tended to begin reviewing in my head the overall context of the past weeks or months while listening as carefully as possible for what the present problem was within the overall context of her personality and our interaction. While I was puzzling in this way she might insist on some sort of immediate response from me. Her demand for immediate responsiveness would catch me off balance. It seemed that under these conditions no response I ever gave was satisfactory and her rage would escalate. Although I'm not sure if any response I might have given would have been more helpful or prevented the escalation, her complaint was invariably that I was inappropriately cold and withdrawing.

In quieter times I seemed to be able to show her the connections and disconnections I was tracking and she seemed to understand them. But in a moment she would tense up. She would feel locked into a fight with me over how I would coldly withdraw, think her complaints to be transference, blame her for disconnecting, and see her as "nuts" and myself as okay and right. There had been a series of interactions that were distressing to both of us. We tended to have different views about what was happening. She believed that I always somehow withdrew when she felt needy and she had a bad reaction to it. She accused me of refusing to examine and to acknowledge that my faulty responsiveness made it impossible for her to trust me or to trust her analysis. She feared I was just going to do it again and worried that there was no point in continuing her relationship with me, that I had a basic personality defect and could not keep from rejecting her. It seemed to me that as she would feel something real in the interpersonal connection or in her body in relation to our connection, something internal would occur causing her to feel that I was cold, isolated, critical, withdrawing, skeptical, and disgusted with her for being so dependent and needy.

My overall tracking for some months had been related to the ways in which she could not allow connection or engagement between us to occur and the ways in which she closed it off when it did occur. I could hear her insistence that at these breach moments the disconnecting problem was with me not her. I could see she needed me to cop to her accusations of my inappropriate emotional coldness and withdrawal. If I did not readily accept the blame for emotional withdrawal, this further escalated her distress because I was in effect saying (like her parents always had) that it was all her fault, that I was right and she was sick, excessively needy, bad, wrong, or pathological.

I became especially interested in tracking how she managed to produce these breaches somehow using features of my personality to relive the anguish of her infancy and childhood. I considered the possibility that my tracking on a more abstract plane than she wanted to be heard on could be an intellectualizing defense, a way of avoiding her connecting overtures. Perhaps my intellectualizing defense was activated when (as she claimed) she was most needy. But whether, or to what extent, I was being defensive, or my moods made me significantly less available to connect with, I had the distinct impression that she was using features in my personality to accomplish transferentially determined disconnections. I tried on several occasions to suggest this but was met with the firm conviction that there was a narcissistic personality flaw in me that I was trying to blame on her. If I was correct in believing that she ferreted out something in me to stimulate and/or attach organizing transference to, how was I to show her that, without seemingly replicating her parents' crime of "shifting the blame" to her and further enraging her? What was going on and how were we to sort it all out? We were both clear about a history of these disruptions that occurred on the day before weekend or holiday breaks.

The precipitating incident leading to our next distress occurred on a Friday afternoon. The week had gone comfortably with her allowing herself more body feeling than usual. I thought Friday might go well also. I was aware, however, that because I was going backpacking I would not be near a phone for forty-eight hours. I might need to tell her this since she often needed to know how I could be reached on weekends. It seemed to me that I was having a good day. I was looking forward to a beautiful weekend in the mountains with close friends with spectacular autumn weather promising.

In the waiting room I felt her penetrating eyes and averted mine (as I usually do). In the hallway she made a full turn around to take me in again, something she has not done before. I felt closely scrutinized and averted my eyes again. The past couple of months it seemed that she had been aware of watching me in the waiting room since I had made the comment about her intense eyes. On a couple of occasions there had been an exchange of what I took to be knowing smiles as we were both thinking about the eye contact and what it might be about. In an instant, as I am reviewing all of this in my mind and am thinking, It is Friday and she is forcing *me* to disconnect, to pull back from her intense, intrusive scrutiny. I feel penetrated and knee-jerk withdraw. She knows this about me. With the weekend coming she is attempting to either break a potential connection or prevent one from occurring by using my instinctive withdrawal from her gaze.

In my consulting room instead of moving to the couch as usual she turns, faces me, and asks if I'm okay. I assure her, "I am, but [and here comes the breach] when you scrutinize me it forces me to withdraw." She was enraged. That's ridiculous. How could she "force" me to withdraw? There it is again, and I'm blaming her for it. She wants that in writing because no one will believe it otherwise. In attempting to explain further (clearly a mistake in these circumstances) I remind her of my aversion to her intense stare and comment that if she wanted to connect with me that's certainly not the way to do it. She was further angered. I attempt a few other rationalizations that fail and then become quiet waiting to hear it all out to see if there is some element I can perhaps take hold of. My silence is further enraging. Toward the end of the session she announces that she had a good week, was overjoyed last night, and wrote an exciting poem that she brought and had wanted to share with me. She is happy with what is happening to her, with our work, with me, and she came to share it all with me today until I ruined it. Instead of waiting to see where she was coming from, I wrecked the session by disconnecting (she never got to the enjoyment of reading the poem).

Every session the following week she sits up to confront me. I always do this to her, just when she is ready to connect I manage to spoil it somehow. I am an unanalyzed analyst. She lists the times I have failed her and then blamed her for being somehow pathological. I have a deep character flaw that I will never get over so what's the point of her trying to relate to me. If every time when she is ready to connect I wreck it, what's the use of continuing her analysis? We need an arbitrator, someone who can show me my part in all of this.

My feeble attempts to talk about our overall context, about her intensity, about eye contact, about her using my discomfort at her scrutiny to achieve a disconnection fall on deaf ears. She is on a rageful roll and nothing I can say engages her in thought about other aspects of what may be happening. Her body is drawn up tight, her eyes are piercing, her voice tense and authoritative, her manner confident and strident. I have done it to her again and it has to stop. As she reviews past incidents that she believes I refused to acknowledge my part in, I repeatedly attempt to correct her, to remind her that I have acknowledged how I have failed to be empathic, but that acknowledgment has not helped. I continue to ask if it is possible for us to notice how she is reacting to my empathic error. Each time she interprets this as my trying to blame her, to hold her responsible for what I have done wrong.

The attack is amplified on Tuesday with her pulling all the stops on her anger, dredging up every complaint and flaw in my nature she can think of, and by mid-session Wednesday I am exasperated and banging my hands on the arms of my chair almost shouting that I did not say she was a bad person, or that it was her fault, or that my response last Friday was the best one. I only said that we are different people with different ways of thinking and responding. I have a real personality that responds to things that she does. She may be using my personal responsiveness for her unconscious purposes. I was angry that she persisted in turning everything I said to mean that I was okay and she wasn't. I was struggling not to defend myself against her harsh attacks, to find some way of validating her feelings. But she still turned my comments into how nuts I think she is, how I think everything is transference, and that I still believe I haven't done anything to deserve her anger and disillusionment.

Toward the end of the session I am able to say as sincerely as I know how that she is absolutely right that I started last Friday's session badly. She is quieter and, I hope, listening to what I have to say for the first time. I try to explain the long-term tracking I am doing. I said that when I felt her gaze and her immediate demand to know if I was okay, I mistakenly responded on the abstract plane I was considering at the moment, rather than waiting to see where she was coming from. She was having a joyous body experience, had written a poem, and wanted to share it with me. A concrete moment of happy sharing was what she wanted. My error, I said, was responding from another plane than the one she was on.

In struggling to explain how, given who I am and our previous discussions about her intense gaze, she can expect me to avert my eyes when she stares at me, I likened it to hugs at the end of the hour that I thought she had previously given an indication of understanding. I explained that if she wanted to interact comfortably with me, neither of these modes would work because they make me uncomfortable. I have shown her I can go along with what she wants, but if her desire is to achieve a mutually comfortable interpersonal connection given who I am, those means will not achieve it. This doesn't make me right and her wrong, it is merely the way I am. The intensity and physical contact are simply not ways of approaching me that she can count on a favorable response to. She had become quiet and thoughtful and left silently. I hoped I had acknowledged the nature of my error, and how it had indeed prevented me from being with her—and how that replicated the numerous times her parents had done just that to her, leaving her isolated and badly damaged as a result.

The next day she arrived utterly devastated. She could see now that I definitely could not be trusted. All along she had believed me. She had hoped that our relationship would be different. She had believed that I could be emotionally honest, but from my response yesterday she could see that there was no hope. No hope for me, no hope for our relationship, and no hope for her. All I could see was "an error in timing." But the fatal flaw remained, I still believed that it was her fault not mine. Further, I had humiliated her by saying I never wanted hugs, that I didn't like them, that they were all her neediness and nothing I cared for. It simply wasn't true, I had engaged warmly in those hugs, she said. Or if it was true that I hated her need of hugs, then I was dishonest when I had hugged her. I managed not to be defensively corrective of how she turned things today, but only echoed her despair and how this was exactly the despair she has experienced all her life with the emotional dishonesty of her parents.

I had encouraged her earlier to go over her concerns with a consultant we both knew. I brought that possibility up again, this time as a suggestion for a way out of her despair. Near the end of the session there was a long silence and slowly tears began to trickle down her cheeks. She was able to whisper, "Betrayal, what a horrible betrayal. To believe someone is emotionally honest and then to find out they haven't been." As she left I mentioned that I would be home all weekend in case she had anything to tell me.

By Monday she was ill with asthma again. Betrayal was the theme. She reviewed her distresses with me. I was allowed to correct the "error in timing" she spoke of to my view that I was badly out of tune with her by being on a plane of abstraction, tracking long-term themes when she was wanting to live together some concrete happiness of the moment. That seemed better. I was allowed to repeat my belief that we were experiencing being different people, not that I was right and good and that she was wrong and bad. We were struggling in this together but not as adversaries. She agreed but expressed that she felt I was trying to send her away to resolve this with a consultant when she had to work it out with me. I agreed that she had to work it out with me, but pointed out that sometimes a third party can shed helpful light.

Then I related the consultation I had had last week regarding my work with her. I told her I had come to understand several things more fully. She listened quietly and intently, but gave little response at the time. I reviewed how I had talked about my dilemma with her. I related that I had shared with my consultant how from her perspective it looked adversarial—and finally, despairing and bleak as she experienced the horror of emotional betrayal. I demonstrated with my hands banging the arm of the chair how I had related how angry I had been that she kept misinterpreting me as saying it was all her fault. I showed her my body freeze-frame that had been caught by my consultant of banging the arms of the chair. I quoted the empathic interpretation of my plight given by my consultant: "Mother, I hate you for not being available to me, for not hearing what I have to say, for misinterpreting my love, for not being there when I need response from you. I thought you understood me and now I find you don't." Our work had succeeded in producing a regressive trend in me that stimulated my response to my own organizing mother.

Her eyes grew larger, but still she was silent. I felt she grasped that I was telling her about my regression in our situation, my helplessness and anger; about how fragile and pained I had become. I continued talking about my consultation. I relayed how I spoke about how what was happening between her and myself was of critical importance. I was tracking the disconnects on one level and she on another and we weren't meeting—how frustrating it was for both of us. I mentioned that I had spoken about how I knew somehow she was doing absolutely the right thing in raging at me, but I still couldn't understand completely what it was all about. I told her I had been sitting in a love seat when the consultant observed another body freeze-frame at the very moment when I was expressing greatest agony about my plight with her. I showed her how I had leaned forward and sideways (toward a fetal position) with my right thumb approaching my mouth. Our session was drawing near an end. She asked a few questions to be sure she understood what I was saying about the oral and fetal body regression I was experiencing. I communicated compassion for both of us in the dilemma we were in and the strength it took on both sides to allow this deep regression to occur at the depth it obviously was.

Several hours later she left word for me to call and I reached her mid-evening. She was sobbing and barely able to whisper, her lungs and throat were unbearably tight and in pain. Her whole body ached. She said she was breaking down and began sobbing uncontrollably. She said Marc was there with her, so she was okay, but very frightened and confused. One thing kept running through her mind that she hadn't told me before. As long as she could remember, whenever her mother was angry, her mother would first scream and yell, but then lapse into a cold, distant, withdrawn silence. Her mother literally wouldn't speak to her for days on end. She wasn't ever sure exactly what she had done to produce the awful silence in her mother, but it was icy and cruel. It felt like what she gets from me when I withdraw into silence. Then she said, "This other I'm not quite sure about—what broke the cold silence. But it seems like after a week or so something would happen, maybe we would be passing somewhere in the house or something, and our eyes would catch and I'd break down. As soon as I'd break down she'd be okay again. But she would hold out until I broke down. It was so cruel. How could anyone do something so unbelievably cruel to a child—holding out until she broke. And I did. I always did. I always broke first. Like it was a battle to see who could hold out the longest. And she always won—even to this day she wins, I have to speak first."

I told her I thought something had happened when I shared my own helpless regressed distress with her. She agreed. We talked about it several ways. She was calming down now, glad for the talk. It seemed that when she could see my pain, my regression, something broke. But for once it wasn't her. When I told her about my body regression in response to her she knew I was connected to her. She knew I had feelings, and that I wasn't her steely mother. That we weren't in an awful battle over who was most sane. She replied, "Right now I feel a tremendous need to be taken care of, to be physically attended to, to be held, caressed, comforted. Like it's been a horrible trauma and I need comforting." I suggested she ask for physical comfort from Marc tonight. She asked if she could call me early in the morning.

When she called the next morning she told me that Marc held her all night. First one side of her body and then the other would get cold and be in terrible pain. He was glad to be there for her and she reminded herself that, despite her various frustrations with him, whenever she has really needed him he has come through. I commented, "He does care deeply for you and he has the patience of a mother who holds on until things are okay again."

This wasn't the first traumatic transference repetition with this woman nor the last as we worked through this organizing transference. But in the aftermath several interesting things were said. She had lunch with a close friend and laid out the whole story of her distress with me and felt very understood. She realized for the first time that I didn't have to be a perfect person to be her analyst. She expressed concern that she had made me feel so bad. I hastened to tell her that I was fine, that my regression was certainly in relation to her, but that it was as much a part of our work together as was my sharing it with her. She said, "I do know that. But all those things I said about you, you know they are true." I explained, "That was the worst part, that you know me too well." "But," she pondered, "I don't know why I said them all to you so meanly. I have to think about that." I said, "You had to remember, and this is the only way. I know we both wish for pictures and stories that are easy to remember, that aren't so hard on us. It would be wonderful if we could simply and easily agree that you had bad parents. It would be altogether too easy to simply confront them about their shortcomings, their abusiveness, the cumulative strain trauma they caused. But this painful reexperiencing kind of memory is more difficult. This cruel and abusive battle, beginning as it did from earliest infancy can only be remembered as trauma, rage, betrayal, confusion, fear, tightening in the throat and lungs, and cold and pain all over your body. The accusations are for the damage they caused you by being preoccupied with themselves."

We then spoke of how fragile her mother must have been to have been so threatened by the relationship demands of a baby. She had always thought of her mother as cold, calculating, strong, and cruel. Suddenly she understood that it was not so—that her mother was desperately clinging to her own sanity. "She could only hold to the false life that he [father] offered. She could hide herself safely in that false life with him. If there had ever been a choice, if it were him or me, it would have been, 'kill the baby.'"

The following week her sessions were quiet, her breathing calm and even, as she several times dozed off on the couch— almost asleep, thinking, dreaming, silently enjoying being with me and not having to entertain me—knowing that I was enjoying her peace and restfulness. I had the fantasy of being a parent lost in timeless reverie in a rocking chair with the new baby.

THE DELUSION DEFINED

The following Monday there was again a despairing rage. It was pointless to continue her analysis. She now knows that she can't trust me emotionally, that I am fundamentally psychotic like her parents and can never provide her with the environment she needs to continue her analysis. "You would just let me walk!" Meaning that I don't care about what happens to her, that I would simply let her walk out in all of her pain and disillusionment. I assured her I could not prevent her from "walking." But that would be a horrible loss for both of us, even as discouraged as she is with me at the moment. Perhaps it would help if she spent some time going over her problems with me with the consultant I had on several occasions urged her to see.

On Tuesday she wordlessly moved the large wing chair she has been sitting in, turned its back to me and sat in silence the entire session. I couldn't tell if it was anger or despair she was feeling.

Wednesday she echoed the uselessness of going on with me, the hopelessness of it all. How psychotic I am and how despairing she is. I struggled to stay with her on how awful it is to feel that there is no one to trust and nowhere to turn. I had occasion to discuss in basic terms a few ideas of Tustin and Klein. It seemed what she had hoped was that I would be able to restore the intra-uterine state of physical at-oneness with her mother's body. Again and again when she bumps into boundaries of myself or of others she is painfully reminded that Eden cannot be regained, that the lost maternal body is lost forever. We discussed the broadest dimensions of how a baby can be slowly led to realize that mother's body is separate and that baby will not die, that basic trust is possible even in an imperfect and failing world. In her case it seems clear that she was abruptly and cruelly forced into the realization that the necessary and loved features of her world were not under her control and that she has been enraged and suffering ever since. She said she had to hold onto this rage and she wasn't sure why—that she mustn't give in. I supported her in this, saying that she should not give in, that she must stay with her intuition. But I was for the first time a bit worried that she might actually attempt to end her work with me.

Thursday she announced that she was mad. She looked more confused than angry. She declared that this situation is impossibly painful and confusing—she can't function, and she doesn't know how she will get through the weekend in this shape. Then came the deepest anguish I had ever heard from her, without the slightest hint of manipulative energy to berate me or to get me to rescue her from it. "I can't trust you because you're psychotic and will emotionally damage me. But I can't let go of you or I'll die." There was a brief silence as we both grasped the impact of her powerful words. The truth had finally been spoken and we both immediately recognized this central definition of the emotional situation in which she has lived since infancy. We talked about it, and how significant this definition of her fundamental delusion is. It was like an enormous boil had finally broken and she was flooded with relief. I agreed to call her each day of the weekend. She immediately and spontaneously connected this central dilemma with the successful business meeting of several months ago which marked the beginning of this lengthy regressive experience. She saw how when her friends and colleagues connected with her she immediately distrusted their sincerity, their warmth, their good will. A series of other situations immediately tumbled out which could be seen in light of this new Rosetta stone. It was as though a key to understanding everything in her life had finally been spoken. She said, "You kept talking about connecting and disconnecting and I suppose that is what this is, but when I put it into my own words it suddenly makes more sense to me."

I emphasized the importance of her finally being able to state the bind she is in with me: that I am crazy and may damage her but that she can't do without me. I added that at least this second time around maybe I wouldn't be so crazy as her first mother! She smiled. She recalled that some years earlier she had attended a weekend "birth regression" seminar. In fantasy she had regressed back to the womb. She had a picture of herself as a "hard-boiled egg." All the other eggs were enthusiastically jumping up and down and she was hard boiled. I interpreted that this was a picture of her psychic life with the protoplasm hardened from the beginning, prohibiting any emotional growth. She said, "It goes back to before conception. My mother didn't want me to develop at all. It happened even before my father appeared." Some deep tension had been relieved, a way to rethink and reexperience everything was now available.

Spontaneously she related this new discovery to a series of distressing situations that have caused her great puzzlement and pain. Now she could see them as somehow arranged by her to prevent contact by experiencing others as untrustworthy or even using the closed off or defended parts of others' personalities to get them to do things that would prove that she couldn't trust them or relate to them. On the way out she said, "And there really isn't anyone I can trust." I said, "Not in the way you have always wished to—they are crazy and may hurt you, but the problem you are stuck with is that even if you can't totally trust anybody, you do need people to relate to and to feel alive with."

7

The Healing Process for Therapists: Some Principles of Healing and Self Recovery

Robert Hilton

In Chapter 3 I talked about the role of the therapist as part of the therapist's self organization. I also talked about the importance of having this role challenged both for the client and for the therapist himself. And that when this role is challenged, since the role is part of the therapist's self organization, the therapist usually responds defensively—moving away, against, or toward the client. For the therapist to respond differently, he must find another process of healing his narcissistic wounds other than through the role of being a therapist.

Like any other person, the therapist unconsciously hopes his defensive role of being a therapist works and also hopes that it breaks down or fails so that he can be freed from it and find again his true self expression. D. W. Winnicott in his 1974 article, "Fear of Breakdown," reminds us that we have all had "breakdowns" as children that produced unlivable states of being, and that what we fear happening in our life today has already happened. He also reminds us that we are inexorably drawn toward what we fear. We unconsciously seek to live through a breakdown in our present life in a different way than we did as a child and thus to integrate that lost part of our self that was sacrificed in service of our defenses. This is also true of the therapist and his role. However, if this breakdown and recovery does not take place in his own analysis, the therapist will not be equipped to help his client face the same process in the therapeutic relationship, but instead will respond defensively, thus retraumatizing the client or leaving himself open to his own retraumatization. I would like to discuss what this breakdown and healing process is like for the many therapists I have worked with around this issue. Alice Miller (1981) summarizes this process:

> I believe then, that it is no less our fate than our talent that enables us to exercise the profession of psychoanalyst, after being given the chance, through our training analysis, to live with the reality of our past and to give up the most flagrant of our illusions. This means tolerating the knowledge that, to avoid losing the object-love (the love of the first object), we were compelled to gratify our parents' unconscious needs at the cost of our own self-realization. It also means being able to experience the rebellion and mourning aroused by the fact that our parents were not available to fulfill our primary narcissistic needs. If we have never lived through this despair and the resulting narcissistic rage, and have therefore never been able to work through it, we can be in danger of transferring this situation, which would have remained unconscious onto our patients. It would not be surprising if our unconscious anger should find no better way than to once more make use of a weaker person and make him take the unavailable parent's place. This can be done most easily with one's own children, or with patients, who at times are as dependent on their analysts as children are on their parents. [pp. 22–23]

Miller is saying that either we, as psychotherapists, in our own analysis work through the way our needs were not met in the past or we will use our role as psychotherapist to act out our unconscious anger on our clients in the present. She suggests that there are certain things we as psychotherapists need to *acknowledge* about ourselves and certain *experiences* we need to have in order to accomplish our own healing and to minimize the acting-out process. What are these?

The first thing that needs to be acknowledged is that we had and still have narcissistic needs. Self psychology reminds us that we all have narcissistic needs and these are present self needs, not just archaic needs left over from childhood. If we deny this, then we will be in denial of the basis of our frustration with the client and he with us. We will not be dealing with reality. We also need to acknowledge that our narcissistic needs were not met by our primary caregivers. We like to deny that we were ever at the mercy of our caregivers. We want to say that they did the best they could or that it really wasn't that bad or whatever else helps us not to stay with how dependent we were and how neglected we felt. Acknowledging that we in fact had needs and that they were not met makes us accept our vulnerability and helplessness. We must recognize how important those needs were to us and how impossible it is ever to make up for what was lost. No amount of success or love in the present takes away the fact that we needed and we lost the struggle to get our needs met. This is very important for a therapist to acknowledge because it has ramifications for how he handles his own clients' disappointments with his role as therapist. We cannot acknowledge that we had needs and that they were not met and continue to hold on to the illusion of omnipotence. However, I did work with one psychiatrist many years ago who held on to the belief that he was like Moses. And, in fact, he looked like Moses and tried to command the attention of others with his illusions of power. One day, during a session in my office, I did a simple exercise with him, which was to have him bend over at the waist, bend his knees and touch the floor with his fingertips. In a very few minutes his legs began to tremble from the strain. I then had him stand up and experience his trembling legs. I asked him how he put together his Moses-like image of himself with his trembling legs. He looked puzzled for a moment and then straightening his back even more and lifting his chin in the air he said, "It takes a very special person to be God on shaky legs!" So if you want to deny that you had needs and lost, I guess you can. But the price you pay is living in the reality of not knowing yourself and your world.

Next we need to understand that the organizing principle behind our role as psychotherapist was the fear of losing the love of the primary caregiver in our lives. The possibility of losing this love in our lives was unthinkable and unlivable. An infant cannot mourn the loss of the primary love object. It must be denied and some form of adaptation created to avoid the terror of the loss. It is one of the things that happens to a child that the child cannot experience. To lose the love of the first object is to lose the person around whom his self organization depends. If this is not available, then another organizing principle must come into play, namely to organize around the needs of the object and not his own self expression. The role of therapist is just such a principle. When who we were could not be mirrored by our caregivers, we became experts at mirroring them and their needs. This at least gave us feedback that we existed and helped us to avoid our own abandonment terror or depersonalization.

> Recently, I was working with a couple in my office. The woman was confronting the man concerning the image he was trying to portray rather than who she saw him to be. He replied that if he was not who he thought he was, then when he looked in the mirror he would expect not to see an image or person there. I asked him to turn and face me and look into my eyes. I then asked him to take my hand and close his eyes and try to contact any feeling he had regarding his contact with me. I had been working with this man in individual sessions for over a year at that time. When he could contact a feeling in regard to his response to my holding his hand, I then asked him to look at me to verify that in fact I was there with him and could respond to his feeling. Slowly, he began to experience his presence in the room as a living being now and not an image in his head and that even if the image were destroyed, he existed. This was particularly relevant for him since he had a very narcissistic mother who was incapable of mirroring him but demanded that he mirror her.

We are here dealing with the most basic rudiments of the organization of a separate self. When the basic mirroring is not present for the child, he learns to be available for the needs of the other. This becomes the basis for the role of psychotherapist. As I mentioned before, once this self-organizing role is established, we hold on to it for dear life, but unconsciously seek a way to fail in this role in order to regain our original lost self realization. Unless the above is acknowledged by the therapist, he will be unable to give up his role when he is challenged and instead will act out defensively with the client as if his sense of self is being threatened, and in some ways it is.

We have said that there are certain things that the therapist needs to *acknowledge*, namely, that he had narcissistic needs that were not met by his parents and that to avoid the loss of their love, he took on a caregiving role and gave up himself. Now we need to look at what the therapist needs to *experience* in order not to duplicate with his clients what was done to him. The first thing that we need to experience in order to recover our true self and not to act out on our clients is to face the loss of illusion. What does this mean? It means no longer being naive about what happened to us as children. It means *experiencing* not just acknowledging that in fact we did not escape unharmed. That we as therapists are wounded healers. No one escapes childhood undamaged. The opposite of illusion is despair. We have held on to our illusions in order to avoid our despair. If we give up our illusions we fear that we will have nothing and we will be nothing. This despair must be experienced in a therapeutic relationship.

The experience of rebellion is also necessary—rebellion against the loss of the love object, rebellion against having to give up our self realization and assume a caregiving role, rebellion against the inadequacy of our caregivers that forced us into this compromise. I believe that we all at one time did rebel. The problem was the consequences of the rebellion were too great to sustain our self expression. The result of our rebellion and saying no to the expectations of others was to be abused, abandoned. Our caregivers could not tolerate this active expression of our lives and felt threatened by it. Taking on a caregiving role was a way of joining them and squelching our own rebellion. This is why I do not trust a therapist who has not rebelled against the role he has imposed on himself. If he has not rebelled in his own therapy, then when the client frustrates his role and rebels the therapist will respond to this self expression of the client in the same manner in which his parents responded to him when he rebelled.

Along with the rebellion, the therapist also needs to have experienced narcissistic rage. Rebellion is taking a stand over and against the imposition of the other, but narcissistic rage is an organismic response to the loss of self-nurturing supplies. These supplies are our birthright and they were withheld from us. The psychic punishment for experiencing this rage is shame. To want the love of the other so desperately, and to feel the rage that accompanies the disappointment, is overwhelming. To have narcissistic rage, we must first experience how essential the love of the other is to our sense of self. To know this and not to have the other acknowledge our desperation or feel the same toward us is to experience shame for needing so much. We try to over-come this shame by attempting to be there for the needs of others and thereby to be valued and wanted. The most important *experience* we need to have in this process of healing is *mourning* our losses. This is perhaps the most difficult. I remember in my own therapy beginning to cry about my losses as a child and then suddenly choking back the tears. The therapist asked me why I stopped and my reply was, "I won't let the bastards win." The reality is, of course, that they won a long time ago. For me to no longer organize my sense of self around the denial of that loss, I must be able to mourn it. But, that means I accept my loss is forever. This can be devastating. But, if I have not faced this in my own therapy, I will not be able to let go of this role with my clients. Also, I will be unable to help them let go of the self-destructive roles they have created to avoid experiencing their losses

In summary, we must experience the loss of illusion around our childhood traumas, own the depth of our rebellion and narcissistic rage, and allow ourselves to feel the mourning and despair that accompany such awarenesses. Only then will we begin to be free of the self organization invested in the caregiving role of therapist and once again find our self organization around our core self expressions. Then will we begin to be free enough to assist our clients on this same journey. We either work through our past in our own therapy or we are at risk of acting out this drama with our clients. Until we have begun this process, we and the clients are in peril and at risk.

RELATIONSHIP BREAKDOWNS
LEADING TO COMPLAINTS

I would now like to discuss how the above principles of healing and self recovery are realized by therapists who have not worked this process through in their own therapy and consequently act out with their clients. In these cases, the therapist is forced to face the above issues because of a breakdown in the relationship with the client. This breakdown often leads to ethical violations and lawsuits. What the therapist was unable to face in his own therapy via the transference with his therapist, he now must face with the client. Of course the client is in no position to serve as therapist for his therapist. This therapist comes to me to face the issues that have surfaced due to the retraumatization of himself or the client or both.

A familiar situation is when a client has filed a claim with the therapist's licensing board regarding an ethical violation. The therapist's life falls apart. It is difficult to imagine the chaos that follows these accusations, whether they are true or false. The therapist is at risk of losing his license, livelihood, reputation, family, friends, and colleagues, and in addition faces a great financial crisis. The stress is often internalized in somatic symptoms of panic, anxiety, sleeplessness, and suicidal ideations. As in any traumatic situation, the therapist begins to obsess about the case. What could he have done differently, what did he do, and what did he not do. The chaos is not dissimilar to that of his childhood. He uses his personal therapy alternately between a confessional and an attempt to justify his behavior. If he is to come through this chaos in a different way than he did as a child, he is finally forced to acknowledge something about himself that he has been frightened to really know and bring to consciousness.

Surfacing in the therapist's awareness is an unintegrated part of his personality. What he has been accused of being by the client is a part of the therapist's character that he had to repress in order to maintain his survival role as a therapist. He is usually accused of some form of self expression that was inappropriate for his role as a therapist and a shock to the client. This expression is always opposite to the image the therapist generally presents. He is accused of being narcissistic, cold, indifferent, sexually inappropriate, seductive, manipulative, exploitative, and so on. What is exposed is the shadow side of the therapist. The part that is unintegrated in his psyche. The negative side of this exposure is that it has been done inappropriately with a client who has been retraumatized by it. The positive side is that unconsciously the therapist has been seeking to express this unacceptable part of himself in order to free himself from the limiting role of being a therapist. This unacceptable part that he is accused of turns out to be the part of the parent that the therapist hated and swore he would never become. This makes it doubly difficult for him to accept and integrate.

As his therapist, I try to help him express directly what was expressed indirectly through his role with the client. A great deal of the time the therapist was trapped around his own unmet needs. The client in the transference relationship often offers, on the one hand, love, sexuality, understanding, support or some other form of contact that the therapist had given up receiving from his initial caregivers and was trying to gain through his role as a therapist. On the other hand, the client resents having to offer this to her caregivers in order to feel loved or safe. The therapist, blind-sided by his own repressed needs, rather than working with the client in the transference relationship begins to accept these gifts at face value and as if they belonged to him. What he had to give up to be a therapist is now offered by the client. Figuratively the client is offering the therapist a breast on which to nurse. And in isolated cases this is literally true. The therapist is extremely vulnerable to this offer since he has not adequately faced this need and loss in his own therapy and is therefore unable to ask for such self-nurturing supplies directly from his wife or lover. He has too much shame connected with needing this form of acceptance and nurture to ask for it directly. Rather, the role of therapist, where he is in charge of the relationship, gives him the false security that appears to make it safe to accept what is offered. Also, not having faced his narcissistic rage in his personal therapy and the subsequent loss of illusion, he still believes these supplies are available in some ideal form, which of course his wife or friends could not supply.

As his therapist, I have him openly ask for what he was indirectly taking from the client through his role. This is done in my office and not with the client. I might have the therapist say in an innocent voice, "I just wanted you to like me," or "I thought you loved me." When he says this, I might ask him to imagine her in his mind and reach out with his arms toward her. As he puts into verbal and physical expression what has been indirectly expressed in his behavior, he becomes in touch with the inappropriateness of his actions and faces deep feelings of shame and vulnerability. He begins to realize that this was the need that he had to give up as a child when he decided to take care of his parents and eventually to become a therapist. I must now help him see the appropriateness of having the longing to be liked as a basic human need and the inappropriateness of using his client to achieve this narcissistic need indirectly through his use of his role as therapist. This is true in regard not only to love and nurturing needs but also to sexuality, aggression, anger, fear, or any other deep core expression of his personality that had to be sacrificed on behalf of the parents' needs or inadequacies. I must help him support his right to have had these needs met by his primary caregivers and then take him through the various experiences I referred to above, namely, the rage, rebellion, disillusionment, despair, and mourning that accompanied that loss but that until now remained unconscious on his part. His innocence was shattered as a child. However, as a result of being unable to accept and mourn that loss, he has used his role as therapist to act out his repressed anger and need on the client and retraumatized her the way he had been traumatized. Once he sees this and accepts it, we enter another stage in the healing process.

When the therapist was a child, the parents' needs were too much for him to handle. He felt overwhelmed and inadequate. Yet, unless he tried to meet these impossible needs, he was left all alone and helpless. Likewise, the therapist in trouble needs to accept that the need of the client was too much for him to handle, that he was frightened by it and that he was also angry that her need exposed his inadequacy. All of this was unconscious on his part. However, instead of being able to own this inadequacy, he activated his role of caregiver, the same as he did as a child, and tried to provide for the client what he felt she needed. Obviously, it was what he needed. Thus, one of the hardest parts of this healing process is for the therapist to admit and to accept that whatever the situation was with the client that got him into trouble, it was too much for him to handle. He has to accept that he failed to do it right. He failed to understand her, provide what she needed, or allow her to be her own person. For the therapist to accept defeat means he is accepting that he can no longer hold on to the illusion that he can heal himself through the client. His role as therapist is limited and so is he. For the therapist to imagine saying to the client, "You are too much for me," is for him to experience his inadequacy with his primary caregiver and that takes him back to feelings of shame and humiliation. However, any therapist who cannot accept that every client will be too much for him is at risk of acting out upon that client his unconscious anger. The healing relationship for the client is in how the therapist responds to his own helplessness, for the client also feels helpless in the same way and for the same reasons.

Once the therapist is able to admit defeat and all that it means, the question comes as to whether or not he will be able to allow himself to receive contact from me in that position. I sometimes use a technique in my office to test this. I ask the therapist to lean against a door and then slowly slide down until he is sitting about three feet from the ground with his feet in front of him. It is as if he is sitting in an imaginary chair. This is an old ski exercise called "wall sitting." In a very short time the muscles in his legs begin to burn due to the stress and if he stays long enough his legs begin to tremble. While he is in this vulnerable no win situation, I ask him to breath deeply with the stress and to make statements like, "I can't do it anymore," "I give up," "I don't know what to do," "I am sorry I let you down." Eventually he has to let himself surrender to gravity and slide the rest of the way down the door and sit on the floor. Some therapists fight hard not to give in; it feels too much like defeat. However, when he is eventually able to do this, and while he is sitting on the floor having acknowledged defeat, I offer him my hand and wait to see if he can take it. He feels alone, inadequate, a failure. This he is finally able to accept. But, can he take my hand and accept my help while being in this position of defeat. This many find impossible to do. They feel shame at having failed and do not deserve to be helped. They cannot be forgiven. My outstretched hand in essence is saying to him, "I am a human being and you are a human being and you have acknowledged defeat; I am putting out my hand as a token of acceptance of you as a person who deserves to live." This is what the client craved from a parent. And the absence of this—or shall I say the defense against ever needing this again—is what started his problems. He reached out to helpless clients, but used them for his own needs because he had to deny his right to have these needs met in order to avoid the loss of the love of his caregivers. If he is able to take my hand, he will break into the deep sadness and pain of what he has lost and what he has now forced his client to face alone without him. If he is able to continue in his contact with me, he will also begin to experience what we have been talking about, namely the rage and despair that he has been living with for years and that he thought being a therapist would cure. Often the therapist at this point feels deeply for the client he has betrayed and may say, "I really wanted the best for her," or "I was really frightened, but I didn't want to hurt her. I did the wrong thing, but I also really cared. I need to receive acceptance of myself, even if I am inadequate and acted inappropriately."

I am reminded of a television program I saw several years ago featuring military personnel that had been captured and made prisoners of war. These men served in World War II, Korea, and Vietnam. They took us back to where they had been imprisoned and told us of the conditions under which they had lived. One Navy fighter pilot told of being shot down over Vietnam and being captured. He said that he knew as a prisoner of war that he would only give his name, rank, and serial number, but he was not prepared for the tortures that awaited him. After several days of excruciating torture that he vividly described, he reported that he finally broke and told the enemy anything they wanted to know. After this experience they put him in isolation so he could not contact any of the other prisoners. He was so filled with shame for having betrayed himself and his country that he knew he could never return to his men or his family. In this state of despondency he could only think of how he could kill himself. While he was in this state of mind, another prisoner was able to smuggle a small piece of paper to him and on it was scrawled, "Hang in there, we have all been broken." This gave him the hope he needed to connect again with his men and together they began to plan their escape.

We became psychotherapists because we were broken and we thought this was a way to find healing. We have tried to heal our families, our society, others, and ourselves. In many ways we have done a good job. However, we have had to pay a very high price for our journey. This price is our self realization, the actualization of our own being, the integration of body and mind. Our clients challenge our roles and give us the opportunity to once again recover our true expression just as we try to help them find theirs. This recovery means going through all the pain and disappointments of the past that we felt we could avoid by being psychotherapists. We must remember that we have all been broken. We need each other to share this important journey. It is essential for the therapist in peril to share his pain and disappointment with me as his therapist and to allow me to accept him in his defeat. For I too know what it is to be broken. He must also share this with his peers and thus form a support group for himself to help him through the difficult times with his clients. I often tell my trainees and supervisees, "Your clients and children will cure you, if you give them a chance."

PART II

TOUCHING, SEXUALITY, DUAL RELATIONSHIPS, AND COUNTERTRANSFERENCE

8

Touching in Psychotherapy

Robert Hilton

SOME PIONEERS IN TOUCHING

Several years ago I was asked by the American Academy of Psychotherapists to participate in their annual meeting and on be a panel discussing the topic "Hands On or Hands Off in Psychotherapy." Participating on the panel was a traditional psychoanalyst representing the "hands off" position while I was chosen to represent "hands on." There were also two other panel members who represented other points of view. Being on this panel forced me to examine why I touch, how I touch, and the many meanings related to touching in psychotherapy, including the transference and countertransference implications. I had to think about touching for psychotherapy in general but also, in particular, I was made aware of its implications in my specialty of bioenergetic analysis. To come to my present position, I had to think back through my personal history and review the meaning of my being touched in therapy. I would like to briefly review that history and draw certain principles that apply to this topic.

In 1965 I received my Ph.D. in counseling, my Marriage, Family, and Child Counselor license, and was a professor in a theological seminary where I taught pastoral counseling. As a theological student I had studied Rogerian client-centered therapy. As a graduate student, in addition to studying all of the various schools of thought, I was particularly attracted to Eric Berne and transactional analysis. I read his books, attended seminars he gave, and began individual and couples therapy with two different transactional analysts. I had also read about Gestalt therapy and its founder Fritz Perls, who was the principal guru at the Esalen Institute, which was a very progressive and humanistic growth center at Big Sur, California.

During this same year, 1965, which was the heart of the humanistic movement in psychotherapy and a time for experimentation and revolution in the field, I decided to go to a week-long Gestalt workshop at Esalen.

The entire atmosphere at that time at Esalen was one of sensory awakening. The institute itself is located on the beautiful cliffs of Big Sur right on the water's edge. Natural hot sulfur water pools have been turned into coed baths for the participants. Needless to say, clothing was completely optional. One of the leaders at that time was Bernie Gunther who was writing his book, *Sense Relaxation: Below Your Mind.* He conducted sensory awareness seminars where physical contact of various forms was the essence of his work. In addition, Esalen was known for promoting and teaching the Esalen sensual massage. Also in the Gestalt therapy groups, participants were not only encouraged to express the various emotions arising in the therapy but to openly confront and embrace various members of the group. These were the beginning days of the group encounter movement.

Well, you can imagine what might happen to me. There I was, a Baptist seminary professor inundated with sensual and physical stimuli and not only given permission to engage in it and enjoy it but taught that the way to true psychological health was to be found in breaking down the rigid defenses I had erected and in participating in the freedom of my body and feelings. Or as Fritz Perls used to say, "Lose your mind and come to your senses."

However, my response to this approach was unexpected. After about the fourth day I was there, I began to be overwhelmed with feeling and started to sob more deeply than I ever had in my life. I was experiencing a profound grief that at the time I could only understand as an awakening in me of the longing for contact and love I had never had. This breaking down was encouraged and I was told I was beginning to let go. In this sadness I found for the first time that I could also reach out to others to be held and comforted in my grief. As the grief subsided I felt a renewal of energy in my body that I had never known before and I was likewise encouraged to feel and express this newfound aliveness. I left there at the end of the week with a new mode of salvation.

I returned to my post at the seminary alive with the excited possibilities of touching. I was ready to introduce this new form of therapy to my students in the pastoral counseling classes. I still remember that the first person I met on campus was the president of the seminary who, up until then, was always greeted as "Dr. Heaton." With great enthusiasm I ran up to him and said, "Adrian!" and gave him a big hug. He responded with shock and stiffness. This was my first clue that the environment was not necessarily ready for my newfound salvation!

However, I found that the students were hungry for this message. I organized encounter groups, conducted sensory awareness experiences, and when it was my turn as a professor to conduct the faculty forum, instead of presenting some dry paper on an obscure theological dogma, I had all of the faculty members close their eyes, wander around a room touching each other and then report their experiences. For awhile I was riding high.

Very slowly, however, the latent resistance in the environment to this new form of expression began to come forth to combat the excitement that was being generated through this process of touching. I did not realize it then, but what was happening was that the environment was responding to my excitement the same way it had responded to me when I was a child. The students were fine, but the faculty and trustees of the school began to express resentment, anger, and suspicion. They were feeling invaded by this process. This eventuated in a special meeting of the faculty and trustees regarding this addition to the counseling program.

I soon realized that I was operating with the naïveté of a child. The result of the criticism I began to receive was to make me feel profoundly depressed. My bubble had burst and I was not grounded enough in this new experience to defend myself. I felt crushed. This new experience had not had time to be integrated. And just as my excitement had been crushed in the beginning of my life, so now I felt it again. And just as then there was no one to defend me, so now also I felt all alone. In addition, the environment of the seminary and ministry, which I had unconsciously relied upon to contain me, was now being shaken. The problem was I could not go back to my previous nonfeeling state, and I could not yet support the new excitement I felt. I could not go back to the previous state of equilibrium I had experienced before I had opened up to the touching and there was no new avenue or means of support for my new expression. My defenses were gone, and the environment I had used to reinforce these defenses was hostile. Within 18 months of these events, I had gotten divorced, left the professorship, left the ministry, and was seeing a psychiatrist who had me on tranquilizers and antidepressants.

About this time I had my first experience in bioenergetic analysis. I had moved to Santa Ana, California and was working as an associate with Everett Shostrom at his Institute of Therapeutic Psychology. One day during our weekly staff meeting, Everett introduced a guest of his from the East Coast. This guest talked to us about a therapy I had never heard of called bioenergetics. He said it had its roots in Reichian theory and that there was a psychiatrist in New York, Alexander Lowen, who had studied with Reich and had an institute where this guest had studied. When he was asked if he could demonstrate this therapeutic technique, he looked at me among my colleagues and said, "You look very depressed. I think I could help you."

He had me stand up, put my fists in my lower back and bend backward assuming a position that looks like a bow. I stayed in this stress position until my body began to vibrate and my breathing began to deepen. Once an energetic streaming began in my body, he asked me to lie on the floor, keep my head still and just look around the room with my eyes. Almost immediately, I went into the deep sobbing I had experienced at Esalen but had not been able to release since then. However, to my surprise, the sobbing led me into a furious, involuntary temper tantrum. My colleagues, having never seen anything like this before, stood around me looking down at what was happening. Suddenly they became members of my family who would not reach out to touch me. In experiencing this rage I knew I had found another avenue of expression besides crying and depression. I had touched another part of my excitement which was my anger. This had not surfaced in my first experiences of touching. The absence of this ingredient had been one of the causes for my deep depression. I also knew in this experience that I had touched the energetic core of my real self. When I got up off of the floor I literally grabbed the guest therapist and said, "You have to help me." He said, "I am on vacation and I haven't any time." Even with his protest I managed to talk him into two more sessions, but I asked him where could I go to receive training in this work. He said Alexander Lowen was coming out to the West Coast to conduct some training workshops. I asked him where they were going to be held. He said, "Esalen Institute."

After attending Dr. Lowen's workshop, I began participating in bioenergetic training sessions with a trainer on the West Coast. I now had a theoretical framework for the expression of my feelings. I also now knew that touching revives all of the repressed feelings in the body and is not a panacea. It revives hope but it also revives pain, rage, and despair. What was missing for me now was a therapeutic relationship in which I could make contact with these feelings and have them mirrored back to me. The trainer was not interested in such a relationship. He was interested in visiting and demonstrating his work. I turned to my new business partner, who was a psychiatrist taking the training with me, and we began to work with each other. In a short time I found that while the work was helpful on one level, it was keeping me from working through my deep transferential issues. One week I felt like a child with my father and the next week I was the child taking care of my father.

This arrangement continued for several years with workshops and training but the deepest issue in my character was not confronted until sometime later. In a session with Dr. Lowen, I faced that as a child I wanted to die. It was the only out I knew. The physical contact through the body work I had experienced mobilized feelings on the surface and elicited the hope of Eden and salvation. However, that hope was always dashed on the rocks of reality. The underlying core issue for me was that I had not touched and embraced my own desire to live. About this time, fortunately, I entered therapy with a woman therapist, where within a relationship I could work through step by step the ambivalence of love and hate that were stimulated by the physical contact in the therapy. I feel that as a result of that therapy I was able to make a deep connection to my own life process, the process that had begun nearly twenty years before. From this brief history I would like to draw attention to the following principles regarding touching and psychotherapy.

TOUCHING IS A NATURAL RESPONSE OF LOVE AND EXCITEMENT

It is impossible to think of loving someone without wanting to be near them and at times to touch them. In fact we as therapists often hear the complaint, "He says he loves me but he never touches me." They don't go together. When you love someone there is an increase of energy in the body that moves toward expression. I was told by a heart specialist that the development of the embryonic arms stem from tiny buds attached originally to the heart. When you love you want to embrace. This is true in passion but it is also true when you love someone who is grieving. Our natural inclination as parents is to touch what is hurt, to kiss it and make it well. We want to hold and comfort those whom we love who are hurting.

Touching is also natural when we share a mutual excitement. Sports enthusiasts are well aware of all of the "high fives" that go on during a game. The team is waiting at home plate for the home run hitter so they can swat him on the rear or hit his hand. When the team wins the series all of the players jump on top of the pitcher or carry him high on their shoulders. When Pat Cash won at Wimbledon, the first thing he did was to drop his racquet and crawl up into the stands to hug his father. As a basketball fan I notice that when a player misses a free throw another one will come over and touch his hand as if to say, "Hey we are here, it's okay." My point is that love and the excitement that accompanies it naturally moves us toward some expression of this excitement through physical contact.

THE LACK OF OR MISUSE OF TOUCHING PRODUCES TRAUMA

We need not belabor the point that being alive without physical contact can be hell. Isolation is a killer. Too much sensory deprivation can threaten our sanity. Isolation has been used in wartime to break the enemy and it is used on children all the time to break their spirits and make them obey.

Studies have been done in orphanages regarding the importance of physical contact for these children, and for infants demonstrating that it is essential to help prevent anaclitic depression. A close friend of my wife, Ann Petrie, produced and directed the award-winning documentary on the life and work of Mother Teresa. A great deal of Mother Teresa's work has taken place in the orphanages of Calcutta. There is one scene in this film that moved me and showed me the essential quality of physical contact. One of the Sisters is shown in an orphanage stroking an emaciated child of perhaps 6 years of age. He had long since given up to the absolute total despair of his situation. There was no life in his eyes and barely any life in his body at all. He was unable to move or eat. In this total abject state, the Sister props him up and has him lean against her while she begins to run her hand in a figure eight motion over the front of his body. Ever so slowly, you begin to see the tiniest flicker of life begin to come back into his body and then as if from the dead, he raises his weak neck to peer into her eyes with wonderment and disbelief. This contact was as essential as food. In fact, without the revival of human contact that comes through touching, the food is meaningless.

Other studies link sociopathy to inadequate symbiosis during the first few months of life. People who commit violent crimes often reveal a history of a lack of physical contact as children or contact that was so brutal that it created a numbness in them toward the pain of others. Because of this lack of or misuse of contact they do not have an empathic awareness of another human being and consequently can be unmoved by their violent actions toward others. We do unto others what was done unto us.

Often, the misuse of contact comes not in deprivation but in manipulation and seduction. As therapists we are painfully aware of the misuse of touching in childhood. The point here is that most of our patients can trace the origin of their problems to some form of frustration in this area. It may take the form of manipulation, smothering, seduction, physical abuse, sexual abuse, neglect, deprivation, or simply lack of awareness of the need for contact. The important step for us as therapists is to understand the nature of the individual trauma and thereby prepare ourselves more adequately as healers for the hurt child in our patients.

THE TRAUMA CREATED THROUGH
THE MISUSE OF TOUCHING PRODUCES
CONTRACTIONS IN THE BODY

The simple example here is an amoeba. When the amoeba extends a pseudopod into the environment and it is stuck with a pin it contracts back toward the nucleus. It then extends in another direction and if pricked again it contracts again. Eventually, if all expansion is blocked it contracts and ossifies. The human organism is much more complex than a simple amoeba, yet this same biological principle is in operation. If a child reaches with its mouth for a breast and it is not there or it sees anger in the mother's eyes, its body involuntarily contracts. If this frustration continues over and over again, the organism withdraws its energy from the source of frustration and holds on to itself for dear life. If this happens too early in life the body can go into a withdrawn, depressive state and die.

Once a person has withdrawn and armored himself around a particular loss or deprivation, while on the one hand he seeks to repair this loss in the world, on the other hand he is highly defended against ever again opening up to the original pain. By studying the contraction patterns in the body, the bioenergetic analyst can help the patient understand when and how he had to protect himself and what fears he must face to free himself again. Figure 3–1 (Chapter 3) is a diagram I use with patients to help them understand this process. Therapists should also understand this process to know what to expect from different patients when they touch or do not touch them. While the principles are general, each person has his own unique pattern.

The straight line on the left indicates the energetic expression of the body as it reaches into the environment. The opposite arrow represents the negativity of the environment that says no to the expansion. When these repeatedly come into conflict, part of the energy of the organism doubles back on itself in the form of muscular contractions, while another part of the energy goes into developing an adaptive self in order to cope with the pain and disappointment.

The purpose of balancing the energy between the contraction and the expansion is to establish a state of equilibrium, which functions to reduce anxiety. If each time I cry you yell at me, which in turn threatens my existence, I find that I must contract the muscles in my throat and reduce my breathing so that I stop crying so I won't be yelled at so

I won't constantly face this threat to my existence. While it is painful to be in this contracted state, it is more painful to feel constantly threatened. I am forced to choose survival over self expression. Thus I develop a "false self," which is acceptable and is used to ward off anxiety. However, this "false self" carries anxieties of its own.

PHYSICAL CONTACT CHANGES THE ENERGETIC EQUILIBRIUM OF THE BODY

When we touch someone we are bringing additional energy into this person's system and are stimulating a particular response in her body. We are inviting this person unconsciously to allow the delicate equilibrium she has established in her own energy system to change and to respond to the environment in a way that may appear to her to be life threatening. Remember, the equilibrium she established is for survival. To change that equilibrium by responding to our touch may be asking the person to experience the anxiety that was, at one time, life threatening. When her life force was originally open, the environment could not support it. Thus, she will be wondering if we really know what we are doing by asking her to trust us in a way in which she has always been disappointed. We also need to ask ourselves if we are ready for the response that may come as a result of our touch.

A good example of this point is that of placing a frost-bitten hand next to something warm. The warmth revives the life in the hand by increasing the blood flow but too much too soon can be dangerous. As the life comes back into the hand, so does the pain. Touching the patient adds warmth to the frozen and contracted areas of her body. This may help to bring her back to life but it will also revive the pain connected with why she had to contract in the beginning. Thus, touching, as it changes the equilibrium in the body, brings back the rage, sorrow, love, and fear that have lain buried in its frozenness. Touching, at times, appears to be cruel because it revives a hope that cannot be fulfilled, and yet not to touch may leave a person lost in her own frozen wasteland. The following are T.S. Eliot's (1950) famous words from his poem, "The Waste Land," which speaks to the point. Here, for Eliot, April with its warm showers, represents the cruel hand of nature that attempts to revive the frozen earth.

April is the cruelest month, breeding
Lilacs out of the dead land, mixing
Memory and desire, stirring
Dull roots with spring rain.
Winter kept us warm, covering
Earth in forgetful snow, feeding
A little life with dried tubers.

Remember as a child when you were angry and pouting and didn't want anyone to touch you. You knew you could hold out as long as you weren't touched. You were afraid that if you were touched you would begin to cry and need the person who had hurt you. And yet you yearned to be touched so you wouldn't be left as a victim to your own frozen stubbornness. This is often the dilemma we find in patients.

TOUCHING INVITES
A REGRESSIVE/TRANSFERENTIAL RESPONSE

Since the original frozenness in our bodies came around early childhood issues, so the melting of that frozenness invites people to once again experience the blocked sensations in their bodies and to express the repressed feeling. This expression always has a regressive quality to it since it is unfinished business from the past. With our touch we are asking the child within the patient to respond once more to the world.

This regressive response is heightened by the fact that we have a transferential relationship with the patient. It is not just anyone who is touching him. The patient receives and interprets our touch from the point of view of their transference to us at the time. Remember the Barbra Streisand song, "He Touched Me." In the song the world was made bright and shiny by the casual touch of someone with whom she was in love. I am sure you remember these feelings as a teenager when you had a crush on someone and they simply looked at you, much less touched you. The excitement was enormous.

Recently a therapist brought a patient in for supervision. She was someone with whom he felt he was doing very well. The patient, indeed, would respond to him however he contacted her, as if on cue. When I observed this happening between the two of them, I looked at her and said, "You would do almost anything for him, wouldn't you?" And with starry eyes she said, "Oh yes!" I said, "It looks as if you are in love with him." She became very shy and he looked rather shocked. He was just assuming that he was doing a good job because his own sense of ego was being reinforced by the response of the patient. He was blind to the fact that the patient had no spontaneous response of her own and that her response to his touch was highly eroticized and thereby kept her attached to him. Her reactions were geared to reinforce his attention. She blocked any spontaneous feeling in order to avoid being separated from him. He needed this kind of response and thus was unable to see her real needs. In other words, he never analyzed her highly eroticized response to his touch because he was too agenda-oriented around accomplishing the task of doing "therapy." She discovered, as she did with her father, that by being a good girl and "doing" what he wanted he would continue to touch her. His touching was being reinforced, the quality of her transferential response was being ignored.

Thus, the patient in a transferential relationship may interpret the therapist's touch quite differently from what the therapist meant it to be. The psychoanalyst on the panel I spoke of at the beginning of this chapter told the following story. He was treating a very depressed young woman and one Friday in his office she was unusually despondent. He feared that she might have a difficult time surviving the weekend. At the end of the session, as they walked to the door, he did something that he had never done before with her and was not accustomed to doing at all: he put his hand on her shoulder and said reassuringly but firmly, "I will see you on Monday." When she came to the Monday session she began by thanking him for his hand of reassurance at the end of the previous session. However, as the hour progressed, he felt her increased resistance to the therapy. As he analyzed the resistance he discovered that she was in reality deeply disappointed that he had touched her reassuringly. In light of the transference he had become her weak father who could never allow her to have her own feelings but contacted her out of his own need for reassurance. The analyst, in touching her, had elicited her hidden contempt for her weak father. All touching has to be understood in light of the transference and frame of reference for the patient.

In preparation for my talk to the American Academy of Psychotherapists, I became aware of how unconsciously, as I began to work physically with my patients, I was reaching over and touching the back of their necks. This unconscious movement on my part was obviously creating different responses in different patients. And yet, being a bioenergetic therapist, it had become second nature for me to reach out and touch my patients in this way. I was losing awareness of the impact of the energy I was bringing to the patients' necks and the response of their body to my touch. When I touched the neck of one of my patients who had been abused as a child, she became frightened as if I were going to take her head off. The same contact, from my point of view, with a more dependent patient caused him to want to lean his head into my hand for support. When I touched the neck of a patient who had a lot of control issues, it stimulated her paranoia and suspicion as if she were about to be manipulated into to doing something she did not want to do. The more compliant patient's response to my touch was to get a pain in his neck and feel burdened. I touched another patient on the back of his neck and his jaw came up with pride as if I were patting him on the back. So, when I touch patients, they have a response that comes out of their particular history, what contact has meant to them in the past, and their transference with me.

Many years ago I was in a workshop with Alexander Lowen and watched him work with a very muscular, powerful man. This man was built like a Turkish wrestler. Dr. Lowen was doing his very best to break down this person's resistance, which was manifested in extremely tight neck muscles. However, all of his efforts were to no avail. About this time Dr. Lowen turned to me and said, "Bob, why don't you try working with him." Not being dumb, I was not going to try the same method as Dr. Lowen. What I did was to sit behind the patient and gently lift his head. It was as if, when he looked at me, he knew he had nothing to fear. Feeling his power with me, which he did not feel with Dr. Lowen, he let go and began to cry. He could not let go with Dr. Lowen because of what he represented to him. He could let go with me. I was not a threat to him. The transferential response to being touched was obvious.

THERAPISTS NEED TO ACCEPT RESPONSIBILITY FOR THE EFFECTS OF THEIR TOUCH

The therapist, with this understanding of transference, must accept responsibility for what response he elicits when he touches the patient.

When I choose to touch a patient who is very desperate for contact or who sees me as a love object, I know I am inviting a relationship that will produce pain. Recently, I chose to make contact with a patient that I knew was in a desperate situation and saw me as a lifeline. Later, when she felt better and was angry at me that I could not fulfill her expectations, she said, "You made me fuse with you and now you tell me you are unavailable." It would be easy to say to her, "I didn't make you fuse with me, I simply touched you when you were desperate. Don't blame me that you interpreted my touch the wrong way or put implications on it that I didn't mean. I'm innocent." And yet from my knowledge of her history and the nature of our transference, I knew that would be exactly what she would feel, and I must accept the responsibility of eliciting that feeling even though I did not create it, nor could I fulfill it. But I can convey to her that I am aware, indeed, that she is not crazy and that is exactly what my touch would do to her and that it was done so that we might successfully live through her disappointment.

Touching does not always elicit fusion. Sometimes it will produce rage, sexual excitement, fear or any other of the basic feeling reactions that were either denied, misused, or encouraged in the patient's family. We as therapists need to be aware of the history of the patient, and the present transference relationship in order to relate our touch therapeutically to the situation. But, above all, we must take responsibility for the effects of touch.

TOUCHING STIMULATES A COUNTERTRANSFERENCE RESPONSE

According to Alice Miller (1981), most of us who are therapists have deep narcissistic wounds that we are trying to heal by listening to others in a way we were never listened to. We became little adults taking care of our parents when we should have been allowed to be children. To the degree that this is true, hidden in our caregiving is the resentment that our own open loving of the parent was not enough to be valued on its own. We had to be productive and, if you will, "perfect," in order to be loved. With this kind of history it is very risky to touch a patient because buried in that touch is our own desire to be received and loved. As long as we stay in our heads and handle our wounds theoretically, we are relatively safe. But if we stimulate through touch our own buried longings, we are open to reexperience our deepest pains. This time our self-worth is dependent on the response of the patient in front of us who no doubt is in many ways not too different from our original parents. The patient's rejection of the extension of ourselves through touch can revive in us our own repressed sadistic rage at our parents and thus make us fully aware of our own countertransference relationship to the patient.

I surprised myself one time in a session when after having my attempts at contacting the patient repeatedly rejected, I said with resignation, "I don't know how to love you." I became aware with this statement of how much having my touching received was an attempt to resolve my own abandonment anxiety. I felt crushed at having my heart/touch rejected. After releasing my sadness I was afraid to touch the patient again. My feeling was that if I tried one more time and was again rejected, the killing narcissistic rage I have around being rejected as a child would be acted out toward him. At that time in my own development, these powerful sadistic feelings overwhelmed me and I could not use them productively in the therapeutic situation without supervision. Today I could reflect back to the patient that this indeed must have been the way he felt about his own parents' rejection of him, but I was too vulnerable to my own feelings at that time to function so clearly.

Countertransference reactions are stimulated in many ways and can be used very productively in the therapeutic relationship. My point here is that just as the transference process is heightened by touch so is the countertransference. In fact, through touch, the countertransference response becomes quite obvious to the feeling therapist and must be dealt with.

Later in this chapter and in Chapter 11 I will talk more about specific countertransference problems that lead therapists into losing their own boundaries and cause them to act out on the patient.

CONGRUENCE BETWEEN FEELING
AND TOUCH ARE ESSENTIAL

Another important issue around touching is congruence. It is important to have a direct relationship between touch and the feeling that is communicated in the touch.

I am aware that we often touch our patients and children with only the awareness of what we intend to communicate and do not actually pay attention to what communication is coming back to us as a result of our touching. An example of this is in a film on mothering that we use in our bioenergetic training program. A group of mothers who had delivered babies at a particular hospital were asked to return to this hospital six weeks later to feed them. They were put in a room and told to feed their infants in their usual manner and that there would be a hidden camera filming the feeding. Some breast-fed their babies and some were using bottles.

In this film you watch the various responses of the mother to the infants. The two psychologists who produced this film, Axelrod and Brody (1968), worked out a system of evaluating the quality of contact between the infant and mother. When they watched the infant–mother interaction they discovered that fewer than 10 percent of the mothers paid attention to the movement of the infant and what the infant was trying to express through physical contact with the mother. The mothers, with good will and pride, were trying to accomplish the task of feeding their babies. However, most of them were unaware that the infant was struggling to make eye contact, that the head of the infant was bobbing back and forth and needed support, and that the infant's hands were attempting to touch or grasp some part of them. The mother was busy touching and feeding the infant while being distracted in her own thoughts. She was responding to her needs and how she was accomplishing her task and not paying attention to the infant's response to her intentions. When you did see an occasional mother that actually paid attention to the impact she was having on the infant through this intimate interaction, a sigh of relief could be felt in the viewing audience as well as a visible sign of relief in the face of the child.

An exercise we use in our training program is to have the trainee/therapist sit next to the trainee/patient and touch the patient around the diaphragm. Meanwhile the person doing the intimate touching is instructed to look around the room. The person being touched experiences the lack of congruence in the touching. The patient feels the touch of intimacy and the indifference on the part of the person making contact and he desperately tries to adjust between those two. This experience is literally crazy-making.

Another problem in congruence and touching is the fact that

therapists often avoid or deny the real feeling that they have in the contact. A patient will sometimes experience my hands as cold. This is an example, often, of my fear or of my being cut off from my feelings. I used to not want the patient to know this. It was embarrassing. I would try to hide it. During a workshop one time I was doing a demonstration with a woman. She reached out and took a hold of my hands and said, "They are so cold." I felt exposed in front of the training group. A bioenergetic trainer should not have cold hands! She said, "Let me warm them for you." Then she looked at me with fright, pushed my hands away and said, "That is what I always did for my mother." Then she said with fear, "My God, you are as scared as I am! What are we going to do?" I looked at her and said, ". What are we going to do?" Together we stayed with this experience of my cold hands and fear and her wanting to warm my hands and thereby take responsibility for me and at the same time not deny her fear. Through my acknowledgment of the congruence of my touch and her perception of reality we both learned something. We learned that we could live through our fears, stay in contact with each other, and find another genuine form of contact where we were both vulnerable and real.

THE THERAPIST NEEDS TO BE AVAILABLE
FOR THE CLIENT'S TOUCH

Alexander Lowen has often said that it is not enough that we touch our patients but that they be able to touch us. I mentioned at the beginning of this chapter that touching was a natural response to love and excitement and that each of our patients has suffered various traumas around the lack of or abuse of touching. As we work with these deep core issues in our patients we are reactivating in them the love and fears that surround these early abuses. To be able to make appropriate physical contact with the therapist today is to help patients complete the cycle that was interrupted. Since our primary ego is a body ego, at times only physical contact can give the patient the experience of our presence that allows him to move from his infantile hysteria to a state of equilibrium.

We as therapists need to provide a safe enough environment to allow the blocked movement in the patient to once again be expressed with appropriate contact. I may be touched and loved by my therapist but I must take the risk of opening and letting my own energy out to her, facing all of the risks that go with that. Reaching to touch from a deeply regressed place may be terrifying. But, it is necessary in order to be freed from the childhood defenses and to be open to new ways of integrating touching today. This is an essential ingredient in self recovery. Otherwise we stay stuck in our transference illusions.

> A colleague of mine was telling me about his own psychoanalysis. He was in a training analysis, with sessions four times a week. He told me of how he went through the transference phase of the analysis and was surprised at his behavior. During one period, when he was in the midst of the positive transference, he saw his analyst driving his car and began to follow him in order to find out where he lived. He was like any other star-struck teenager even though he himself was a therapist. He was afraid to let his analyst know how much he wanted his love and affection, knowing that to receive this would be inappropriate and not within the "frame" of the therapy. As a good patient he eventually resigned himself to the reality of the situation. Then came the last session of a three-year analysis. As he was walking out of the office for the last time, the analyst for the first time put his arm on my friend's shoulder and told him how much he enjoyed working with him. My friend said it was as if none of the therapy had happened. All of the feelings he thought he had worked through surfaced in his body as he felt the touch of the analyst. He said, here he was leaving when he felt for the first time he was beginning.

AS THERAPISTS WE MUST UNDERSTAND OUR PERSONAL RESPONSES AND BOUNDARIES IN REGARD TO TOUCHING

As a former minister I am aware of the conflict between human nature and the dictates of the church. As a therapist, I am aware of the difference between insight and the powerful life and death forces in the body. More than one minister has preached against the evils of sexual freedom only to be trapped by his own passions. Likewise, many therapists, denying or disregarding the power of their own feelings, have been trapped in acting out against patients. The problem is that prohibition does not stop acting out, even when your reputation and career are at stake. The powerful life forces in the body must be recognized and integrated into the personality. Otherwise they wait like the soldiers in the Trojan horse ready to overwhelm the unsuspecting citadel of the ego. The greatest safeguard against the misuse of touch is to know your own responses and boundaries in regard to touching and being touched.

As therapists we are called upon to deal with the intensity of people's passions and yet we have had very little training on how to recognize and deal with our own. When we have been taught simply to control these feelings with our wills, we are subject to great anxiety and failure in the presence of their power. This is especially true when we open ourselves and our patients to physical contact. And yet, touching is part of being human and the way the child in us learns to integrate and trust our feelings.

There are many reasons why touching is misused and abused in therapy. We have suddenly been flooded with studies indicating how dual relationships and sexual abuse are abundant. This is true wherever there is a misuse of authority. Ministers, lawyers, doctors, teachers, therapists are all guilty. We have recently had articles indicating the types of therapists who are vulnerable to this misuse. I would like to draw our attention to two particular problem areas.

The problem in touching is not the touching itself any more than the problem with the sexual abuse of children is that children desire contact and are vulnerable. The problems come when the unfulfilled needs in the therapist are acted out on the patient. Among the therapists I have worked with who have had problems in this area, I have found that they have mainly gotten into trouble with two types of patients. The first is the "understanding" patient. In this situation the patient offers to the therapist what the therapist never received from his own parents and what he has been trying to give to others. The vulnerable patient who offers to touch the therapist and invites the therapist to touch him or her in return is making an offer to the child in the therapist that many therapists find impossible to resist. The therapist feels loved and not having expressed his own anger and disappointment over not being loved as a child he now wants to believe that this offer to him is real. Soon the therapist is touching the patient more and more out of his own needs. Eventually this either leads to sexual contact or the patient begins to realize that he or she is paying for the therapist's therapy.

The second problem area is working with the "innocent" patient. Here, the patient has a childlike, defenseless quality that opens the heart of the therapist and he begins to touch the patient as you would a small infant but without the awareness that this "infant" is in an adult's sexual body. The boundaries are soon blurred because once again the therapist, in touching the patient without accepting the reality of the situation, is reliving his own deprivation. He feels like he is loving the patient and that the touching is coming from an "innocent" place. However, there are no "innocent" patients or therapists, only naive, and the "innocence" of the therapist's affection is still coming from his own wounded child. Eventually, the repressed anger that has kept both people naive surfaces and reality is faced. The patient is not a child but a sexual adult and the therapist is not a giving parent but a hungry child in a parental role.

Guntrip (1964), discussing the nature of psychotherapy, says,

> The key to the nature of psychotherapy . . . is the search, not for the "ideal mate" but for the "ideal parent-substitute" who will do for the "little needy ego" inside the adult what the actual parents failed to do at the right time. One may say that the relationship between the psychoanalytical therapist and the patient lies midway between the parent–child relation and the husband–wife relation. It is not a relation between an actual parent and an actual child, nor is it a relation between two adults on terms of equality. It is a relation between the unhappy and undermined child in the adult patient and a therapist whose own "internal child" ought to have been taken care of by his own training analysis so that he is free to be the stable adult parent-substitute to the lonely "little needy child" in the patient. Only this kind of therapy can promote regrowth of personality from the depths. [p. 75]

Herein lies the problem, "a therapist whose own 'internal child' ought to have been taken care of by his own training analysis, so that he is free to be the stable adult parent-substitute to the lonely 'little needy child' in the patient." We as therapists must be open to the issues in ourselves that we are trying to work with in others. In order not to misuse the sexual feelings of our patients we need to accept and know the power of our own sexuality and this needs to be done within a therapeutic relationship. Otherwise, we are hit on the blind side with our patients' intense feelings and are over our heads before we know it. The same thing applies to touching. Just as one of the major problems regarding child abuse is secrecy, so it is with therapists in regard to when they are feeling inadequate around the issues of personal intimacy with patients. *Each therapist who touches patients must have lived with and through his own regressive behavior in this regard with his own therapist and must now have a supervisory group to which he can turn when he feels overwhelmed.* Avoiding touching is not the answer; understanding and integrating the meaning of touching for you personally will give you the solid basis from which you can be the "stable adult parent-substitute" that is needed. But first your own needy little child must have been acknowledged and allowed to grow up.

In summary, it was the misuse of touch that created our pain and forced us into developing our defensive structures. It is with the hope of the release of that pain that we have, as patients and therapists, risked touching again. The heart of that recovery is to be found in the reenlivening of our deepest needs within a safe relationship. To be in our body is to live with the desire to love, to touch, and to be touched.

9

Sexuality in the Therapeutic Process

Virginia Wink Hilton

Clients' stated reasons for seeking therapy often include some degree of sexual dysfunction or dissatisfaction. Unless the therapy is of short duration and narrowly focused on a specific, nonsexual issue, it is almost inevitable that some aspect of sexuality will emerge in the course of the treatment process. And, in a large percentage of cases, some degree of sexual attraction will be experienced, consciously as well as unconsciously, by one or both members of the therapeutic dyad (Pope et al. 1986, 1993).

As therapists, we face the challenge of dealing with sexuality and sexual issues in clinical practice without, in most cases, having been adequately trained, and from a completely vulnerable position. We must respond to this task without having support of any kind: without the support of the "sex-negative" culture that is preoccupied with sex on the one hand and frightened by it on the other, and without the support of the profession that has perpetuated an "antilibidinous atmosphere" (Pope et al. 1986). And most often we are not supported by our own personal history, which after all, can be at best little more than a reflection of the collective attitude.

The task for the therapist is formidable. The failures are most painfully apparent in the statistics revealing the prevalence of sexual intimacies between therapists and clients (Gartrell et al. 1986, Holroyd and Brodsky 1977, Pope et al. 1979, 1986, 1993). The damage done by such violations is extensive and profound (Bouhoutsos et al. 1983, Brown 1988, Butler and Zelen 1977, Feldman-Summers and Jones 1984, Pope et al. 1993, Sonne 1985, Vinson 1987).

For too long there was a tendency in the profession to overlook or deny the indiscretions of its members (just as there was in the culture at large around incest and child abuse). In recent years there has been a change. The literature on the issues is steadily growing, and awareness has increased many times over. The result is apparent through the increase in filing of claims and civil suits, and the establishing of criminal laws (Pope et al. 1993).

SUBTLE VIOLATIONS BY THERAPISTS

While there is evidence that the heightened awareness of and action against sexual violations has resulted in a decrease in such incidents (Pope et al. 1993, Strausburger et al. 1992), another level of sexual behavior continues. It is a range of *subtle* behavior that is unlikely to result in a formal complaint or civil suit. Yet the client feels violated by it at worst, and misunderstood at best. Sometimes the feelings evoked by this behavior are vague and inchoate, but always uncomfortable; the client often feels he/she has no real "right" to question or object. And the therapeutic process founders. In such "subtle" situations, the therapist likely has no idea of what the offending attitude, comment, or gesture may have been, and has no awareness of any inappropriate behavior on his or her part. Two examples come to mind:

A woman intern told her therapist that her supervisor always gave her a "full body" hug at the end of their weekly sessions. She felt he had no conscious seductive intentions, but she was always disturbed and left with uncomfortable feelings. She did not want to jeopardize her position with him by making an issue of it.

A trainee confided his distress over the fact that his former therapist whom he occasionally saw in social situations, would at those times give him a "social" kiss on the cheek, as was customary in such situations. I happened to have observed this behavior, and I had no doubt that there was no seductive intent on the part of the woman therapist. But for the man, this action was confusing and disturbing.

There seems to be a surprising and ubiquitous lacuna around the effects of certain "mildly" seductive or invasive behaviors on the part of the therapist. Unfortunately, there is rarely the opportunity for therapists and teachers to learn about such effects, to receive feedback about them, or to process and understand their impact.

The most common failure of therapists, however, is likely to be one of omission rather than commission: the avoidance of sexual issues altogether. The whole subject of sexuality is enormous, baffling, confusing, overwhelming, exhilarating, and—in spite of the cultural preoccupation with it—a little-understood aspect of human existence. Given the complexities and the dangers (including an underlying threat of legal punishment and professional censure), there is no wonder that when possible, we professionals choose to focus on another issue. Such a choice seems to be made by writers and educators in the field as well.

Yet, sexuality is central to human existence, and therefore it is central to the therapeutic process. Whether we are comfortable with it or not, our task as therapists is to be present with our *feelings* as well as our awareness, when the client's sexual issues emerge in the relationship. And the task is to intervene effectively on behalf of his/her truest needs.

The greatest help to the therapist for dealing appropriately and effectively with sexual issues can come from a thorough exploration of the dynamics of transference and countertransference. It is my contention that failures of abuse—erotic acting out anywhere on the continuum from "harmless" flirtation to actual sexual involvement—frequently occurs because of *an inadequate understanding of the nature of transference*. The failure or avoidance of sexual issues and feelings in the therapeutic process is often due to the *fear of countertransference feelings*.

The transference phenomenon was first observed and elucidated by Freud (Breuer and Freud 1893–95, Freud 1912a,b, 1915), and it became the central focus of the practice of psychoanalysis. Analyzing the transference became the key to understanding the unconscious and the means of effecting the cure. Over time, countertransference, the therapist's feeling response to the client, was increasingly recognized as significant—

and for many, crucial—to the process. While the definition and development of these concepts and their application has largely evolved within the psychoanalytic community and its body of literature, most other psychodynamically oriented therapies recognize their significance and incorporate them in their training, at least to some extent. Most therapists, regardless of their approach, have some superficial knowledge about the meaning and functioning of these dynamics.

Transference and countertransference are relational phenomena, present to some degree in all human interactions. They are present in a particular way in relationships involving any kind of authority. Therefore, whether or not the transference and countertransference are directly utilized in the treatment, the dynamics warrant recognition and understanding by all who work therapeutically with people. This has particular relevance in regard to sexual feelings and sexual issues. The vague and partial "popular" awareness of the terms *transference* and *countertransference*, however, is not adequate.

Understanding the concepts is one thing. Becoming familiar with the implications and ramifications, and how these are manifested specifically in one's self and one's clients is another. In working with sexuality and sexual feelings we are dealing with dynamic interactions that create profound responses and intense reactions. Therapists have been offered too few opportunities in their education, supervision, and training to become familiar with the possible range of sexual responses of clients, or to become more at ease with their own sexual feelings (Holroyd 1983, Kenworthy et al. 1976, Landis et al. 1975, Pope et al. 1986). This chapter points to some ways of becoming better prepared to fulfill our task of responding ethically, appropriately, and adequately to our clients' sexual issues.

TRANSFERENCE

Understanding the Transference Phenomenon

Definition

Transference is the term applied to an unconscious process of displacing onto a person in the present feelings and responses that were originally evoked by a person or relationship in the past. Therefore, transference responses are a repetition of the past and are to some degree inappropriate to the present (Greenson 1978).

Freud's colleague Joseph Breuer had a patient who came to be known in analytic literature as "Anna O." (Breuer and Freud 1893–95). In the course of her analysis, this woman responded to her analyst with great erotic intensity, which was judged unwarranted by the reality of the situation. Freud (1912a), reflecting on this case recognized that the passionate feelings of the patient were not primarily evoked by any realistic attributes of her doctor, but instead were being displaced onto him from an earlier source. He then came to understand that the individual's early interactions with parental figures provided a proto-type for later love-object responses. Part of the early feelings and impulses remain unconscious or undeveloped, and only part become conscious and directed toward reality. It is the *unconscious* material that is transferred to the doctor. Therefore, through the patient's response to the analyst, the unconscious and the effects of his early relationships to his present reality become accessible to the analytic process. Thus transference became, and still remains, the very center of classical psychoanalysis.

Transference is seen to be "always present, active and significant in the analytic situation" (Bird 1972, p. 52). But the phenomenon is not limited to this relationship. Freud (1925) stated that transference "is a universal phenomenon of the human mind . . . and in fact domi-nates the whole of each person's relations to his human environment" (p. 76).

The Function of Transference

What is the function of the transference? According to Fenichel (1945), the patient misunderstands the present in terms of the past, and then, instead of remembering the past, he strives without recognizing the nature of his action *to relive the past and to relive it more satisfactorily than he did in childhood.* He "transfers" past attitudes to the present.

Silverburg (1918) provides the following formulation:

Transference may be defined as a repetitious attempt to rectify in action a traumatic situation which, though it is in a sense "remembered," cannot be recalled; it is the attempt to learn, by a series of rehearsals, how not to be helpless or powerless in a situation which originally found us so—the original situation being "remembered" (implied in acting out) although not consciously recalled. Such attempts continue to be made in a variety of forms throughout the patient's life, until he has learned to understand the nature and purpose of his behavior and becomes convinced of its futility. [p. 309]

The function of the transference phenomenon, according to this formulation, is to replicate the past *in order to rectify it*. In the therapeutic process, one could say, the patient is unconsciously attempting finally to find the "right" responses to his/her feelings or actions.

Erotic Transference

Freud on the Erotic Transference

In his treatise, "Observations on Transference-Love" (1915, 1959), Freud makes clear the importance and the dangers of the erotic transference. He communicates understanding and a kind of empathy for the difficulties that await the analyst in working with the erotic transference, and for the temptations that may beset him:

One has no right to dispute the "genuine" nature of the love which makes its appearance in the course of analytic treatment. . . . The transference-love is characterized, nevertheless, by certain features which ensure it a special position. In the first place, it is provoked by the analytic situation; secondly, it is greatly intensified by the resistance which dominates this situation; and thirdly, it is to a high degree lacking in regard for reality, is less sensible, less concerned about consequences, more blind in its estimation of the person loved, than we are willing to admit of normal love. We should not forget, however, that it is precisely these departures from the norm that make up the essential element in the condition of being in love. [p. 388]

Freud speaks eloquently of love between the sexes, and says that "the combination of mental and bodily satisfaction attained in the enjoyment of love is literally one of life's satisfactions" (p. 389). Yet he is clear and unequivocal about the correct response of the analyst to the patient:

When a woman sues for love, to reject and refuse is a painful part for a man to play. . . . And yet the analyst is absolutely debarred from giving way. However highly he may prize love, he must prize even more highly the opportunity to help his patient over a decisive moment in her life. [p. 389]

In spite of the fact that the formulation of transference as central to the psychoanalytic process emanated from Freud's reflections on the *erotic* transference most of the attention in subsequent writing, particularly in recent years, has focused on other aspects. Ethel Person (1985), in one of the rare articles on the subject, may give the reasons why: "Compared with other types, [erotic transference] has always been tainted by unsavory associations and continues to be thought of as slightly disreputable. It remains both *goldmine and minefield*" (p. 163, emphasis added).

Differences in Male and Female Responses

In the same article, Person also emphasizes that while erotic transference is considered a universal phenomenon its development occurs in differing degrees among patients. Women in treatment with men are much more likely to experience strong erotic feelings than in the reverse situation.

Person suggests that women tend to use erotic transference to resist the analysis, whereas men tend to resist the *awareness* of the erotic transference.

She points out that rarely in the literature are there references to male patients having strong erotic transferences to their female analysts (Bibring 1936, Lester 1982).

With female patients and male therapists, the erotic transference is more often overt, consciously experienced, intense, long-lived and directed toward the analyst, and focuses more on love than sex; in the [male patient–female therapist dyad], it is muted, relatively short-lived, appears indirectly in dreams and triangular preoccupations, is seldom consciously experienced as a dominant affective motif, is frequently transposed to a woman outside the analytic situation, and most often appears as sexual rather than as a longing for love. . . . Like women, they may idealize the analyst, but the idealization is not merged with erotic longing. [Person 1985, p. 170ff]

What accounts for these differences between male and female responses to the erotic transference?

> For the male patient, to feel erotic urges toward the female analyst would be to emphasize his overall need for her, a need that apparently undermines his sense of autonomy. To the degree that he can, the man preserves or juggles his autonomy and independence by separating sex from dependency (and intimacy) and controlling his sex object. He fears dependency connected to sexuality insofar as it represents weakness and loss of control. [Person 1985, p. 172]

On the basis of these observations it would be worth pointing out that the "lopsided" statistics around sexual misconduct do not indicate, as might be superficially assumed, that women therapists are morally superior, or more able to contain their impulses than their male counterparts. The pressures are generally not as great upon women; for the most part they are not faced with the same intensity and powerful erotic affects as their male colleagues encounter. And if and when they do, it is more likely that impulses toward acting-out behavior will not be as compelling for either client or therapist.

Conclusions

The client–therapist relationship is an intense, intimate dyad wherein the therapist, in most instances, is perceived to be in control and has the power. The client is perceived to be in a dependent position. There is no real mutuality; the therapist reveals comparatively little of himself, leaving huge blank spaces that invite projection. The dyad is removed from the social context of each person; there are no comparisons readily available, no checks and balances. Each views the other primarily against a backdrop of powerful emotions that are evoked through the process. The stage is set for the client to project onto the therapist the aspects of the longed-for parental object. When the transfer of erotic feelings and desires takes place, the therapist may be faced with powerful affects, such as unrestrained adoration and passion. It is not always easy, at such a time, for the therapist to remember, as Freud admonished that, ". . . the patient's falling in love is induced by the analytic situation and is not to be ascribed to the charms of his person, that he has no reason whatsoever therefore to be proud of such a 'conquest,' as it would be called outside analysis" (Freud 1915, 1959, p. 379).

The patient's reexperiencing of erotic strivings is an attempt not to fulfill the incestuous longings but to correct and heal the initial situation, which in some way blocked the natural maturation process.

In the therapeutic process the therapist is relating to an adult person in an adult body. Yet the client's feelings may be those of a 3-, or 5-, or 15-year-old in relation to a parent. They may be the feelings of an infant. It is for this reason that sexual involvement with a client is likened to incest (Marmor 1972), and the effects are often similar to those of child abuse (Pope 1988, 1990, Pope et al. 1993).

Male therapists are at greater risk than females, due to the nature of male–female erotic relationships and the culturally defined attitudes toward power and dependency of both men and women.

Treatment Implications

Erotic Response to the Client

Freud (1915, 1959) was clear about the effects on the therapy of responding "in kind" to the patient's transference feelings: "If her advances were returned, it would be a great triumph for the patient but a complete overthrow for the cure" (p. 384). Yet any sense of triumph in the patient, according to the data (Bouhoutsos et al. 1983, Holroyd and Bouhoutsos 1985, Pope 1988, 1990), is destined to be short-lived. Even in the heat of passion clients often know *consciously* as well as unconsciously that they do *not* want their advances returned. They know that to "win" is to lose. One client illustrates this point with the following reflection on her therapy experience:

> "I came to understand that, in order to work through my sexual problems, what I needed was to find a male therapist in whose presence I could be 'turned on to the max' and be absolutely certain he wouldn't come on to me. He would just be there and enjoy my feelings and not want something from me for himself. That was what I didn't get from my father. I had bad experiences with two male therapists. The first I fell in love with, and the second I just felt wildly attracted to. Both came on to me one way or another. I hated them for that, for not understanding what it was I really needed." [V. Hilton 1987, p. 81]

Human beings are quite remarkable at achieving replication of their primary relationships. As has been stated, the manifestation of the transference feelings in the therapeutic process is an unconscious attempt to re-create the original situation and to find a different—and better—solution. The therapist must remain clear that a better solution requires his or her intervening *only on behalf of the patient's truest needs*.

Setting Clear Boundaries

Clients need to know that their transference feelings for the therapist can be experienced and expressed in absolute safety. This necessitates the establishment and the maintenance of clear boundaries. To get a firm idea of just how important this is, one needs only to consider the effects upon the child of a parent's unclear boundaries around sexuality. In therapy the process inevitably goes awry when the limits are not clearly defined and stated.

Over the years I have found not infrequently that male clients will make some humorous comment that is a veiled request for a verbalization of the boundaries around sexuality, even though they clearly know the rules. I have understood this to be an expression of the need to be reassured that I am on the side of protecting their vulnerability as well as containing their impulses. The verbal reinforcement of what is rationally assumed is often crucial to the establishment of the trust that is necessary for dealing with erotic feelings and the intimacy of the relationship.

Following is an account of one female client's experience with unclear boundaries:

> "In the initial session I found the therapist attractive. When I told him about my childhood, he pointed out certain things we had in common. It felt like a bond. By the fourth session, I began by telling him that for the first time I was in touch with anger and dissatisfaction toward my husband. At this point the therapist said to me that he wanted to put his cards on the table. He was attracted to me and I was the kind of woman he was looking for. He said he wouldn't act on his feelings because that would ruin the therapy. I was terrified! But by the next session I felt hopelessly in love. After that he never made any advances that could actually be called sexual. But there was never a patient scheduled after

me, and frequently after the session he would invite me to talk about his current fascination with astrology or to listen to music. Once we lay on the carpet, side by side, listening to Ravel's "Bolero."

"An enormous conflict was raging inside me. I was experiencing feelings of intense passion for my therapist, feelings I didn't have in my marriage. I was psychologically aware enough to know that my relationship with my father was all mixed up in this. I knew I couldn't tolerate the guilt of having an affair with him. So I struggled for several months, fighting my passion, wanting to set it free. Finally one day I came into a session ready to declare the love I felt. When I spoke about my feelings, the therapist replied that he wasn't available. He went on to say that over the previous weekend he had renewed a relationship that had broken off just before I had come into therapy. I felt stunned and hurt and betrayed.

"From then on there was a marked change in his behavior toward me. There was always a client in the hour after mine. I tried to be understanding and rational. I found myself being protective of him. But soon the hurt changed to rage. I couldn't release it. Finally the therapist and I met with a consultant, who lent enough support that I could vent my feelings. In the discussion that followed, my therapist came to the realization that while he had decided not to seduce me, unconsciously he felt that if I seduced him it would be okay! I realized my childhood experience had been repeated. *I* was made responsible for keeping the limits. [V. Hilton 1987, p. 85ff]

Here was a situation where the therapist *verbally* set limits, of sorts: "I won't have sex with you." Yet because he unconsciously decided he could be seduced he was constantly leaving the door open, so to speak, and was really seducing her to seduce him. When he suddenly behaves more professionally after resuming a personal relationship, it is clear that the "limits" were defined more by his needs than by his client's.

Self-Disclosure

Another issue that is demonstrated in the above account is the effect of the therapist's "confession" of his feeling for the client. The appropriateness and usefulness of self-disclosure by the therapist is an issue that has been debated at length in the psychoanalytic literature; for example, Winnicott (1975) and Heimann (1981) take opposing viewpoints. Many therapists of all types take the stance that revealing honestly personal feelings and reactions is a valid, therapeutic response.

Yet in my experience as teacher and supervisor, the consistent feedback gathered through role playing, discussion, and clinical data confirms that in regard to *erotic feelings* clients do not want that information from their therapist. It is always at best disturbing and confusing, and often (as in the account above) it is terrifying. And it automatically renders the boundary ambiguous.

Clients, in the course of dealing with erotic transference and oedipal issues, may ask the therapist, directly or indirectly, "Are you attracted to me?" The need being addressed is *to have their sexuality acknowledged and affirmed.* What they want from the therapist/parent figure is to hear, "You are an attractive person." Such a response from the therapist has the sense of being "objective," and is not experienced as threatening. My experience has led me to conclude that, no matter how the question is put, what the client does *not* want to hear is "I am attracted to you." The difference is subtle but crucial: "You are attractive" is about the client; "I am attracted to you" is about the therapist's feelings. The latter response violates the boundary and changes the relationship instantly. As in the process recounted above, the client is no longer able to focus entirely on his/her own feelings, but now has the overwhelming burden of relating to dangerous feelings of the therapist. The task of the therapist is to contain his erotic feelings and "unburden" them in supervision or in his own therapy, until and unless he is able to *use* them in the service of the therapeutic process.

A Male Client's Experience

Following is a client's story—this time a young man with a female therapist—that illustrates the effects of a therapist's "disclosure."

> CLIENT: After we had been working together for some time, my therapist picked up on the fact that I had some sexual feelings for her. I think she wanted to validate them, but it came out wrong. She said to me that if she were younger she would be my lover. It was a real awkward moment. I was flattered and felt good and kind of special. But it was like the way I felt in my relationship with my mother: Gee, I'm special! And it also made me feel really strange around her from then on. I kept wondering, what does this mean? Are we going to have sex sometime,

or what happens when the therapeutic relationship ends? Where are the parameters or the boundaries for this, and what about *my* sexuality? At that time I didn't know what to expect. I was very naive and vulnerable.

CONSULTANT: What effect did this have on your therapy?

CLIENT: It contaminated it. It took it to another level. We crossed a boundary with that statement. And then because I felt special, it made me a sort of pseudo-sexual man. . . . I started to feel frightened of being seduced, of having a sexual relationship. Since the therapist was an authority figure, like a mother, in essence I would be having sex with my mother. And I would be castrated or demeaned in some way for not being manly enough for her. Sometimes I would just wonder, What would happen if she seduced me? Would I or wouldn't I? It was a real conflict. It was all in me, but God, it was a terrifying place to be in. Yet I couldn't run away, because this was my therapist, and this was a person I believed in and felt connected to. It wasn't as if I could stand up and say, "Well, she screwed this one up!" I couldn't even say, "This is not right." Because she was the authority figure who had the answers. That put me in a real predicament.

CONSULTANT: Were your feelings ever dealt with?

CLIENT: I never talked about them, and she never said anything again. I wouldn't dare even bring up the subject of sexuality after that. As a matter of fact, we finally just came to an impasse because we could not talk. I literally sat with her at the last session without being able to say anything at all. I could bring up no images or words, and I knew that I had to leave. . . . That was years ago, but as I talk about it the feelings come up almost as strongly as if it were yesterday.

Duration of Transference—Sex After Termination

The strength and power of the transference phenomenon is evident in its duration. Once established, it seems to last forever. The lack of general awareness of this characteristic of transference has only recently been challenged by the therapeutic community at large. A not uncommon attitude was revealed in the response of one indignant psychiatrist to the sexual acting out of a resident with his patient: "If he wanted to sleep with her he should have terminated the therapy!" The inference, of course, is that termination changes everything. Recent studies indicate otherwise.

If, as has been clearly demonstrated, the presence and nature of the transference itself proscribes sexual acting out, then sex between therapist and client would be a violation as long as transference exists.

Does transference end with termination? The indications are that even after a long and successful therapy, transference is never fully resolved (Bird 1972). Gabbard and Pope (1988) assert: "Even in formal analysis, where detailed interpretation of the transference neurosis constitutes the cornerstone of treatment, transference residues of varying intensity always remain" (p. 21). They cite a number of studies that substantiate this observation (Buckley et al. 1981, Carlson 1986, Norman et al. 1976, Oremland et al. 1975, Pfeffer 1963).

Not only is there no indication that the transference disappears or even lessens in intensity after termination, but some data indicate that the "transference residue" in fact peaks five to ten years after termination (Gabbard and Pope 1988, referring to the study by Buckley et al. 1981).

Herman and colleagues (1987) make reference to the "timeless nature of the unconscious. The intrapsychic attachments to incestuous figures, whether a parent or therapist, know no time limits" (quoted in Gabbard and Pope 1988, p. 22).

The very essence of psychoanalytically oriented psychotherapy, say Gabbard and Pope, is to give up the incestuous childhood wishes, mourning their loss, and moving on to appropriate and mature object relatedness. If there is a possibility of gratifying these wishes "someday," then this process may be stopped by holding on to a fantasy.

For a therapist to argue that the sanction against therapist–patient sexual relations can be broken at some future date once he/she is not seeing the client in therapy would be just as absurd as an argument suggesting that the taboo against parent–offspring sexual relations can be broken once the child has left home (Gabbard and Pope 1988).

Vulnerability of the Client

The client seeks therapy because he is experiencing the need for help of some kind. He/she is expressing some degree of vulnerability in making the initial appointment. She is dependent by virtue of the nature of the relationship. The transference magnifies and intensifies the dependency and therefore the vulnerability. Even the most sophisticated, knowledgeable and otherwise independent person can find herself feeling certain that the "therapist knows best," unable to question his interventions, even when they do not match with an inner knowing. Thus the client is an easy prey to the exploitation, whether subtle or blatant, of the unconscious, as well as the intentional perpetrator. Those therapists with character disorders who will likely be repeat offenders on many levels of exploitation should somehow be apprehended at the training level. But what about the rest of us? What about the unconscious exploitation of a "minor" sort? What about those who would not think of acting out sexually, but who would subtly seek affirmation of our own sexual attractiveness? Or those who encourage the expressions of the erotic transference feelings for our own gratification? Any using of the client to meet one's own needs is exploiting the transference feelings and violating the client–therapist relationship. The same can be said for all relationships of authority (Gabbard 1989, Rutter 1989).

COUNTERTRANSFERENCE

Once the therapist has come to understand the nature of transference in the therapeutic relationship, the most important task thereafter is first to understand and then to appropriately and effectively utilize the *countertransference*: his/her response to the client.

While Freud mentioned countertransference only twice in his writings, a vast and ever-increasing portion of the psychoanalytic literature has been devoted to this subject. Over the years since Freud's time the classical definition of countertransference has been challenged, and a broader perspective has evolved. [For a review of the literature see Bollas (1983), Ernsberger (1979), Gorkin (1987), Kernberg (1965, 1980), Langs (1976a), Orr (1954)]. I have stated that fear of countertransference responses contributes to the avoidance of sexual issues. Appreciating the classical position, as well as highlighting the departures and developments is necessary for understanding the significance of countertransference in the therapeutic process.

The Classical Definition

Freud's attitude toward countertransference is evident in his first mention of the concept:

> We have become aware of the "counter-transference," which arises in [the analyst] as a result of the patient's influence on his unconscious feelings, and we are almost inclined to insist that he shall recognize this counter-transference in himself and overcome it. [1910, pp. 144–145]

In his only other direct reference to counter-transference Freud states:

> Our control over ourselves is not so complete that we may not suddenly one day go further than we intended. In my opinion, therefore, we ought not to give up the neutrality towards the patient, which we have acquired through keeping the counter-transference in check. [1915, 1959, p. 383].

So from the beginning there was a pejorative connotation attached to the concept of countertransference; it was something that one should keep under control and "overcome."

Since Freud did not elaborate upon this concept of countertransference, what precisely he meant by it has been the subject of debate throughout subsequent decades. However, a majority have concluded that by countertransference Freud referred to the *analyst's transference to the patient* (Gorkin 1987). The implication is that the countertransference, the analyst's response to the patient, contains unconscious and conflict-laden material. Insofar as the proper stance of the analyst, according to the classical perspective, is to be a "blank screen" and to remain a neutral observer, it follows that responses emanating from his/her own unconscious material would be inappropriate and a *hindrance* to proper handling of the analytic situation.

The Analyst as Participant

Early on there were departures from the Freudian perspective. Ferenczi's (1926a, b, 1931, 1933, Ferenczi and Rank 1923) approach to psychoanalysis included direct and emotional interaction with the patient. He saw the responses of the analyst as significant in the treatment.

Michael and Alice Balint (1939) held a similar position:

> The analytical situation is the result of an interplay between the patient's transference and the analyst's counter-transference, complicated by the reactions released in each by the other's transference on to him. [p. 218]

They maintained that accurate reflection of the patient did not require a sterile or "inanimate" approach to the analytic process (p. 220).

While the mainstream continued to accept Freud's position of neutrality as the correct stance for the analyst, a significant departure came from the school of thought established by Harry Stack Sullivan, known as the "interpersonal" school (Sullivan 1953). In Sullivan's approach, the analyst was clearly seen as participant, not just observer.

Countertransference as an Instrument of Research: Paula Heimann

The greatest challenge to the classical position on countertransference came from the British object-relations school. Paula Heimann is generally credited with being the first to view countertransference as constructive (Langs 1981). She begins her brief and pivotal paper (read in 1949) with an observation about what may be the effects of the classical stance toward countertransference:

> I have been struck by the widespread belief among candidates that the counter-transference is nothing but a source of trouble. Many candidates are afraid and feel guilty when they become aware of feelings towards their patients and consequently aim at avoiding any emotional response and at becoming completely unfeeling and "detached." [Heimann, in Langs 1981, p. 140]

In the same article Heimann goes on to define countertransference as *all* the responses the analyst experiences toward the patient. This, then, was the first enunciation of what Kernberg later referred to as the "totalistic" point of view (Kernberg 1965).

Heimann states:

My thesis is that the analyst's emotional response to his patient within the analytic situation represents *one of the most important tools* [italics added] for his work. The analyst's counter-transference is an instrument of research into the patient's unconscious. . . . Our basic assumption is that the analyst's unconscious understands that of his patient. . . . Often the emotions roused in him are much nearer to the heart of the matter than his reasoning, or, to put it in other words, his unconscious perception of the patient's unconscious is more accurate and in advance of his conscious conception of the situation. [p. 141]

In her paper, "Counter-transference and the Patient's Response to It," Margaret Little pushed the challenge further by introducing the concept of *using* the countertransference:

Both [transference and countertransference] are essential to psychoanalysis, and countertransference is no more to be feared or avoided than is transference; in fact it *cannot* be avoided, it can only be looked out for, controlled to some extent, and used. [Little 1981, p. 49]

Reliving the Patient's History: Harold Searles,
Christopher Bollas

Harold Searles is one of the most powerful proponents of counter-transference as an indispensable source of information and understanding of the seriously disturbed patient. But he also says (1979) that "the countertransference gives one the most reliable approach to understanding patients of whatever diagnosis" (p. 309). Searles speaks of the characteristically intense feelings of borderline patients that will be experienced intensely in the countertransference. He indicates that the analyst will find himself experiencing the emotions, not only of the projected parent, but *of the child as well*.

A more recent writer, Christopher Bollas (1987), speaks of the importance of "countertransference readiness," a state of availability and emotional sensitivity to the feelings aroused in us by the transference: for "in order to find the patient *we must look for him within ourselves*" (p. 202, emphasis added). Bollas says that the patient creates a unique or "idiomatic" environment in which he and the analyst will "live" and recreate the various aspects of his early object experience.

Varieties of Countertransference Responsiveness: Hedges

Lawrence Hedges' view of countertransference (1983, 1992) challenges the psychotherapy field to embrace a far-reaching paradigm shift in order to put psychoanalytic thinking and practice into the quantum age. He points out that the concepts of transference and countertransference, beginning with Freud, were formulated out of a framework based upon biological determinism and Newtonian physics, and that our continued usage of outmoded language limits our creative possibilities. He suggests that, consistent with contemporary thought systems, the search for truth "out there" has to be replaced by a systematic study of subjective "vantage points" an observer selects from which to make observations. The new paradigm that Hedges elucidates features different ways of listening and responding to the various developmentally determined modes in which the self is experienced in relation to others. Each of four developmental stages of "self and other representation" requires a distinctly different way of listening and responding, which Hedges calls "listening perspectives." Further, Hedges (1992) specifies how countertransference responsiveness can be differentially used in response to each stage of relatedness development. Thus, according to this approach, the countertransference—the therapist's response to the client—and its use is determined by the developmental stage from which the transference and the therapeutic work issues.

Summary

We have, then, in this crucial area of the therapist's responses to the client, the evolution of thought from (a) Freud's "hindrance" formulation, to (b) countertransference as an important tool for understanding the experience of the client, and to (c) using the countertransference responsively according to the developmental level of the client's process. Viewing countertransference from these several perspectives has different and profound implications for the therapist when confronted with erotic feelings for (and from) the client.

Erotic Countertransference

Michael Balint (1949) writes, "It is obvious that every human relation is *libidinous*. So is *the patient's relation to his analyst . . .* but *the analyst's relation to his patient is libidinous in exactly the same way*" (p. 231).

In his article "Countertransference Neurosis" (1953), Heinrich Racker maintains that, just as transference is always present and always reveals itself in the analytic process, so likewise is countertransference present and reveals its presence. Just as the original neurosis and the transference neurosis is centered in the Oedipus complex, so is the countertransference neurosis (which he defines as the pathological expression of the countertransference). "At this level every male patient fundamentally represents the father and every female patient the mother" (p. 107). These observations from the psychoanalytic literature support the conclusion that not only is countertransference a ubiquitous phenomenon, but sexuality, too, is always present in the therapeutic relationship, and so, therefore, is erotic countertransference.

Keeping the Countertransference in Check: The Hindrance Perspective

While there is a general theoretical agreement that therapists, given the nature of countertransference, will experience erotic feelings for their clients, research further confirms this position. Studies also show that therapists are quite troubled by sexual feelings toward their clients.

In a 1986 national study (Pope et al. 1986) 87 percent of the respondents reported experiencing sexual attraction to clients (95 percent of the males, 76 percent of the females, 88 percent of the females under 45). Eighty-two percent said they never seriously considered acting out (7 percent reported having acted on their feelings). Sixty-six percent said they felt anxious, guilty, and bewildered by such feelings.

Extreme discomfort is experienced in our culture when we have sexual feelings that, to act upon, would be inappropriate. Therapists, too, are subject to the ubiquitous "if I'm not supposed to *do* it I shouldn't *feel* it either" response, which leads to denial or repression.

Impact of the Classical Definition

Along with the general problem we have as a culture of integrating sexual feelings, it has been suggested that as therapists our difficulties have been exacerbated by the classical and still prevailing definition of countertransference. Pope and colleagues (1986) point out the implications in this classical view around therapists' attraction to clients—that feelings of attraction are countertransference, and as such represent a distortion of which he or she is unaware; and because it is an inappropriate response to the client's transference, it represents a mishandling of the phenomenon; therefore it is something to hide and to be ashamed of.

One teacher, commenting recently on the reluctance of therapists to bring up such issues in supervision, said: "When a supervision group member *does* bring in sexual transference material everyone becomes absolutely silent; when sexual *countertransference* material is mentioned, the tension in the room becomes palpable!"

Reticence around sexual countertransference may be reflected in the paucity of writing on the subject. Gorkin (1987) notes that "in spite of the burgeoning interest in countertransference issues, scant attention has been paid in the literature to the therapist's sexual feelings and fantasies toward patients" (p. 108). If sexual feelings for clients are difficult enough to acknowledge, then surely it would be considered risky to expose oneself in writing about such responses in the therapeutic process.

Avoidance of sexual countertransference is reflected in education. Research has revealed that most graduate schools and training programs in the mental health professions do not provide sufficient training for their students in this area, leaving them with a feeling of inadequacy (Holroyd 1983, Kenworthy et al. 1976, Landis et al. 1975, Pope et al. 1986).

In addition to the culturally ingrained "dis-ease" around the subject of sexuality and sexual feelings, the classical view of countertransference that reflects it so well, and the inadequate attention to sexual feelings in literature and education, there is another currently powerful deterrent to dealing with sexual countertransference. The considerable attention in recent years to the problems of sexual abuse by therapists, and the burgeoning of legal suits against therapists for malpractice make it seem all the more unsafe and even dangerous for clinicians to acknowledge, let alone explore, their sexual feelings for clients.

While there is no way to determine just how often the sexual issues of the client are avoided in the therapy process, given the general discomfort with sexual countertransference, the inadequacy of information and training, and the current litigious atmosphere, it is easy to see how they may be avoided, deflected, or suppressed more often than not. Pope (1986) cites studies where male therapists reacted with "anxiety and verbal avoidance of the material" when a female "client" discussed sexual material (Schover 1981, p. 477). Another study (Abramowitz et al. 1976) suggests that female therapists actively avoid treating attractive male clients. Pope et al. (1993) cites Reiser and Levenson (1984), who give an account of a resident psychiatrist who handled his attraction to an unusually attractive female client by inappropriately directing his interventions to "early" issues and by incorrectly pronouncing her "borderline."

I recall a male therapist who, in a training session on sexual transference and countertransference, maintained that he had no clients in his large practice who showed any indications of having erotic feelings toward him. He was a warm, sensitive, and appealing young man. It was objectively inconceivable that erotic transference feelings were not present in his clients, but also unlikely that there were no perceivable indications of such feelings. However, many of his clients came from a religious community where celibacy was the rule. Erotic feelings were problematic. In the course of the training sessions, he came to realize that discomfort with his own sexuality and sexual feelings, reinforced by that of his clients, caused him to effectively select out all perception of erotic feelings—his and theirs. Veiled verbal references were ignored, and body language was not even registered. As the trainee began to accept "permission" to experience his own sexual feelings in the therapy session, he found that his clients "suddenly" were exhibiting signs of erotic responses.

Exploring Sexual Issues

While the "hindrance" view of countertransference may have contributed to our uneasiness with and inhibition around sexual feelings and sexual issues, the classical definition impels us toward a deeper examination of our own issues and how they may impinge upon the therapeutic process in the form of countertransference. The necessity of such an awareness is apparent and inarguable.

Therapists and therapists in training would benefit from engaging in a process that would explore in depth and detail his or her sexual history and all related issues. Such a process might be stimulated by questions that would focus on the following issues:

> *Childhood*—birth data, care in infancy, childhood sexual experience and feeling response, parental attitudes toward sex, experiences of abuse, sex education;
>
> *Adolescence*—relationships to parents, attitudes toward body, attitudes toward sex, sexual fantasies and dreams, autoerotic activity, attitudes toward homosexuality, homosexual experience, heterosexual experience;
>
> *Adulthood*—self-perceptions related to sexuality, sexual attraction, sexual activity, intimate relationships and committed relationships, communication about sexual issues, and sexual satisfaction.

Further topics for exploration: How do themes in the personal story recur in relationships and choices? What type of woman and man is a person attracted to and why? What type of man and woman does one dislike and why? By thus drawing together old awarenesses and familiar data and focusing them in such a way, therapists may gain new and invaluable insight into their relationship to sexuality, both their own and that of others. It is likely that such a thorough and linear survey would unearth new issues to be dealt with in personal therapy.

As therapists gain greater familiarity with and clarity about issues regarding their own sexuality, they then can relate this information to the countertransference responses. Robertiello and Shoenewolf (1987) suggest some of the pertinent questions to raise: What kind of countertransference am I prone to? (In other words, what kind of client will push which buttons?) Are there certain types of clients that I should not treat at this point in my life? What clues do I have that I am experiencing countertransference (material from my own unconscious)? What do I do when I get the clue? What are the parts of my father, mother, and siblings that I did not like or gave me problems?

Pope and colleagues (1993) provide an excellent guidebook for exploring sexual responses in the therapeutic setting without offering solutions and answers. Numerous situations and scenarios are offered whereby the clinician may consider how he or she would respond.

The importance of paying attention to and concern for one's own personal issues is clear. And such familiarity and clarity with the issues should facilitate for the therapist the further step of utilizing effectively his/her feelings on behalf of the process.

Countertransference as Tool: Heightened Awareness

A Case Illustration

To illustrate how the countertransference feelings can provide a tool for better understanding the client's needs, I offer a failed example from my own practice. I have chosen this case because it also illustrates some of the problems discussed above: discomfort with sexual feelings and resultant avoidance, lack of awareness of my own sexual issues, a limited understanding of the meaning of the countertransference, and the resulting inability to utilize it on behalf of the process. The result was a missed message and an aborted process. (Circumstances have been altered to protect confidentiality.)

> Early in my practice a young man was referred to me who was a producer in the entertainment industry. He had experienced a meteoric rise to a powerful position in his company. But he sat on his success with great discomfort and insecurity. He was at once grandiose and felt himself an undeserving fraud who could lose everything in an instant.
>
> Mike was physically quite attractive, charming, quick witted, and seductive. He was also a self-proclaimed "wise-ass" who couldn't contain his "smart" remarks. He was married and had two children.
>
> Mike had seen many therapists—briefly. According to him, none of them was helpful or "any good." He had felt insulted by the last one, a psychoanalyst, because he took notes during the sessions. He had a positive response to me and frequently told me how much better I was than all "those guys who are out there ripping people off."

Mike complained that he never felt anything. The exception was the aggression and anger that erupted toward other drivers when he was on the highway in his very expensive sports car. Sexually he was impotent with his wife. In addition to occasional sexual encounters with women he knew, he had a practice of seducing aspiring young actresses into his office to give him oral sex. This happened routinely. He stressed that his one point of integrity was, "I always told them up front that this wasn't going to get them anything." He felt disgust and contempt for the women who succumbed, and disgust for himself for being trapped in this obsession.

After a couple of months of working together, Mike began to tell me that he was quite attracted to me. He would go on to say, in effect, that to go to bed with me would solve his problems. He would insist, with a teasing tone and a seductive-little-boy manner, that surely if I really wanted to help him I would be willing to do what would get the job done! At other times he would tell me how I compared to the glamour girls he had had. They were fluff, they were phony; I had substance, I was real.

This was heady stuff for a woman who, at the time was a divorcee without a committed relationship, and had passed a fortieth birthday! Yet the fact that this young man was definitely not "my type" made matters easier for me. I was very clear that I would not under *any* circumstances have had an intimate relationship with him. I was also clear that under any *other* circumstances he would not have wanted a sexual relationship with me; in other words, I was clear about the transferential nature of his feelings toward me. I also knew better than to take his flattery seriously (although in another sense, that was where I missed the boat). Yet I was affected by the flattery. I became aware that I took a little extra care about my appearance before his sessions. One day he said to me, grinning, "Well, you've really got it together today! You know that, don't you?" Indeed I did! I became quite dismayed at the way I was reacting. I was uneasy at the anticipation I felt before his visit, and of the increased excitement I experienced.

In spite of my clearly laying out the boundaries with him about sexual acting out, he persisted in his seductive urging, sometimes with humor and sometimes seriously. I really did not know how to handle this, and so I sought a consultation with a colleague. I recall telling the consultant that I felt I was being affected by the flattery, but I doubt that I talked about the increased attention to my appearance, or about any of the other subtle ways I was being seduced. It also appears likely now that my colleague was caught in some of his own issues. The result was that we did not focus much on the countertransference. Based on the information that I gave him, my colleague picked up on the "little boy" quality of the client, and he suggested that I take a confrontive-reality approach: Tell him when he persists, "You're not man enough for me." At some unconscious transference-countertransference level his formulation did point to a truth, but just how in transference he might not be "man enough" was not clear.

To my credit I will say that such a response sounded wrong to me. However, I was ungrounded and uncomfortable enough not to be able to trust my intuitive sense or even to be in touch with it. So when given the cue, I delivered the line. Shortly after, Mike left therapy by simply canceling his appointment.

In his last session, Mike was able to contact deep feeling for the first time. He got in touch with a longing for contact with his father. At the time I attributed his precipitous departure to his anxiety around the emergence of those feelings. To some extent that may have played a part. But clearly my intervention had been a blow that had severed any possibility of a connection between us. Mike would have been able to tolerate the vulnerability of his deeper, authentic feelings only if he could have been sustained by a connection with me. I destroyed that possibility by delivering a blow to his very damaged ego, and by discounting his plea for a connection in the only way he knew how to ask for it. What dynamic features were operating I never got to understand.

Now many years later, there are a number of things I wish I had done differently. What if I had taken my response as an opportunity to learn more about my own issues? I could have explored my desire to primp and preen, to be admired and desired while being well out of reach. I might better have recognized the humiliating, masochistic position Mike was putting himself into; begging and pleading inside the cool, seductive propositioning, knowing that I was unavailable. It was the same position he put the young actresses in who got on their knees to give him oral sex. And interestingly enough, the contempt he felt for them he got from me in my remark, "You're not man enough for me!" The fact that my rebuff set off intense longings for father suggests either a replication of mother rejection and turning toward father or that, in transference, my "strength and substance" represented fatherly traits he had been unable to identify with so that he still felt like a little boy, impotent and passive.

One of the most important areas I could have explored was his "flattery." He never told me I was gorgeous and glamorous. He talked about substance and depth, those qualities he could not find in himself or in anyone else in his life. He longed to feel real, to be authentic. The longing was real, and I brushed off his expression as flattery. If I had been able to honor those feelings, to see through to the deeper, subtler meanings of the transference, we would have been on a very different footing. But I was uncomfortable with *my* response, so I didn't really look at it, and allow the countertransference to teach me more about myself and about Mike.

When the therapist experiences erotic feelings for the client, he may be receiving a "message" from that person's unconscious: he or she *may* be experiencing the feelings of the overstimulated infant or small child in the hands of an unbounded, seductive mother or an abusive father. How unfortunate if the therapist, in the presence of such feelings gets tense and frightened, preoccupied with his or her "inappropriate response," and completely misses the message!

Countertransference Responses to
Sexual Transference: Role Play

One of the most difficult tasks for the therapist, it seems, is the countertransference response to the client's erotic transference when it initially appears in the therapeutic process. An effective technique for elucidating such issues, I have found, is that of role playing. In training settings I often ask two persons to play the role of client and therapist. A scenario is established wherein the client is experiencing erotic feelings for the therapist. Periodically, as the dialogue proceeds, the supervisor asks for the "subtext" from both "therapist" and "client." Each responds with what he/she is *really* thinking or feeling behind the words that are being spoken. The process yields up a great deal of information: the trainee has the opportunity to experience how he/she would respond in the presence of erotic transference situations, what happens in his/her own body and feelings, and how his/her issues inform the verbal process. The trainee learns of the client's inner (unspoken, rarely revealed) responses to the interventions, and can experiment with alternative interventions. Videotaping of the role-play sessions gives the added important benefit of observing the body language and its ramifications.

Below are two sample role plays in which two trainees improvise a therapy session wherein the client expresses sexual feelings for the therapist. The subtext appears in all-capital letters, the "dialogue" in lower case. The therapists in these examples struggle with the discomfort aroused by their inner responses to the erotic feelings of the "clients" and attempt to find a way to accept the feelings, establish boundaries, and connect to the real need of the client.

Role Play Between a Female Client and Male Therapist

> CLIENT: Gee, I feel really embarrassed to say this, but, you know ... I mean, I really love my husband, but I just have such good feelings toward you.
> THERAPIST: Oh? (SUBTEXT: GOOD FEELINGS—IN WHAT SENSE? WHERE IS THIS LEADING? I ALREADY FEEL THE ANXIETY IN ME. ARE YOU TALKING ABOUT ATTRACTION?) Let me know more about those feelings.
> CLIENT: This is really embarrassing. I don't even know if I can talk about it. I had this dream about you the other night and it was so embarrassing, but it was full of feeling. I just felt a lot of sexual attraction. It was such a vivid dream, and I don't know if I should even talk about that in here.
> THERAPIST: Is it scary to talk about it?
> CLIENT: Yeah.
> THERAPIST: It's not okay? It doesn't feel safe?
> CLIENT: Well, I don't know.
> THERAPIST: What do you fear would happen if you talk about it?
> CLIENT: I don't think I *can* talk about it. . . . I could never tell you the details. It's bad enough just to tell you that I had the dream.

THERAPIST: Why is it embarrassing? Does it seem bad to have sexual dreams or feelings about me?

CLIENT: About you, yeah. I mean it was so strong. The feelings were so strong I just couldn't believe it. I wish I had never dreamt it.

THERAPIST: (SUBTEXT: I'M FEELING ANXIOUS. WE ARE INTO ANOTHER DIMENSION NOW. I'M RECOGNIZING THAT THIS IS REALLY IMPORTANT TO GET INTO AND TALK ABOUT. I'M SENSING YOUR ANXIETY, AND I WANT TO ASSIST YOU. BUT I FEEL A LOT OF TENTATIVENESS. I DON'T WANT TO BLOW IT HERE. I WANT YOU TO FEEL SAFE TO TALK ABOUT SEXUALITY.)

CLIENT: No, I would never tell the dream. It's uncomfortable. Just telling you that I had the dream is a big thing for me.

THERAPIST: Talking about this is like taking a big risk.

CLIENT: Well, yeah. I've never talked about this before. I'm not sure I want to now.

THERAPIST: Could you tell me a little bit about your sexual feelings in terms of your father?

CLIENT: (Laughter) With my *father*? Oh, *no*!

CLIENT and THERAPIST: (SUBTEXT: AGHHHH!!!)

CLIENT: (SUBTEXT: I CAN BARELY HEAR WHAT YOU'RE SAYING. I'M GONE. I'M SITTING HERE BUT I'M REALLY SITTING BACK THERE. I'M MORE LOOKING AT YOU THAN LISTENING TO YOU. I'M REALLY WATCHING AND I SEE A LOT OF DIFFERENT THINGS GO OVER YOUR FACE, AND EVERY TIME I SEE SOMETHING THAT'S TENTATIVE, MY HEART FLOPS OVER, AND I FEEL, THIS IS REALLY DANGEROUS, THIS IS SCARY. I JUST NEED TO FEEL SAFE.)

THERAPIST: (SUBTEXT: I WANT TO RETRACT MY QUESTION ABOUT THE FATHER. I REALIZE HOW TOTALLY INAPPROPRIATE IT WAS. WHEN I'M ANXIOUS I INTELLECTUALIZE TO GET AWAY FROM THE FEELING. WHAT I NEED TO DO HERE IS SIMPLY MAKE IT SAFE FOR YOU TO TALK ABOUT THIS. IT'S JUST THAT I'M NOT SURE WHERE THIS IS GOING TO GO.)

CLIENT: (SUBTEXT: WHEN I FIRST BROUGHT THIS UP I COULD SEE THE TENSION IN YOUR FACE. THEN YOU RELAXED MORE AND SEEMED MORE AT EASE. I GUESS THAT'S WHAT I REALLY NEED TO HEAR— AND SEE, THAT YOU'RE OKAY WITH MY TALKING ABOUT THESE FEELINGS. BECAUSE ACTUALLY I HAVE SOME OTHER ISSUES I WANT TO TALK ABOUT THAT ARE REALLY IMPORTANT. THIS WAS LIKE A TEST. . . . I'LL THROW THIS DREAM OUT AND SEE HOW HE RESPONDS. THEN I'LL FILE THAT AWAY, AND MAYBE LATER WE'LL TALK ABOUT IT SOME MORE. BECAUSE, REALLY, I HAVE THIS RAGING CRUSH, BUT I'M NOT GOING TO SAY THAT NOW!)

THERAPIST: There are two things that I want to say here. One is that your feelings and your sexuality are *okay*. Even having sexual feelings for me is okay. The other is that I can stay within myself and be here with you. My desire is to make it safe for you so that you can have whatever feelings are there, and we can deal with whatever comes up for you. That's how I really feel.

CLIENT: What you just said feels good to me, really nice. (SUBTEXT: I'M GLAD IT SEEMS TO BE OKAY ALSO FOR ME TO PUT THIS SUBJECT ASIDE FOR NOW. THIS IS ALL I CAN HANDLE AT THE MOMENT.)

THERAPIST: I'm feeling a lot of respect for the quality of your feelings. This is somehow kind of precious, delicate, and fragile.

CLIENT: Yeah. It really isn't easy.

THERAPIST: And yet sexual feelings are so important, so central. We want to deal with them and understand their meaning. When the time is right.

CLIENT: I feel good now.

The therapist, following the role play, commented that his initial anxiety had caused him to disconnect from the client, so that his interventions were more on behalf of his becoming comfortable than on helping her to feel safe. Gradually he was able to respond to her need (to be assured that her feelings were accepted).

Erotic Transference Role Play Between
Female Therapist and Male Client

THERAPIST: How have you been this last week?

CLIENT: A little better. I'm selling a lot of cars now. Making a lot of money.

THERAPIST: (nods).

CLIENT: I think this stuff is working between us . . . isn't it?

THERAPIST: (SUBTEXT: *WHAT'S WORKING BETWEEN US?* I FEEL ON THE DEFENSIVE ALREADY!)

CLIENT: (SUBTEXT: I WANT TO CHARM YOU AND SEDUCE YOU SO I CAN BE IN CONTROL HERE.)

THERAPIST: (SUBTEXT: [LAUGHING] YOU GOT ME!)

CLIENT: (SUBTEXT: I'M PLAYING . . . PLAYING AND FLIRTING.)

THERAPIST: I have two responses: first, your success must feel really good to you. But I also sense a real playfulness in you around it.

CLIENT: Oh, do you? Do you like it?

THERAPIST: Yes, I like the playful quality in you. I can see the little boy in you.

CLIENT: (SUBTEXT: THAT THREW IT WHEN YOU SAID, "A LITTLE BOY . . ." I DON'T LIKE THAT. NOW I'M STARTING TO FEEL A LITTLE BIT UNCOMFORTABLE.)

THERAPIST: (SUBTEXT: [LAUGHTER] GOOD!)

CLIENT: (SUBTEXT: I DON'T WANT YOU TALKING ABOUT A LITTLE BOY. I WANT TO GET TO SOMETHING ELSE WHERE I CAN FEEL MORE IN CONTROL.)

THERAPIST: (SUBTEXT: GEE, DID I BLOW IT? I DON'T WANT YOU TO FEEL TOO UNCOMFORTABLE, BUT AT THE SAME TIME I DON'T WANT YOU TO CONTROL THE SESSION. YOU CAN'T BE IN CONTROL AND SEDUCING ME, GETTING ME SUCKED IN, AND THEN EXPECT TO GET ANYTHING OUT OF THERAPY. THE WHOLE THING WOULD BECOME POINTLESS. SO, IN THAT WAY I DON'T MIND GETTING YOU A LITTLE

BIT OFF TRACK.) I can see a little bit of the little boy and I like that playful quality in you.

CLIENT: (SUBTEXT: OKAY, WELL THAT FEELS ALRIGHT.) How was your weekend?

THERAPIST: It was fine.

CLIENT: What did you do?

THERAPIST: (SUBTEXT: WHAT DID I *DO*? IT'S NONE OF YOUR BUSINESS! I'M NOT GOING TO TELL YOU. . . . BUT THEN I HAVE THE IMPULSE TO TALK ABOUT IT. . . . YOU GOT ME AGAIN! EVERYWHERE I MOVE I FEEL SO SUSCEPTIBLE!)

CLIENT: (SUBTEXT: I WANT TO GET YOU AWAY FROM DEALING WITH ME.)

THERAPIST: Why do you ask about my weekend?

CLIENT: I'm really interested to know what you do. You're really an exciting person. I'm real curious about you.

THERAPIST: But this hour is about you, Norman, not me.

CLIENT: You know, I'd really like to spend more time with you.

THERAPIST: You want to spend more time with me?

CLIENT: Yeah. Things are going so good. I mean, I'm doing well, and you're doing well. It would be nice to spend some time together.

THERAPIST: Do you mean spend time here or outside of therapy?

CLIENT: Whatever. You like to play, right? You'd like to go to the beach this weekend, have a little wine or something, right?

THERAPIST: I see what you mean. Well, no, because this therapy really has to be for you. It wouldn't be right to have a relationship outside of the therapy. (SUBTEXT: ARE YOU CONVINCED BY WHAT I'M SAYING?)

CLIENT: (SUBTEXT: NO, NOT REALLY. YOU SOUNDED TENTATIVE, AND IT ENTICED ME. IT MADE ME WANT TO SAY, "THIS THERAPY STUFF IS REALLY BULLSHIT, MAN. YOU KNOW, THIS IS REAL LIFE. WE'RE TALKING ABOUT YOUR FEELINGS AND MY FEELINGS. COME ON. I'M ATTRACTED TO YOU, YOU KNOW THAT. LET'S WORK THINGS OUT.")

THERAPIST: There's no way we can have a relationship outside of the therapy, Norman. I want you to understand that. This therapy is for you—in this hour, this time, and this place. There's no way we're going to have a relationship outside of here at any time. After the therapy is over or while the therapy is going on. I really want you to hear that.

CLIENT: (SUBTEXT: WELL, NOW IT'S STRONGER. I'M FEEL-ING DEFENSIVE AGAIN. I CAN GO EITHER OF TWO WAYS: I CAN KEEP TRYING TO SEDUCE YOU OR SAY THAT I DIDN'T REALLY FEEL THAT WAY. I WAS JUST TRYING TO SEE HOW YOU REALLY FELT AND IF YOU HAD INTEGRITY. I COULD THROW IT BACK AT YOU.)

THERAPIST: I'm interested in what you're feeling right now.

CLIENT: Well, I think we're missing out on each other and a nice relationship. I mean, let's face it. This therapy stuff is, you know . . . it's not real life.

THERAPIST: No, it isn't real life. But it's important because you are important. Your life is important and this is your time. Just for you.

CLIENT: Yeah, but I'm interested in spending more time with you.

THERAPIST: That's not possible outside of this therapy, Norman. Not while the therapy is going on and not even when it's over. There will never be a time when we'll have a relationship out-side of the therapy.

CLIENT: (SUBTEXT: THAT'S EVEN STRONGER. IT'S HARD TO GET AROUND THAT. I'M LOOKING FOR A WAY, BUT I CAN'T FIND IT NOW.)

THERAPIST: (SUBTEXT: I WAS WISHY-WASHY BEFORE BECAUSE I DIDN'T WANT TO BUY INTO THE SEDUC-TION, YET I DIDN'T WANT TO WOUND YOU, EITHER. ANOTHER PART OF MY SUBTEXT WAS, HOW CAN I PUT THIS IN A NICE WAY SO THAT YOU'LL HEAR IT, BUT YOU WON'T BE HURT BY IT. AS I FELT STRONGER I THOUGHT, THIS IS GOING TO HURT YOU BUT YOU'VE GOT TO HEAR IT!)

CLIENT: (SUBTEXT: NOW WITH THESE PARAMETERS, MY THOUGHT WAS, OKAY, I WANT TO LEAVE THE THERAPY IF I CAN'T CONTROL YOU. SOMETHING HAS TO ENGAGE ME FURTHER, AND I DON'T KNOW WHAT THAT IS.)

THERAPIST: As I talked about the limits just now, I saw a real change come over you. It looked as though you had some feelings about that.

CLIENT: Yeah, I feel disappointed.

THERAPIST: Disappointed that you didn't get what you felt you wanted.

CLIENT: Why won't you go out with me?

THERAPIST: Because this is your time. It's not about us. It's not about a social relationship. You have lots of relationships out in the world, but you don't really have a time and place that's just for you.

CLIENT: I don't really understand this, you know. What are you driving at?

THERAPIST: That this a place where you can share what's going on with you, and really be in touch with yourself here.

CLIENT: I'm in touch with myself.

THERAPIST: (SUBTEXT: I'M STUCK. IF YOU'RE IN TOUCH WITH YOURSELF, WHY ARE YOU IN THERAPY?!) Norman, do you have a sense of what you really *do* need here?

CLIENT: What do I need? I need some love. I need to be loved. I need to be cared for.

THERAPIST: I do care about you.

CLIENT: I need to stop playing this game. I'm really sick and tired of playing it. (SUBTEXT: SOMEHOW I FINALLY HEARD BOTH THAT THE BOUNDARIES WERE DEFINITE AND SECURE—YOU WEREN'T GOING TO GIVE IN TO ME— *AND* YOU CARED ABOUT ME . THAT'S WHAT GOT THROUGH. I COULD FEEL A SHIFT IN ME. NOW I FEEL VULNERABLE AND A LITTLE SHY AND SAD.)

In the discussion that followed the role play, the "therapist" could further see how her desire not to "wound" the client undermined her communication of the absoluteness of the boundaries. The client could only begin to give in to his real feelings when he felt certain that she would not be seduced, but at the same time had genuine caring feelings for him. The therapist was also able to identify the source of her countertransferential responses in specific psychic issues, and was alerted to areas that needed deeper investigation in personal therapy.

In both of the examples, the therapists, using hypothetical scenarios, had the opportunity to become familiar with situations that were usually suppressed in the therapeutic relationship, due to their own discomfort with sexual material. They could explore optional responses and get otherwise unavailable feedback as to the "client's" reaction. The therapists indicated that engaging in these and other role plays lowered their anxiety considerably, and gave them more confidence to begin working with sexual issues as they emerge in the process with their clients.

Using the Countertransference in the Therapeutic Relationship

A Role Play in Supervision

The following is a portion of a supervision session during a training seminar for the staff of an inpatient treatment center. The case discussed involves erotic transference, the countertransference elicited by it, and one form of utilizing the therapist's response in the treatment. Through role play, the countertransference feelings are highlighted and participants explore the reactions and responses of the client. Names have been changed and identifying data deleted.

Felicia, a skilled and experienced clinical psychologist, has asked for help with a patient who, she says, "I don't know quite how to deal with." The patient, Megan, is a 27-year-old woman with a schizophrenic diagnosis and a history of incest with an older sibling. She considers herself a lesbian, though she has never acted on her homosexual feelings. She has a delusional system wherein she proclaims her ardent love for Felicia (loudly, dramatically, constantly); she intends someday to marry her and have their child. She is confused about whether she has sperm or ova to contribute to that process. Megan presents in a masculine manner, and identifies with Felicia's "masculine" side, admiring her leadership qualities, strength, and power. She is seen to be very intrusive, violates other people's physical boundaries, and is often socially inappropriate.

Felicia agreed to do a role play, and another staff member enacted Megan. The supervisor periodically interrupted the dialogue to ask the person speaking for the subtext, the thoughts or feelings behind the words spoken. The person then verbalized those feelings. (The subtext appears in all capital letters.) Staff members joined in the discussion.

> PATIENT: Felicia . . . (she begins with a breathless, dramatic and intense voice), you are *such* an outstanding therapist here. I feel you all time, and I *know* that we're meant for each other.
>
> SUPERVISOR (to THERAPIST): Before your reply to Megan, can you give us your subtext? What are you feeling at this moment?
>
> THERAPIST: (SUBTEXT: IT'S REALLY HARD FOR ME TO STAY IN THIS.)
>
> PATIENT: You are the perfect woman, the woman that I've been looking for all my life. And even if you say you don't want me, I know you do . . . I know.
>
> THERAPIST: It sounds like there's something that you need from me that's less dramatic than this. I'd like to focus on what it is day to day that you'd like from me.
>
> PATIENT: I'd like you to hold me. I want to feel your arms around me, holding me tight.
>
> SUPERVISOR (to THERAPIST): Stay with your feelings now. Focus on exactly what's going on inside.
>
> THERAPIST: (SUBTEXT: I FEEL INVADED.)
>
> SUPERVISOR: I sense a lot of anxiety.
>
> THERAPIST: (SUBTEXT: YES, THE ANXIETY IS BECAUSE WHEN SHE TALKS ABOUT WANTING ME TO HOLD HER I ALMOST FEEL LIKE I'M BEING RAPED. . . . SO HOW DO I RELATE TO HER IN A NURTURING KIND OF WAY WHEN I'M REALLY FEELING LIKE SAYING "GET AWAY FROM ME!" I CAN'T TOLERATE PHYSICAL CONTACT WITH HER.)
>
> SUPERVISOR: The last thing Megan consciously wants to hear is, "Get away from me!" But that is clearly the response that was elicited in Felicia and in everyone in the room. Felicia, let's go back and see if you can say to Megan what you *are* feeling.
>
> THERAPIST: Megan, I'm feeling scared and overwhelmed by the amount of energy you're putting out here. I feel invaded.
>
> PATIENT: I know you want me. I think you are afraid of what we have.

THERAPIST: I'm not available to you to be sexual with you. And I'm concerned that if I hold you and make physical contact with you, you would misconstrue that. So I would like to find a way that I can make contact with you so that your need for contact with me and your sexual feelings don't get mixed up.

PATIENT: Would you hug me when I see you?

THERAPIST: Many times when you want a hug I feel like you are aroused.

PATIENT: That's just how you make me feel. How do I stop what I'm feeling with you?

SUPERVISOR: Now let's stop here for a moment. Felicia has told us what she experiences, and we've all agreed that as we listened to the dialogue between Felicia and Megan we, too, experienced the same feelings of being overwhelmed and invaded and the desire to flee. Now what might we assume is being communicated from some deep level in Megan?

STAFF PERSON: That that was *Megan's* experience . . .

SUPERVISOR: Yes! In some way Megan, as an infant or very young child may have felt absolutely overwhelmed and invaded. So, Felicia, perhaps you can begin to separate out a bit from being the beleaguered therapist who has to deal with this most troublesome patient, anxious about your own responses. Ask yourself the question: What do my feelings tell me about what it was like to be Megan, early in her life, long before she had any possibility of dealing with her situation or even forming words about it. And then, with this kind of awareness, when she says these things, how would one respond? Let me demonstrate this. . . . Give me a line or two.

PATIENT (in a seductive voice): You are a magnificent woman. You give everything to everyone. Everyone gets what they need from you.

SUPERVISOR: Megan, when you talk to me like that sometimes I get this feeling of absolutely being invaded and I feel in my body this desire just to pull back from you. It feels overwhelming. . . . And it makes me wonder . . . could it be that those are the kinds of feelings *you* had as a child . . . ?

PATIENT (her voice becomes soft and quiet): Yeah, I was real afraid, real afraid when I was small.

SUPERVISOR: It must have been overwhelming for you.

PATIENT: Yeah, it was.

SUPERVISOR: Maybe you can tell me more about that. . . .

FELICIA: When you talk with Megan and you hit upon what she considers to be the truth about her childhood she immediately says, "Yes!"

SUPERVISOR: Now that is the point. I find that when you observe what you're feeling, in certain situations you can turn it around and say, "This must be the way it was for you." If it connects, then suddenly you've hit upon the truth that the person wanted to convey. Yet she couldn't do it in her own words. The experience was too early, too inchoate, too inaccessible to reflection. But she *can* create her experience in you. When you put words on what *you* experience, then you, the therapist, have given her words for *her* experience. The person has finally gotten the message across. Then there may be no longer the need to act out in the same way. . . .

STAFF MEMBER: I was thinking, Felicia, if you were talking to Megan and the revelation of your feelings connected to what *she felt*, it would remove her sense of isolation—and therefore the need to behave the way she does. "Because you're letting me know—more than just understanding, you're conveying to me that you feel what I'm feeling—this hell that I live in, call it sexuality or not. I'm no longer alone in this state that I go around in, trying to get someone else to pull me out or help me stop feeling." That revelation is what's the bridge to her isolation!

SUPERVISOR: That's right. Because you are reflecting not her current behavior but the deeper feelings that she cannot communicate directly. And, again, you are giving her, not just a sense of connection, but also a way to begin to understand her experience.

STAFF MEMBER: Could you say in situations like this, her behavior is really not even about sex?

SUPERVISOR: I would say that it is and it isn't about sex, both at the same time. Megan wants a connection, but much more she wants to merge. Her wanting to have a baby seems to be expressing a very early symbiotic need to merge. Undoubtedly she did not have that symbiotic connection as an infant. Then when she gets to the oedipal phase and wants the affection and recognition from the father, she brings to that phase all the un-resolved symbiotic material. Well, sex would fix everything, wouldn't it? On a primitive level, sex is perceived as a way to have the merging/mother needs and the oedipal/father needs met all at once.

STAFF MEMBER: Megan was undoubtedly eroticized through the incestuous activity with her sibling.

SUPERVISOR: All the more reason why she would choose some-one who is not going to violate her boundaries. She chooses Felicia because she senses that Felicia is not available. In spite of all her pleading and imploring, on some level the last thing she really wants is that kind of violation by Felicia.

FELICIA: And yet she'll argue about that.

SUPERVISOR: Yes. To put it another way, these earlier issues are "living" in an adult body and when they are activated they will get expressed in a sexual, "adult" way.

STAFF MEMBER: So then the way to work with Megan would be to acknowledge—"okay, you're having sexual feelings, but what's it about?"—rather than working with the sexual feelings themselves?

SUPERVISOR: Again, I feel that in regard to this issue the most effective way to work is for the therapist to reflect back to the patient the feelings that she evokes; to communicate to her the countertransferential response—certainly not as a "confession," but as the possible reflection of the patient's early experience. In other words, this is really *using* the countertransference. And then all the little ploys, the delusions, perhaps the psychotic system itself may become relatively unimportant and unneces-sary at that moment. That really simple connection has been made and the patient is no longer in an isolated position, as we said earlier. And this allows Felicia, by ceasing to focus on guilt and confusion about the countertransference, to get unstuck, and bring the focus back to where it belongs: on the experience of the client. Then from this point of contact, the therapist and patient can begin to work on the deeper issue, which now has been experienced by both.

In this example of supervision utilizing role play, a therapist and staff members reenact an actual dilemma. Through the role play and discussion, they begin to see how, as Searles (1979) had indicated, they were experiencing through their countertransference responses the projected emotions of the patient as a child. The supervisor interpreted the erotic transference as an expression of the merging needs emanating from the symbiotic stage of development. The appropriate use of the countertransference, or "listening perspective" for this stage, according to Hedges, is the reflecting to the patient the therapist's feeling responses as a way to connect to the patient's experience that is or cannot be verbalized.

It may be noted that the countertransference expressed in this case did not include erotic feelings. Their emergence at a later date in the process may signal another level of developmental issues and therefore require a different use of the countertransference.

Conclusions

Numbers of people with some degree of sexual dysfunction or dissatisfaction, together with victims of child sexual abuse, make up a large portion of the client population in psychotherapy today. The majority of psychotherapy clients, regardless of what their presenting problems may be, will thus have some degree of sexual dysfunction or dissatisfaction, or will have been victims of child abuse or incest. These clients are asking for awareness of and responsiveness to their sexual issues. Avoidance by the therapist—whether consciously or unconsciously, because of inhibition, fear, or inadequate training—might be considered another form of abuse. It is at least a serious failure. To ensure against such failure, we as therapists—whether trainees, interns, or seasoned clinicians—need to be fully prepared in the following ways: (1) to understand the nature and power of the client's transference with all its implications; (2) to become fully comfortable with our own sexuality and sexual feelings, aware of our own sexual issues and how they may impinge upon the therapeutic process in the form of the countertransference; and (3) to learn how to use the countertransference feelings both to understand the client's issues and to intervene on his or her behalf.

10

In Praise of the Dual Relationship[1]

Lawrence E. Hedges

INTRODUCTORY COMMENTS: THE RISE AND FALL OF THE "DUALITY" CONCEPT

In 1973 the American Psychological Association (APA) code of ethics, in an effort to curb sexual exploitation in the psychotherapeutic relationship, opened a Pandora's box when it coined the term *dual relationship*. Since then, like Pandora's miseries that spread evil throughout the world, the psychotherapeutic relationship has been colored with continual concern, frustration, and doubt. The faulty shift of ethical focus from "damaging exploitation" to "dual relationships" has led to widespread misunderstanding and incessant naive moralizing, which has undermined the spontaneous, creative, and unique aspects of the personal relationship that is essential to the psychotherapeutic process.

---

1. This chapter is adapted from a three part article published in *The California Therapist*, 1994.

The atmosphere in the community of practicing psychotherapists that has been created by ethics committees and licensing boards now amounts almost to hysterical paranoia. It is as though some sort of witch-hunt is afoot, and no practicing therapist has a clean conscience when guilt is being dished out about the subtle potentials of dual relating! The bottom line is, dynamic and systems-oriented psychotherapies cannot be practiced without various forms of dual relating and every therapist knows this. But we have wrongly been told that dual relating is unethical.

The good news is that the pendulum has started swinging back and a lengthy dialogue lies ahead of us. The APA Insurance Trust states, "not all multiple roles are dual relationships." But the implication is still that "duality" may be unethical. The recent code of ethics for the California Association of Marriage, Family, and Child Counselors categorically states that "not all dual relationships are unethical." And the revised (December 1992) APA Code of Ethics at last returns us to sanity:

> In many communities and situations, it may not be feasible or reasonable for psychologists to avoid social or other nonprofessional contacts with persons such as patients, clients, students, supervisees, or research participants. Psychologists must always be sensitive to the potential harmful effects of other contacts on their work and on those persons with whom they deal. . . . Psychologists do not exploit persons over whom they have supervisory, evaluative, or other authority such as students, supervisees, employees, research participants, and clients or patients. . . . Psychologists do not engage in sexual relationships with students or supervisees in training over whom the psychologist has evaluative or direct authority, because such relationships are so likely to impair judgment or be exploitative. . . . Psychologists do not engage in sexual intimacies with current patients or clients. . . . Psychologists do not accept as therapy patients or clients persons with whom they have engaged in sexual intimacies . . . [and] do not engage in sexual intimacies with a former therapy patient or client for at least two years after cessation or termination of professional services. . . . The psychologist who engages in such activities after the two years following cessation or termination of treatment bears the burden of demonstrating that there has been no exploitation, in light of all relevant factors.

Thus, after twenty years of grief, the term *dual relationship* as an ethical definition has been entirely eliminated from the revised APA code. The current ethical focus is on remaining mindful of the ever-present possibility of damaging exploitation. But the malignant concept of dual relationship that the APA had introduced and has now eliminated has infected ethics committees, licensing boards, and malpractice litigation everywhere. We still have a major battle ahead to undo the severe damage done to the psychotherapeutic relationship by the pejorative use of the term.

THE CASE FOR DUAL RELATIONSHIPS

As the pendulum swings back, such writers as Kitchener (1988) and Tomm (1991) argue that dual relationships need to be considered more carefully. Here are the main points that have emerged to date. (1) Dual relating is inevitable and offers many constructive possibilities. (2) Dual relationships are only one way an exploitative therapist or an exploitative client may take advantage of the other. (3) Metaphors are mixed when duality is treated as a toxic substance that "impairs judgment." (4) A priority of emphasis on the professional *role* serves to diminish personal connectedness, thereby fostering human alienation and endorsing a privileged role hierarchy. (5) Exploitation in relationships is always exploitation and unethical, regardless of whether it occurs in a dual context. (6) Multiple connections that cross boundaries between therapy, teaching, supervision, collegiality, and friendship can be celebrated as part of the inevitable and potentially beneficial complexities of human life. (7) The power differential in any relationship can be used to empower the personal and/or professional development of both parties as well as to exploit them. (8) A frequent therapeutic goal involves helping students, supervisees, and clients understand and negotiate the multiple and shifting layers of human relatedness and human relational systems. (9) It is preferable to humanize and to democratize the therapeutic relationship rather than to encumber it with unnecessary trappings of professional expertise and higher authority. (10) The therapeutic role can be misused by cloaking it in paternalistic, patronizing attitudes of emotional distance and myths regarding superior mental health of practitioners. (11) Incompetent and exploitative therapists are the problem, not dual relating. (12) What is needed by therapists is classification and discussion of the subtle kinds of exploitation that can occur in professional relationships, not a naive injunction against dual relating. (13) To categorically prohibit dual relationships reductionistically implies that there is no continuity or overlap in roles in relationships and that therapy can be separated from the person of the therapist. (14) Dual relationships are inevitable and clinicians can conduct them thoughtfully and ethically, making whatever happens "grist for the mill." (15) Dual relationships represent an opportunity for personal growth and enriched human connection that benefits both parties. (16) Human connections evolve spontaneously and change over the course of time naturally and unpredictably, and therapy need not block this natural process. (17) Duality provides an important pathway for corrective feedback, potentially offering improved understanding and increased consensuality. (18) Duality opens space for increased connectedness, more sharing, greater honesty, more personal integrity, greater responsibility, increased social integration, and more egalitarian interaction. (19) Dual relating reduces space for manipulation, deception, and special privilege, gives more opportunity to recognize each other as ordinary human beings, and reduces the likelihood of persistent transferential and countertransferential distortions. (20) Interpersonal boundaries are rarely rigid and fixed, but rather fluctuate and undergo continuous redefinition in all relationships, including the therapeutic relationship, which deliberately focuses on developing consciousness of boundary fluctuations and discussing such changes. And (21) dual relationships represent, after all, the exact kinds of complex interpersonal situations that our professional skills were developed to study and enhance, so as to increase the beneficial possibilities of human interactions and transformations. These points have been discussed at length by the writers mentioned above. Various considerations of duality have emerged over time in the psychoanalytic literature. These ideas seem relevant to consider in all dynamic and systems-oriented therapies.

PSYCHOANALYTIC CONSIDERATIONS OF DUALITY

Duality: The Essence of Transference Interpretation

The very heart and soul of psychotherapy, transference and transference interpretation, by definition always constitute some form of dual relationship. Freud's (1912a,b, 1915) initial definitions of psychoanalytic technique revolve around the "love" relationship that begins to form between physician and client in the course of psychoanalytic free association. Freud suggests the image of an opaque mirror to describe the neutral stance that the analyst seeks to achieve vis-à-vis the patient's neurotic conflict. Freud's images make clear the ultimate impossibility of ever attaining perfect mirroring or perfect neutrality. Despite the analyst's attempt to form a real relationship based on mirroring and neutrality, relationship expectations brought from the client's past would inevitably begin to make their presence felt. *The decisive moment in psychoanalysis, and in all derivative psychotherapies, is that in which the duality is at last recognized and successfully interpreted by the psychotherapist.* There exists at this moment the "real" relationship that has evolved over time between two people. But another reality is suddenly recognized and defined by the transference interpretation. In the former reality the analyst has a caregiving, curative role and the client has an obligation to relate to real needs of the analyst including fees, attendance, and respect for the setting, which supports and protects the personal and professional life of the analyst as well as the client. But when transference reality can be discerned and discussed by the two, the therapist functions in a completely different relationship to the client—one of professional interpreter of the emotional life of the client that is brought to the real relationship set up by the analytic situation. At the moment of interpretation the analyst steps into the role of a third party viewing the realistic interaction of the two and comments on a heretofore hidden reality, the transference—or the resistance or the countertransference.

The Working Alliance

The nature of this dual role of the analyst has received considerable attention in the psychoanalytic literature. Greenson (1965), acknowledging the real developing relationship speaks of the "working alliance" to acknowledge the *realistic collaboration* and mutual respect of the two. Greenson's formulations stand as a correction of the faulty belief that the client's attitudes and fantasies are mostly transference distortions—when in fact a significant real relationship develops quite apart from the professional task of transference interpretation.

"Acting Out" Childhood Transformations

Bollas (1979) further clarifies the nature of the real relationship by pointing out that Freud (unwittingly and forgivably) designed the psychoanalytic listening situation in order to "act out" with his patients the earliest caregiving roles of parenting in order to promote the transformational aspect of psychotherapy. The transformational role of the analyst is a realistic role distinctly different from that of transference interpreter. Psychoanalytic transformation occurs by means of this dual transforming/interpreting relationship. Following Winnicott's (1975) developmental approach and Modell's (1976) notion of the "holding environment," Bollas places the transformative element of psychotherapy less in a context of interpretive correction and more within a context of the therapeutic experience as it actually, realistically evolves. He refers to this transformative process as "psychoanalysis of the unthought known."

Transference Experience Arises from Realistic Relating

Schwaber's (1979, 1983) clarifying work arises from an orientation emphasizing the subjective aspects of self. Her ideas focus on the role that the reality of the analyst and the analytic relationship play in evoking transference. She, following Kohut (1971, 1977), emphasizes the reality of the ongoing nature of the relationship that evolves in the psychoanalytic listening situation. Transference from past experience is to be discerned on the basis of something the analyst did or did not do and the emotional reaction that the analyst's activities elicited. Schwaber highlights the real relationship based upon the analyst's effort to listen and to respond as empathically as humanly possible. Transference is then thought to be perceivable against the backdrop of failures in the analyst's empathic understanding. That is, the analyst engages or fails to engage in real interpersonal activity, the disruptive results of which the analyst could not have possibly foretold. According to this view, the working through of the "selfobject" or narcissistic transference constitutes a new edition, a novel interpersonal reality that the analyst and client now have to address with new and different understanding and interpretation. Thus, not only is transference discernible by virtue of aspects of the real relationship coming up for discussion, but the working through is seen as an entirely new and evolving form of personal relationship.

The Transference Neurosis

The notion of cure in psychoanalytic theory revolves around Freud's definition of *transference neurosis*. The (neurotic) conflicts from the past come to be actually reexperienced in the present and are experienced by the client as the realistic situation. They are, by Freud's definition, complex unconscious features never fully interpretable as such. The ultimate unresolvability of the transference neurosis is widely misunderstood by those who wish a happy sunset at the end of analysis. But in Freudian analysis there are always interminable aspects to analytic work and the transference neurosis in certain respects lives on indefinitely (for discussion see Hedges 1983, Chapters 3 and 4).

Mutative Interpretation

Strachey (1934) quotes Melanie Klein as saying that analysts are generally reluctant to give mutative interpretations (those that promote change) because full instinctual energy would thereby be directed realistically at the person of the analyst. This situation is feared and avoided by analysts who fail to interpret so the full power of transference comes into focus in the here and now. Thus, the two key "curative" agents in psychoanalysis, the establishment of the transference neurosis and the mutative interpretation, both function to bring past emotional experience to bear on and to intensify the reality of the present interpersonal relationship. These two realities will never become completely sorted out. One's past emotional life forever colors present relationships. Thus, psychoanalytic doctrine holds that the duality between the realistic present and the transferential past can never, in principle, be eliminated from human relationships. Psychoanalysis serves the purpose of shedding light on many aspects of these dual realities.

The Corrective Emotional Experience

Another other line of psychoanalytic thought revolves around the notion of "corrective emotional experience" (Alexander 1961). Various realistic and active procedures may be introduced into the relationship for the purposes of promoting or maintaining the analysis (Eissler 1953, Ferenczi 1952, 1955, 1962). But the need for such reassurance, suggestion, or gratification, later will have to be analyzed as transference. According to this view, the client's emotional past was flawed and the therapist is (realistically) going to be able to provide a better (corrective) emotional experience. The analyst by this view may step out of his or her usual role as analyst and "do things," intervene in active ways to help the client relate to the therapist and to stay in therapy.

Classical analysts who oppose active techniques maintain that the refusal by the analyst to engage in active, helpful interventions (which serve to strengthen the ego by support and suggestion) is what makes psychoanalysis different from all other "more supportive" psychotherapeutic and counseling techniques. Analysts who advocate the need for active intervention under certain circumstances implicitly recognize that the therapeutic action of psychoanalysis requires various forms of duality to become effective. This line of thinking asserts that psychotherapy and counseling, as distinguished from classical psychoanalysis, definitely and inevitably include the duality that characterizes the more active psychoanalytic techniques. Bollas (1979) pointed out that even classical technique implicitly includes a setting in which transformational experiences from early childhood are "acted out" in a supportive way by the analyst. Dual relationships thus form the backbone of all dynamically oriented psychotherapies.

The Development of Ego Functions

Another line of psychoanalytic thought relates to ways in which ego functions are formed in early child development. It has been well documented that ego skills such as perception, memory, judgment, and signal anxiety evolve as a function of the realistic presence and actual interest of the early (m)other. Likewise, through various activities of the analyst the development of failed, arrested, or defective functions may be facilitated. Ego deficits associated with many psychological conditions including learning disorders can only be activated for therapeutic study and transformation through the emergence of realistic learning situations in which the therapist realistically functions as the observing auxiliary ego while the learning deficit involved in limited or arrested functions is being made good. If early development of basic ego skills was favorable, they are thought to be "autonomous" from neurotic conflict, but in all preneurotic conditions ego skills have undergone various limiting, constricting, or warping influences that are subject to correction by realistic attention in the analytic relationship. Winnicott has spoken what many believe, that when early developmental issues are involved, the therapist does not function like the mother but realistically is the mother in certain ways for certain periods of time as early ego functions are restored.

Absence of the Eye of the Third Party

A European way of viewing dual relationships is clarified in Clavreul's (1967) notion of the "perverse couple" that exists when the social structure is taken as blinded to the mutual need fulfilling nature of private relationships such as the analytic one. Clavreul's argument asks, "Can the activities necessarily involved in analytic growth be carried on publicly before an all-seeing eye that is not blind to mutual personal needs, that is, in an atmosphere of duality? Or is the therapeutic effort forever tinged with hidden incest and perversity?" Merged parent–child relatedness is incestuous unless it occurs within a context of third parties, that is, social regulation (dual relating). The implication is that duality is an essential aspect of all human relatedness situations in which favorable development occurs. It is the essence of duality that fuels creative development. The absence of duality is seen from this angle as incestuous or perverse.

In summary, beginning with Freud's initial images of the analyst functioning as an opaque mirror and as a neutral transference interpreter, psychoanalysts over eighty years have come to recognize the many aspects of dual relatedness that are essential to the psychoanalytic task. The concepts of the working alliance, the transformational other, transference arising from realistic relating, the transference neurosis, mutative interpretation, the corrective emotional experience, the evolution of ego skills, and the function of the third party all form the basis of contemporary psychoanalytic thought and practice. All of these foundational understandings underline in various ways the fact that dual relating is the heart and soul of the transformational experience as well as the essence of transference interpretations. There can be no psychoanalysis or psychotherapy without the dual relationship.

Essential Dual Relatedness in Developmental Psychotherapy

It is a moot question whether psychotherapeutic clients today are more primitive or disturbed than in the past or whether our therapeutic knowledge now enables us to see more clearly the more regressed aspects of human nature. In either case, people who come to psychotherapy today present for analysis many very early developmental issues that have come to be called "borderline," "narcissistic," and "character" problems.

In general, the earlier the developmental issue, the greater the subjective sense of reality in the analytic relationship. Winnicott (1949a) points out that the earlier in development the impingement on the infant's sense of "going on being" is, the shorter the span of the ego—meaning the less that can be considered at any one moment in time. Thus, when early developmental issues arise in therapy, there is less ordinary reality testing available, and only a greatly narrowed picture of the world and the analytic relationship is possible. In today's psychotherapy, many early developmental issues are activated. Consequently, a narrow, concrete subjective experience may well take on a fully formed reality sense, when in fact only a small segment of the overall reality context is being considered.

At the psychotic or primary organizing level of human personality there is the risk of a complete breakdown of the sense of complex shared realities when the "transference psychosis" emerges in the therapeutic relationship for study (Little 1981, 1990). All people have deep layers of psychotic anxiety that may need to be activated at some point in therapy. This means that in any analysis a psychotic core may emerge for brief or extended periods of time during which the client's usual capacities to test reality and to abstract from broad experience may be impaired, such that the analyst may become part of a delusional transference experience—possibly one that can threaten the therapist emotionally and realistically.

At the opposite end of the developmental spectrum, psychoanalysts early learned that symbolic interpretation (oedipal, 4- to 7-year-old level) serves in neurosis to permit a return of the repressed, which is recognized as one's own self that has been declared to be nonexistent for so long. In neurotic issues the capacity for reality testing and high-level abstraction and symbolization make the work easier to think about and safer for both parties.

At the selfobject (narcissistic, 3-year-old) level the analyst is perennially responsible for and often blamed for realistic empathic failures. Technically, the analyst takes responsibility for the activities in question, at which time the person in analysis can generally be helped to distinguish between interpersonal realities as they have actually occurred and the emergence of selfobject transference. Kohut (1977, 1984) is clear that actual, realistic, resonating understanding is the key therapeutic feature at this level. Interpretive verbalizations ("summarizing reflections") follow realistic interactional understanding. Kohut's (1971, 1977) selfobject transference concepts demonstrate that blurring of self and other boundaries is prerequisite to being able to analyze the narcissistic transferences based upon selfother failures in early childhood that left the self with structural defects.

At the level of symbiotic (borderline, 4- to 24-month-old) issues, dual realities are more difficult to tease out. It requires considerable time and actual relating to establish interpersonal symbiotic scenarios as visible in transferences that become somehow replicated in the therapeutic relationship. In my work I have dealt extensively with the complicated interactional sequences and dilemmas that therapists encounter in responding to symbiotic (borderline) transferences (Hedges 1983, 1992). Interpreting the countertransference becomes a critical aspect of responding to the many projective identifications encountered in this work.

Thus, at each of the four major levels of self and other relatedness the dual relationship mechanism is required for psychotherapy, although just how duality operates is different at each developmental level.

The Necessary Interpenetration of Boundaries

The theoretician exciting the most interest today in clinical circles is Winnicott (1958, 1965, 1971), who in his studies of the early mother–child relationship demonstrates the way the boundaries between the two mix and mingle and how this mixing and merging must be replicated when studying early developmental issues in the transference/countertransference relationship. Infant research (Stern 1985) further underlines this mixing of boundaries at early developmental levels. Little's (1990) deeply moving account of her own analytic work, which led to a complete psychotic breakdown in her analysis with Winnicott, demonstrates this aptly. No one makes clearer than Winnicott the importance of the reality of the therapist and the setting. His work demonstrates that the therapist must be realistically available to the client for long periods while restricted areas of the personality have an opportunity to expand. In his focus on early developmental issues he demonstrates that interpretation can only follow actual involvement and improvement. This kind of duality is essential to the transformation of all primitive mental states.

Loss of Reality Testing in the "Negative Therapeutic Reaction"

When aspects of the organizing (psychotic, schizoid) level become activated, the person in analysis often develops the conviction of special, privileged understanding regarding the reality of the therapeutic exchange. Reality no longer is a matter for mutual discussion, or for consideration by various standards of social consensus, or for contradictory or varying viewpoints. "This is real, don't give me any bullshit, you are shooting secret cosmic rays from behind your chair at me." "This is incest, you have damaged me irreparably by allowing me to feel close to you." "Because you have stepped out of your neutral role and given me advice, opinion, suggestion, or help, you are in a dual relationship with me. I cannot seek consultation with a third party as you have asked because I would be ashamed at how I seduced you into actually helping me grow. You are the guilty party because you have the power and should have known that revealing personal aspects of yourself and reaching out to me in realistic and 'helpful' ways would be experienced by me (in transference) as incestual and abusive. Your 'good nature' and 'willingness to help me grow' are devious things you do for self aggrandizement, to make your own ego swell with pride. You have exploited me for the sake of your own ego, your narcissism. You have damaged me by overinvolving yourself in my therapeutic growth. I demand recompense for the violations you have indulged yourself in and the damage you have done. You seduced me (or let me seduce you). Now you will pay." No amount of objective feedback, attempts at rational discussion, or weighing of considerations are possible at such a shocking moment and there may not be another moment in which these psychotic transference convictions can be discussed before an ethical complaint or a lawsuit is filed.

At the moment of the negative therapeutic reaction symbolic speech and discourse are replaced by destructive concretization. Rage or lust is mobilized and with it a clarity of understanding about reality that is subjectively experienced as right, good, monolithic, absolute, and beyond dispute or discussion. A moral crusade characterized by vengeance and righteous indignation is on. The therapist is the enemy, the perpetrator of crimes, the exploiter. Evidence is gathered, much as one gathers evidence to support a paranoid pseudocommunity, in order to support and bolster his or her views against the alleged misbehavior of the therapist. If no moderation or mediation softens the position before accident intervenes, we see suicides, destructive mutilation and homicides, as well as legal and ethical claims facing the therapist as a result of good therapeutic mobilization of unconscious organizing affects. The therapeutic activation has succeeded. But the cure has failed and the therapist is in realistic danger. Our focus for the future must be on how to understand and prevent such dangers.

Freud (1918, 1923, 1933) has formulated that the failure to deidealize the analyst in time leads to a "negative therapeutic reaction." The dual relationship becomes not one in which transference and countertransference realities can be secured and discussed as a special reality that two can share as somewhat different from or resultant from other aspects of the real relationship, but as *the* reality that the person in analysis is privileged to know, a reality in which the wickedness and self-interest of the (parent) therapist is believed to have gotten out of hand.

As our experience with the emergence of psychotic transference (even in better-developed personalities) expands, the need becomes increasingly clear for the presence of a case monitor of some sort to follow the course of treatment so that when reality controls are lost by the client in psychotic transference, a third party who is knowledgeable about the course of the treatment and who has some relationship with the client is able to intervene to prevent such a dangerous and destructive negative therapeutic reaction.

Since all people have experienced an early developmental (organizing or psychotic) period with constricting limits and constraints, all people are subject to psychotic anxieties and transferences—meaning that the therapist is, in principle, never safe from the destructive emergence of an abusive psychotic transference that is experienced as very real by the client and aimed at the therapist's person. No amount of good judgment ahead of time is fail-safe protection against such potential disaster. Viewed from this angle it is always an error to trust the good will, good nature, and truth searching qualities of the client since they can suddenly be reversed in a psychotic episode.

The analyst is always in danger of becoming the target of psychotic anxieties that cannot be surmounted. If the patient received abuse as an infant or young child, this abuse will likely emerge as some form of primary identification in the psychotic transference. The subjective experience is so real it cannot be interpreted successfully and the therapist becomes the victim. Therapists facing misconduct charges regularly report that they "never would have dreamed therapy could have produced such a miscarriage. She (the client) seemed like such a trusting person of good will, and of upstanding moral character. She was so involved in her therapy, so respectful of her analytic partner. How could such vengeance and hatred be directed at me, the very person who has probably done more for her in terms of opening herself up than anyone she has ever known." This is the problem. The therapeutic work did succeed in loosening the moralizing and idealizing defenses and in easing up the stifling rigidity of the symbiotic character structure. Indeed the traumatized, annihilated true self began to emerge with all of its raw, infantile power, lust, and rage, but while it was still identified with its aggressor in a very primitive way. The transference interpretation not only succeeded, but when the therapist (according to transference script) failed, the structure opened to the murderous psychotic rage of infancy. The idealizing tendency, which has made for such an angelic self and unshakable idealization of the analyst, collapses suddenly and the way things have been going the analyst is in deep trouble if he or she has in any way trusted the good nature of the patient and extended various active interaction measures that can appear to a third party as not avoiding an unethical dual relationship:

The Dangers to Therapists Rage on Unchecked

As our therapeutic tools for bringing out early traumas improve, practicing psychotherapists are headed for deeper and deeper trouble. The dual nature of psychotherapy cannot be denied or minimized and the active role of the therapist required in working with earlier developed layers of the personality moves the dynamic psychotherapist inexorably toward an ill fate. Social consciousness raising increasingly holds the teacher, minister, physician, and psychotherapist accountable for their activities. Deep-working, well-intentioned psychotherapists face the danger that their best, most well-conceived efforts to help will be experienced as violent or incestuous intrusions that they should have known about in advance and should have taken measures to forestall.

Perhaps we should ask where the phrase *should have known* appears in any single piece of responsible therapy research or even in a single theoretical tract on the nature of psychotherapy? Such a claim is completely untenable and unsupportable. The literature on predicting violence and suicide has repeatedly demonstrated how poor our best-trained experts are at ever predicting even very strong variables. No one who seriously practices in-depth psychotherapy is likely to use such a phrase as "should have known." What may evolve in psychotic transference is never known in advance. Who are those who would tell us what we should or should not have known? After the fact, like Monday morning quarterbacks, they sit in armchairs saying what we should have known or done; meanwhile strange and idiosyncratic transference configurations unfold hourly in our consulting rooms.

The misplaced focus by licensing boards and ethics committees on dual relationships when damaging exploitation is the issue has meant that therapists can no longer simply consider what such events as attending a client's wedding, attending a lecture or social event in a client's presence, offering a helpful book or cassette, giving or receiving token gifts or touch, or sending a birthday or sympathy card may mean to a client in the context of the therapy. Rather, the dual relationship witch-hunt has come to mean that we must concern ourselves with what precautions to take so that legal and ethical questions can never arise. The only tool we have at our disposal in psychotherapy—the spontaneity of ourselves—has thus been tarnished and is in danger of serious damage.

Given the absurd state of affairs currently prevailing, the orientation now required by therapists who think developmentally and who work dynamically (a) begins with the realization that depth psychotherapy always depends on the successful evolution of a dual relationship, (b) realizes that heretofore questions of meaning and interpretation have been foremost in our practice, and (c) concludes that now (considering the dual relationship panic) we must reorient our thinking to protect ourselves from accusations that could dangerously be held against us for doing exactly what we aim to do—exploiting the potential of dual relatedness for the purpose of studying human nature and freeing our clients from the bondage of the past. What a fine kettle of fish this is!

Fortunately, the pendulum has begun to swing back to a position where we can rely once again on clinical considerations rather than naive moralizing and absurd misconduct rulings to guide our therapy. But, for the present we are stuck having to water down what we do for fear of censorship by ethics committees and licensing boards. We are in the midst of a major crisis in the practice of our discipline.

Our growing expertise in elucidating the deepest, most primitive and crazy aspects of our clients and of ourselves is expanding at the very moment when the therapeutic dimension we most depend on—dual relatedness—has come under social, legal, and ethical censorship. It is by no means clear how we will come to grips with these and many related issues.

Regulatory boards and ethics committees in their eagerness to provide rules for the practice of psychotherapy have rapidly moved toward positions that, if allowed, threaten to obliterate the essence of clinical work that relies on the dual relationship. Viewed from this vantage point our fear of the boards and therefore our tacit support of their trends register a resistance on the part of therapists to enter the new terrain of enriched psychotherapeutic relatedness.

Unavoidable Duality

The essential duality involved in psychotherapy can be considered from many angles. The views on duality presented here serve to contrast (a) the real, moment to moment, spontaneous, mutual need-fulfilling aspect of the contractual relationship that evolves over time between two people, with (b) the symbolic, interpretive relationship in which the two gradually come to stand apart, as it were, from their real, spontaneous relating and speak in such a way as to characterize from a third-party point of view the manner and quality of their relating. The two create pictures and stories that describe (as if from an outside or objective point of view) what is happening between them and why. This interpretive, third party, symbolic relationship that the two share enables each to speak his or her subjective reactions arising from within the real relationship in such a way as to consider the emotional load (left over from past emotional relationship) that each may be adding to their ongoing appreciation of the other and the relatedness.

The essence of the interpretive art at the symbiotic, borderline, character level is a confrontation of the person's refusal to have such a dual relationship with the therapist and therefore with all emotionally significant others (Hedges 1983, 1992). The merger sense that lies at the root of virtually all clinical syndromes in treatment today resists treatment by relegating the reality of the therapist and his or her personality functioning to one of relative unimportance. This resistance functions to prevent the actualization of the symbolic duality that makes human development possible. The decisive interpretive move with symbiotic (borderline) issues comes when the therapist can say, "But I am not you and I am not your wished for (or feared) other. I am a real person relating to you. I am unique, different from anyone you have ever known. I have shown you that I can relate more or less as you wish me to. But for myself, I do not think or react as you might expect or wish me to. It is not necessary for you to be disappointed, enraged, or hurt as you once were when you were on the verge of discovering your mother was a separate person. Differentness is something that can be celebrated. It is possible for you to learn to relate realistically to me and to others in ways that are different from your experience of the past. You are perfectly capable of seeing the two of us as we realistically relate to each other and to form ideas and feelings about us and our ways of relating."

Necessary Subjectivity

We no longer believe there is any such thing as an objective analyst (Natterson 1991). No one knows in advance how transference and countertransference will unfold, and therefore unconscious transference and countertransference feelings cannot be limited and regulated in advance. This is especially true for the evolving countertransference that is projected into the therapist at the level of the spontaneous interaction that recapitulates the early (borderline) mother–child symbiotic relationship. What evolves as a second relationship to the one based upon conscious contract is a joint fantasy relationship that the two collaborate in creating (Spence 1982).

Natterson's (1991) text illustrates how patient and analyst communicatively achieve an intense oneness and fusion, how subjective features from the analyst's past come into play in the countertransference, and how at the same time each is able to individuate and differentiate more completely from the experience than either was able to do before their work together. Natterson shatters the myth of the value-neutral therapist, exposing it as a fictive assumption:

> All human two person transactions share fundamental meaning: *each party attempts to influence the other* with his or her view of the universe, to persuade the other of the rightness of his or her view. . . . This basic power orientation of dyadic relationships makes it natural for moral influences to be invariably significant components of the therapist's activity. [pp. 21ff, italics added]

The interaction of the basic beliefs of patient and therapist are inseparable from the human fantasies and yearnings of each. Natterson views the psychoanalytic encounter as a dyadic impingement in which each person influences the other. "Then respective fantasies and desiring, values and goals, are engaged in continuous struggle, through which both persons are continuously changing. . . . This intersubjective experience should be regarded as the basic precondition for any theoretical understanding of psychoanalytic processes" (p. 23). Natterson's brilliant work highlights the duality between the real relationship and the emerging transference/countertransference relationship.

The nature of transference, countertransference, resistance, and interpretation as we have come to understand them, de facto rest upon the existence of a dual relationship. It behooves us to remember that all beneficial effects of psychotherapy arise in consequence of the dual relationship.

An Anthropological Insight into How Psychotherapy "Hooks into the Flesh" through Dual Relationships

The French anthropologist Claude Levi-Strauss (1949) undertakes a penetrating definition of the psychoanalytic task, revealing from an anthropological and sociological viewpoint the necessarily dual nature of the psychotherapeutic endeavor. Levi-Strauss reviews the first available South American "magico-religious" text, an eighteen page incantation obtained by the Cuna Indian, Guillermo Haya, from an elderly informant of his tribe (original source: Holmer and Wassen 1947). The purpose of the song is to facilitate unusually difficult childbirth. Its use is unusual since native women of Central and South America have easier deliveries than women of Western societies. The intervention of the shaman is thus rare and occurs only in the extreme case of failure to deliver and at the request of the midwife.

The song begins with the midwife's confusion over the pregnant woman's failure to deliver and describes her visit to the shaman and the latter's arrival in the hut of the laboring woman, with his fumigations of burnt cocoa nibs, his invocations, and the making of *nuchu*, sacred figures or images carved from various prescribed kinds of wood that lend them their effectiveness. The carved *nuchu* represent tutelary spirits who become the shaman's assistants. He leads the *nuchu* to the abode of *Muu* (inside the woman's body). *Muu* is the goddess of fertility and is responsible for the formation of the fetus. Difficult childbirths occur when *Muu* has exceeded her functions and captured the *purba* or soul of the mother. The incantation thus expresses a quest for the lost soul of the mother that will be restored after overcoming many obstacles. The shaman's saga will take the woman through a victory over wild beasts and finally through a great contest waged by the shaman and his tutelary spirits against *Muu* and her daughters. Once *Muu* has been defeated, the whereabouts of the soul of the ailing woman can be discovered and freed so the delivery can take place. The song ends with precautions that must be taken so that *Muu* cannot pursue her victors (an event that would result in infertility). The fight is not waged against *Muu* herself, who is indispensable to procreation, but against her abuses of power. After the epic saga, *Muu*'s words to the shaman are, "Friend *nele*, when do you think to visit me again?" (p. 187), indicating the perennial nature of psychic conflict that can be expected to interfere with childbirth.

Levi-Strauss comments that in order to perform his function the shaman is, by cultural belief, assigned supernatural power to see the cause of the illness, to know the whereabouts of the vital forces, and to use *nuchu* spirits who are endowed with exceptional powers to move invisibly and clairvoyantly in the service of humans.

On the surface the song appears rather commonplace among shamanistic cures. The sick woman suffers because she has lost her spiritual double, which constitutes her vital strength. In traveling to the supernatural world and in being aided by assistants in snatching the woman's double from a malevolent spirit and restoring it to its owner, the shaman effects the cure. The exceptional aspect of this song making it of interest to anthropologists and psychoanalysts alike is that "'*Muu*'s way' and the abode of *Muu* are not, to the native mind, simply a mythical itinerary and dwelling-place. They represent, literally, the vagina and uterus of the pregnant woman, which are to be explored by the shaman and *nuchu* and in whose depths they will wage their victorious combat" (p. 188). In his quest to capture her soul, the shaman also captures other spirits, which govern the vitality of her other body parts (heart, bones, teeth, hair, nails, and feet). Not unlike the invasive attention of the psychoanalyst, no body part is left unattended to.

Muu, as instigator of the disorder, has captured the special "souls" of the various organs thus destroying the cooperation and integrity of the main soul, the woman's double who must be set free. "In a difficult delivery the 'soul' of the uterus has led astray all the 'souls' belonging to other parts of the body. Once these souls are liberated, the soul of the uterus can and must resume its cooperation" (p. 190). It is clear that the song seeks to delineate the emotional content of the physiological disturbance to the mind of the sick woman. To reach *Muu*, the shaman and his assistants must find "*Muu*'s way," the road of *Muu*. At the peak moment when the shaman has finished his carvings, spirits rise up at the shaman's exhortation:

The (sick) woman lies in the hammock in front of you.
 Her white tissue lies in her lap, her white tissues move softly.
 The (sick) woman's body lies weak.
 When they light up (along) Muu's way, it runs over with exudations and like blood.
 Her exudations drip down below the hammock all like blood, all red.

The inner white tissue extends to the bosom of the earth. Into the middle of the woman's white tissue a human being descends. [Holmer and Wassen, cited in Levi-Strauss, p. 190]

"*Muu*'s way," darkened and covered with blood is unquestionably the vagina and the dark whirlpool the uterus where *Muu* dwells.

Levi-Strauss comments that this text claims a special place among shaman cures. One standard type of cure involves an organ that is manipulated or sucked until a thorn, crystal, or feather appears, a representation of the removal of the malevolent force. Another type of cure revolves around a sham battle waged in a hut and then outside against harmful spirits. In these cures it remains for us to understand exactly how the psychological aspect "hooks into" the physiological. But the current song constitutes a purely psychological treatment. For the shaman does not touch the body and administers no remedy. "Nevertheless it involves, directly and explicitly, the pathological condition and its locus. In our view, the song constitutes a *psychological manipulation* of the sick organ, and it is precisely from this manipulation that a cure is expected" (p. 192).

Levi-Strauss observes that the situation is contrived to induce pain in a sick woman through developing a psychological awareness of the smallest details of all of her internal tissues. Using mythological images the pain-induced situation becomes the symbolic setting for the experience of conflict. "A transition will thus be made from the most prosaic reality, to myth, from the physical universe to the psychological universe, from the external world to the internal body" (p. 193). The mythological saga being enacted in the body attains sensory and hallucinatory vividness through the many elements of ritual—smell, sound, tactile stimulation, rhythm, and repetition.

What follows in breathless (hypnotic) rhythm and rhyme are more and more rapid oscillations between mythical and physiological themes "as if to abolish in the mind of the sick woman the distinction which separates them, and to make it impossible to differentiate their respective attributes" (p. 193). Spirits and events follow one another as the woman's total focus becomes the birth apparatus and the cosmic battle being waged there by the invasion of the shaman and his spiritual helpers who bring "illuminating light" into the birth canal. The presence of wild animals increases the pains that are thus personified and described to the woman. Uncle Alligator moves about with bulging eyes, crouching and wriggling his tail. He moves his glistening flippers that drag on everything. The octopus arrives with sticky tentacles alternately opening and closing, contracting and expanding passageways. The black tiger, the red animal, the two colored animals are all tied with an iron chain that rasps and clanks against everything. Their tongues are hanging out, saliva dripping, saliva foaming, with flourishing tails and claws tearing at everything.

According to Levi-Strauss the cure consists in making explicit a situation originally existing on an emotional level and in rendering acceptable to the mind pains that the body otherwise refuses to tolerate. The shaman with the aid of this myth encourages the woman to accept the incoherent and arbitrary pains, reintegrating them into a whole where everything is coordinated and meaningful. He points out that our physicians tell a similar story to us not in terms of monsters and spirits but rather in terms that we believe like germs, microbes, and so forth. "The shaman provides the sick woman with a *language*, by means of which unexpressed, and otherwise inexpressible, psychic states can be immediately expressed" (p. 198). The transition to the verbal system makes it possible to undergo in an ordered and intelligible form an experience that would otherwise be chaotic and inexpressible. The myth and its hypnotic power enable the woman to release and reorganize the physiological processes that have become disordered in the woman's sickness.

The Dual Relationship Cure

Levi-Strauss explicitly contextualizes this shamanistic cure as psychoanalytic in nature. The purpose is to bring to a conscious level conflicts and resistance that have remained unconscious with resulting symptom formation. The conflicts and resistances are resolved not because of knowledge, real or alleged,

> but because this knowledge makes possible a specific experience, in the course of which conflicts materialize in an order and on a level permitting their free development and leading to their resolution. This vital experience is called *abreaction* in psychoanalysis. We know that its pre-

condition is the unprovoked intervention of the analyst, who appears in the conflicts of the client *through a double transference mechanism* as (1) a flesh-and-blood protagonist and (2) in relation to whom the client can restore and clarify an initial (historical) situation which has remained unexpressed or unformulated. . . .

The shaman *plays the same dual role as the psychoanalyst*. A prerequisite role—that of listener for the psychoanalyst and of orator for the shaman—*establishes a direct relationship with the patient's conscious and an indirect relationship with his unconscious*. This is the function of the incantation proper. But the shaman does more than utter the incantation; *he is its hero, for it is he who, at the head of a supernatural battalion of spirits, penetrates the endangered organs and frees the captive soul*. [pp. 198–199]

The shaman, like the psychoanalyst, is thus enabled by the dual relationship to become (a) the transference object induced vividly in the patient's mind, and (b) the real protagonist of the conflict that is experienced by the patient as on the border between the physical world and the psychical world. In this dual situation in which pain is deliberately induced by the practitioner, the psychoanalytic client eliminates individual myths by facing the reality of the person of the analyst. And the native woman overcomes an organic disorder by identifying with a "mythically transmuted" shaman.

Levi-Strauss notes that the shamarita cure is a counterpart to psychoanalytic cure. Both induce an experience through appeal to myth. The psychoanalytic patient constructs a myth with elements drawn from his or her personal past. The shamanist patient receives from the outside a social myth. In either case the treating person fosters the emergence of a storyline that cures by giving language to experience. The effectiveness of symbols guarantees the parallel development in the process of myth and action.

Levi-Strauss provides a fascinating argument that aligns shamanism of ages past with the modern activities of psychoanalysis and psychotherapy. His arguments go considerably beyond Freud and into areas being explored in psychoanalysis and psychotherapy today in which an inductive property of symbols permits formerly homologous structures built out of different materials at different levels of life—organizational processes, unconscious agency, and rational thought—to be understood as profoundly related to one another. Levi-Strauss points out that the individual vocabulary of the cure is significant only to the extent that the unconscious structures it according to its laws and thus transforms it into language. Whether the myth is a personal re-creation or one borrowed from tradition matters little, the essential structure of language and the unconscious is the locus of the power of the symbol. Any myth represents a quest for the remembrance of things past and the ways those remembrances are structured in the unconscious. *"The modern version of shamanistic technique called psychoanalysis thus derives its specific characteristics from the fact that in industrial civilization there is no longer any room for mythical time, except within man himself"* (pp. 203–204).

The purpose of reviewing this anthropological analysis of psychoanalysis and psychotherapy as knowledge of the symbolic function inherited from shamanism is to highlight the inherently *dual* relationship involved in psychological cure. The shaman/analyst is first of all realistically involved with the person in conscious and unconscious ways so as to evoke a second-order relationship, the mythical transference in which the shaman/analyst becomes hero, protagonist in an inner drama, a conflict, a quest for possession of the soul. The drama proceeds by putting private experience into symbols that have the power to transform the inexplicable, the unintelligible, the inchoate, and the irremediable in a series of epic narrations that the two can share together. It is only the extent to which the shaman/analyst succeeds in establishing a real relationship that the epic journey in search of the soul through mythic transference, resistance, and countertransference becomes possible.

If an attorney should happen into the hut midway in this woman's process to cure with papers for her to sign, she no doubt would produce a stillbirth or die in childbirth from inability to stay with the symbolic. He would be on hand to bring action against the shaman for negligence. A judge and jury with no way of understanding the power of the symbolic or the subtle operations of transference could hardly be expected to show much mercy for the poor shaman left with only the incantations bequeathed him by wise forefathers, a handful of hand-carved stick figures, and cocoa incense. Perhaps his songs, smoke, and hocus pocus will be viewed as harmless enough. But that he had formed a dual relationship with the woman, had become by virtue of his social role an authorizing personage in her life, and furthermore was actually fraternizing with her family and midwife thus (no doubt) exploiting the hapless victim for personal aggrandizement of his narcissistic needs may indeed be dimly viewed by administrative judges as he is charged with responsibility for stillbirth, a faulty delivery indeed.

Or should this woman by chance attend an incest survivors or Adult Children of Alcoholics (ACA) group midway in the move to the symbolic, she may come to recognize the very real sense of penetration she feels from her shaman/analyst and begin reliving the traumas of the past that have been revised by this penetrating therapeutic relationship of the present. The therapeutic relationship may become so terrifyingly real that she enters a negative therapeutic reaction with her heretofore idealized shaman. She soon is encouraged by well-meaning group members to file suit against him for failing to maintain his boundaries by his attending her wedding, sniffing cocoa incense with her, failing to stop her from reading his journal articles, and not preventing her from attending his classes at the local university. The shaman is judged negligent because he "should have known" that dual relationships are damaging. He should have known that she would in the long run prove insufficiently motivated, insufficiently endowed for the process, or easily derailed by accidental outside influences so that she would be unable to move to the level of the symbolic required for cure. The tragedy: the dual relationship, which is the primary vehicle requisite for carrying the symbolic cure, had been put securely in place, but patient constitution, concentration, or motivation to effect a transition to the transferential symbolic proved insufficient. Outside instigators empathically tapped into her negative psychotic transference feelings toward the shaman and urged her to file a complaint to avenge herself—as it turns out, for childhood abuse now attributed by transference to the shaman.

Those who know little or nothing of the subtleties of psychological cure can only point to what remains from aborted processes and rush in with judgments. How are we who are charged with the sacred function of utilizing the power of the transferential symbolic for benefit of suffering humans to protect ourselves from tribal administrators who have little or no knowledge of our function and no awareness that our art involves wielding the symbols of the gods in *real* relationships, such that people forget the difference between ordinary reality and the mythic in order to bring to bear the power, function, and effectiveness of the symbol for the purpose of relieving psychological and physiological suffering. Caught midway when only the reality aspect is so far in play, or stopped short because the willingness or capability to enter the symbolic is lacking, we can indeed look like negligent fools! But if we give up the dual relationship we relinquish the wisdom of the ages! Then we become reduced to the same sense of impotence of those who seek to reaffirm their self identifications and power by sitting in judgment over people and processes they cannot hope to understand.

Personal Opinion

For over twenty years my primary business has been consulting with therapists and analysts about difficult clinical work. I have witnessed a rising swell of horror and fear among professionals as stories circulate about atrocities perpetrated by governing boards under the name of "administrative justice" and acts of ethics committees that appear to be operating as kangaroo courts. If even a small portion of the rumors that reach me are accurate (and I believe they are) we are all in a precarious position.

The shocking findings of the social consciousness movement regarding real abuses by therapists have taken us all by surprise. Our professional organizations have reacted as quickly as possible in order to recognize the hazards of damaging and exploitative dual relationships and to take measures to rectify wrongs and to prevent future abuses. Only now are there beginning signs that boards and ethics committees are coming to appreciate the extreme subtleties and complexities of dual-relationship issues.

I have hoped in this chapter to bring to the attention of the community of practicing therapists the central position of duality in our work in order to challenge thinking further so that injustices can be prevented and so that future regulatory efforts can take into account the inevitable blurring of boundaries that transference and countertransference interpretation necessarily entail.

I offer the following suggestions for consideration in evolving safeguards against abuse while honoring the dual relationship inherent in the practice of psychotherapy.

1. When any direct or indirect contact outside the formal therapeutic setting exists between therapist and client, a consultant be sought out regularly (at two- to six-month intervals) to evaluate and comment on the course of therapy. This is especially

important in training programs where the trainee is likely to see or hear much that will necessarily color the therapeutic relationship. It would also seem critical in small communities where various forms of outside contact are inevitable.

2. Any roles that might be unavoidable outside the formal therapeutic relationship need to be kept somehow "in the public eye." Some provision for periodic review with a third party should be obtained to evaluate how the therapy is proceeding.

3. In the name of protecting privacy and confidentiality, all *appearance* of dual relationship that might potentially be seen by third parties and conceivably reported to boards and committees for open investigation should be avoided. It is understood that "pure" work is to be preferred to "complicated" work but that work with various outside influences and complications (spouses, insurance companies, employers, government agencies, etc.) tends to be the rule rather than the exception. Complications cannot be assumed to be damaging exploitations. Multiple roles do not constitute unethical relationships that are exploitative and damaging. But avoidance of appearances and third-party consultation can help keep the distinction clearer and work to avoid confidentiality breaks through investigation.

4. Qualified experts should render opinions to regulating bodies. At present most individuals serving on regulatory boards and ethics committees, so far as I can tell, do not possess advanced specialty training that qualifies them to make judgments about the subtleties of the dual relationship necessarily involved in depth transference and countertransference work without expert consultation. If this is true, then these individuals are operating unprofessionally and unethically. For most purposes persons serving on regulatory boards and ethics committees need not possess advanced expertise in the dual nature of transference/countertransference work to be able to identify therapist's abuses of the professional relationship. But when subtleties are involved, when therapists have sophisticated and enlightened rationales for various interventions based on the dual nature of transference work, or when a therapist's professional reputation and personal life are to be profoundly affected

by claims that they do not honor as valid, we cannot afford as a profession to allow people without advanced training and professional expertise to stand in judgment of matters they cannot possibly be qualified to understand.

One way to correct the current threat that therapists live under as a result of cries and accusations of unethical dual relationship would be to create a panel of expert consultants who can demonstrate advanced understanding of the complexities of transference/countertransference relationships. Experts in panels of three could be called upon to evaluate aspects of investigations in which subtle aspects of dual relationship are in play and to render expert opinion to regulatory boards and ethics committees.

5. An alternate approach to the expert consultant model would be for the therapist needing protection to have some recourse to having the dispute settled in civil court where discovery and due process is guaranteed—as it is not under administrative law. We know that all too often ethics committees and governing boards are prey to political pressures and various preestablished biases so that a therapist acting in good faith and on sound judgment may not get fair treatment. Governing boards are certainly in a dual relationship position! Consumer interests and fear of publicity resulting in adverse political effects are too apt to color judgments against the therapist when subtleties of depth work are involved. While a judge and jury certainly do not constitute peers in terms of depth understanding, at least there is some hope of an unbiased, unpolitical, fair judgment. With either the client or the governing board as plaintiff the therapist de facto loses the civil rights guaranteed by the constitution of the United States. As it stands we have no civil rights and no recourse to due process. We are potential prey of political pressures and victims of governing hierarchies without recourse to adequate defense.

6. Some therapists have pointed out that a jury does not represent peer opinion, so that arbitration panels of persons sophisticated in aspects of depth therapy are to be preferred over civil courts.

Defining Qualified Experts

There are many kinds of transferences, countertransferences, and resistances that operate silently in psychological treatment. Cure itself is dependent on the successful discernment and utilization of dual relationship variables. There is no provision in any currently existing licensing law that insures that training or licensing as a psychotherapist involves expertise in understanding and interpreting transference and countertransference phenomena. The California Research Psychoanalyst Law[2] does, however, specify compliance with a set of nationally and internationally recognized standards for such training. Expertise in transference, countertransference, and resistance analysis as reflected in this law is thought to be attained by exposure to (a) extensive (five years) didactic training *beyond* ordinary licensing requirements, (b) a minimum of 400 hours of personal didactic transference analysis, and (c) a minimum of three apprentice training cases with at least fifty hours of supervision each for a total of 200 post-licensing supervisory hours studying transference, resistance, and countertransference phenomena as they operate in three specific cases and two years of case conference supervision. When an individual becomes certified at this level and practices analytically for an additional five years, he or she attains the status of training analyst and is only then a fully qualified expert with enough experience to teach, supervise, and analyze others in the refined aspects of transference interpretation. This is the level of training and experience recognized the world over by psychoanalysts that constitutes expertise in transference and countertransference analysis.

Other schools of psychotherapy have yet to codify in law what comparable level of experience might qualify one with expertise to make judgments in this highly technical area of knowledge. Can we name any single board or ethics committee member with ten years of comparable advanced training and practice (as specified in law) that might ethically qualify him or her to render the professional opinions now being made in this area? Administrative judges have no training at all and yet cavalierly remove licenses based on their evaluation of

---

2. Business and Professions Code, *Research Psychoanalysts*, Chapter 5.1 (added by Stats 1977, Ch. 1191), Section 2529—2529.5.

subtleties that in the profession require roughly fifteen years of advanced training to be considered qualified evaluators. A person would certainly not have to be a registered psychoanalyst to have sought out extensive and intensive training and practice in understanding the power and subtleties of transference and countertransference, but to date this law stands as the only public recognition of what such expertise might look like, or of how qualified individuals might be legally and ethically identified.

CONCLUSION

I hope the spirit of this chapter will not be misunderstood as accusatory in nature or tone. Blame is hardly appropriate at the level of peer review or professional regulation. We have been rapidly overtaken by a rush of new and important social consciousness issues. I have already suggested it may be our own reluctance to enter deeper therapeutic involvement, which so many of our clients desperately need, that accounts for our fear at present.

I hope my thoughts on the inevitability of the dual relationship in psychological cure will sound a precautionary note in quarters where it is sorely needed. I am calling for a more careful examination of the nature of duality, not only for therapist protection but, more importantly, in order to focus our attention on the dual nature of our work so that we can develop even further its importance and potency for the benefit of those who seek out our professional skills.

11

Countertransference: An Energetic and Characterological Perspective

Robert Hilton

In the passage quoted in Chapter 7, Alice Miller (1981) refers to the essence of *subjective* countertransference. The therapist attempts to gain from the patient the narcissistic supplies that he was denied by his parents. *Objective* countertransference is when the therapist, having worked with these narcissistic needs in his own therapy, is able to experience in his body what it is like to be the patient. With this somatic knowledge of the patient he is better able to build a bridge for empathic contact with him and thereby move toward the resolution of the transference relationship.

In this chapter I outline what I feel is the energetic basis for these two forms of countertransference. This chapter is germinal. It contains the distillation of my thoughts on these two subjects. The practical applications of these ideas are not specifically spelled out; however, the theoretical and energetic bases of these concepts are delineated.

THE ENERGETIC PERSPECTIVE

Figure 11–1 demonstrates the energetic basis of character development as well as the foundation for transference and countertransference. This diagram is my version of Reich's original concept of the unity and diversity of life energy that is seen in the mind–body duality and oneness. The diversified aspects of this life energy I have labeled the adaptive, contracted, negative, and primal selves (Table 11–1). The unified gestalt of these various selves I am calling the characterological self.

The primal self is the basic psyche/soma self expression in the world. When this is met with repeated negativity from the environment, part of the life-affirming energy doubles back on itself in the form of muscular contraction. The energy that sustains this contraction is the unreleased rage at being constantly frustrated by the environment in the attempt to get the basic organismic-psychic needs met. This contraction forms the basis of the contracted self.

The contracted self inhibits the life force of the primal self from further direct expression toward the environment in order to reduce the physical and psychic pain that accompany continued rejection. This contraction expresses the wish to die rather than continue in constant frustration. The physical form the contracted self takes in the body depends on when the frustration takes place in the developmental sequence of the person and how much energy is available in the organism at the time.

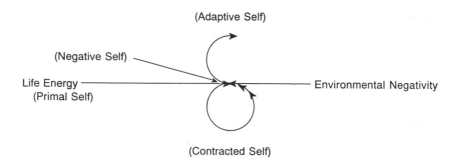

Figure 11–1. The energetic basis of character development.

Table 11–1. Self Formulations

Primal self	Characterological self	Adaptive self	Contracted self	Negative self	Real self	Actualized self
being/need	understands	interprets	withdraws	annihilates	fear	excitement/movement
need/dependence	love	incorporates	depresses	abandons	longing	desire/connection
dependence/autonomy	guidance	manipulates	disconnects	humiliates	inadequacy	vulnerability/separateness
autonomy/freedom	support	smothers	collapses	crushes	guilt-shame	aggression/possession
freedom/sexuality	commitment	confronts	controls	rejects	heart break	love/sexuality

Just as part of the survival of the organism depends on contraction so also does its survival depend on developing an adaptive self. As
strong as the wish to die is invested in the contracted self, so the will
to live continues in the adaptive self. The person no longer able to get
his needs met through direct organism self expression now adapts the
methods used against him in order to get them met indirectly. "If you
can't beat them join them," becomes his theme. However, since the organism is physically blocked from receiving by the contracted self, the
victorious efforts of the adaptive self do not nourish it.

When these contracting and adaptive efforts are recognized as
fruitless, the energy invested in the adaptive self and contracted self find
expression in the negative self. At this time the person once again
asserts his rights to life in the environment. When this expression is
released, since it has been bound up behind strong muscular walls and
psychic inhibition, its entrance back into the world is rageful and
sadistic. The person responds as if he has nothing to lose. Trying to stop
the pain hasn't worked, doing it "their way" hasn't worked, and now
the negative self expresses the life of the organism with the same
aggressive-negative intensity of which it at one time had been the
recipient. The environment usually responds with increased negativity or withdrawal and the person responds with guilt or shame and
retreats back behind the fortress of the blocked expression.

The overall characterological self functions in such a way as to
maintain an energetic equilibrium between these various aspects of the
personality. It helps the person walk the tightrope between the strong
organismic impulsivity of the primal self and the environmental negativity toward that self expression. It is the form one has created for survival and the prison in which one lives. It serves to bind the person's
anxiety. This anxiety arises if too much energy is built up in the body-
block and wants expression, or too much impingement from the environment occurs that threatens the defenses. One of the results of this
organization of energy is to present to the world an image that is
expressed in the form of a role that the person plays, a character, if you
will in the drama of life. The person playing this character attempts to
offer what he never received and thus hopes to repair his own narcissistic wound by being the idealized parent to others.

In life, this frustration of expansion and contraction between the
various selves continues until a safe-enough environment is created

wherein the person can receive support for the primal self and negative self along with an empathic analysis of the adaptive and contracted selves. A break in this cycle usually occurs when the negative self is acknowledged by both the person and the environment. What happens energetically is that in the expression of the negativity, the "glue" that has held the original block together gives way and the primal self is given another chance to return to the environment. This time around the primal self has more energy and help in confronting the environment and more flexibility in responding to frustration.

To the degree that the efforts of the primal self are recognized and supported, a real self (Figure 11–2) is formed that takes the place of the characterological self. Under stress the characterological self, like a role one has played for years, will return. However, it will become ego dystonic and not acted upon unconsciously. Likewise, each of the selves will function from time to time in the old roles. The difference now is the awareness of their defensive-survival function and the capacity to assert more directly the needs of the real self.

CHARACTEROLOGICAL SELF

In the beginning the patient consciously or unconsciously is attracted by and responds to the characterological self of the therapist. This self, as we have just mentioned, was created by the therapist as a means of survival in his own family and now acts as a way of guaran-

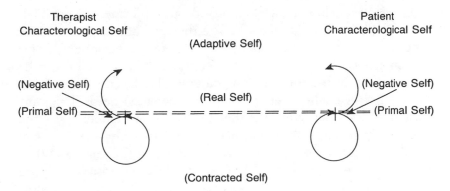

Figure 11–2. The characterological perspective: subjective countertransference.

teeing the replenishing of the narcissistic supplies that he lost with his parents. The patient, like any narcissisticly wounded child, senses the wound in the therapist as well as the way in which the therapist covers this up and idealizes himself as a healer. The patient, as he did in his own family, learns how to find solace for his own wounded self by appealing to the therapist for help without threatening the therapist's narcissistic investment in "helping" him the therapist's way, which of course is the "right" way.

This narcissistic collusion on the part of the patient and therapist continues until the primal self of the patient impinges on the carefully organized energetic balance of the therapist. This occurs when the patient needs more than the therapist can give or no longer rewards the therapist in the usual manner. For the therapist this is experienced as the withdrawal of valuable narcissistic supplies and he begins to react to this withdrawal of contact in the same manner that he did as a child. The difference now is that he has someone who needs him and he has an armamentarium of techniques in which to reconnect to the patient and bring him back under his control. The utilization of these techniques on behalf of the therapist's own needs requires that the therapist activate his adaptive self.

ADAPTIVE SELF

The main tool the therapist has in which to bring the patient and thus his narcissistic supplies back under his control is the functioning of the adaptive self. For each characterological self there is a specialized function of the adaptive self. The therapist now appears to give more of what the patient originally wanted from the therapist only now the "giving" is under the ego direction of the therapist and is for the therapist, not the patient. This last point must be cleverly disguised lest the patient feel as if he is being used for the therapist's needs. This same caution was experienced by the therapist in his own family. Since the parent of the therapist was not available for the therapist's needs he had to learn to pretend to be there for the parents in the same way they pretended to be there for him. The function of the pretense was to ward off the anxiety of isolation or disconnectedness. This pretense is now being carried out with the patient. If this works and the patient returns with the proper appreciation, the therapist's anxiety is reduced and the therapy continues on as before until another crisis arises. However, if this employment of the adaptive self does not work, the therapist experiences the contracted self.

CONTRACTED SELF

In this state each therapist begins to manipulate his energetic involvement with the patient. This manipulation is very much like what happened to the therapist when he was a child and he did not reward his own parents with what they wanted from him. This kind of contraction is felt as a unconscious threat to the patient. He feels as if he is in danger of no longer having the therapist available to him as he once was and that in some way, of which he is not aware, the sudden change of personal investment on the part of the therapist is his fault.

If this action on the part of the therapist works and the patient, unconsciously sensing the danger, once again changes his needs to meet those of the therapist, all is well. However, if the patient continues to insist on his own way or challenges the therapist in regard to this new behavior the therapist may move toward expressing the energy behind the block, which is the negative self.

NEGATIVE SELF

The essence of the negative self is the release of aggression toward the patient in the same manner that the therapist experienced his parents' reaction toward him when he insisted on his "rights" as a child. At this time it is evident that the therapist is out of control and the response of the patient varies from great satisfaction to terror. Since each patient expects the environment to respond with negativity in regard to the assertion of his needs, this form of countertransference is often accepted by the patient and justified by the therapist as a reality response of the environment toward the patient's movement. The patient, believing that he has "magically" changed the characterological self of the therapist into this negative self by persisting on expressing his opposition or by not giving, usually retreats with shame or guilt and thereby restores the original contract. If this does not work and the patient withstands the therapist's negativity or fights back with his own aggression, the therapist is in danger of collapsing and exposing to the patient the primal self.

PRIMAL SELF

The primal self consists of the original need the therapist had with his own parents. The inability to have this need met left him with a deep injury to the primal self. The various other forms of self were then constructed to attempt to deal with this loss. However, in each person there is a hope that the defenses will not work and that the original trauma can be reexperienced with a different ending. Unfortunately for the therapist in this case the primal self is exposed to someone, namely the patient, who while being rewarded with the unusual power of bringing the idealized parent to his knees, nevertheless is in no position to welcome or accept this primal need of the therapist. Thus by fate it would seem the original trauma has been revisited and the patient, like the original parent, angry that he has been betrayed and that his own needs have not been met responds with rejection or even disgust. This response on the part of the patient reinforces the original rejection that the therapist had experienced as a child and thus reinforces the therapist's need to shore up his defenses in the form of the characterological self. The patient is left with the dubious victory of having done to the idealized parent what had been done to him and the therapist is left with the possibility of seeking supervision and help in breaking this cycle. In so doing, the therapist builds the foundation for the real self.

REAL SELF

The therapist in his supervision and personal therapy acknowledges his inability to give to the patient what his characterological self had consciously or unconsciously promised. What the therapist had promised is what he had wanted from his own parents, the absence of which created such pain in the therapist that he developed the characterological self in an attempt to prevent this from happening again. Now he is faced with reliving this initial trauma. This time, with the proper support, he will be able to acknowledge the failure of the characterological self in its attempts to rectify his childhood position. With this acknowledgment of failure comes the grieving of the original loss and the strength to face that the patient will also have to, with his help, grieve this same loss. With this new awareness and grounding in reality comes the possibility of hearing the patient in a new light. And the patient, unable to use the therapist as a solution to his narcissistic wound, loses his power over the therapist and gains a real person who will be able to help him grieve his loss and recover his true dignity. This prepares the therapist for the experience of objective countertransference.

CHARACTEROLOGICAL PERSPECTIVE: OBJECTIVE COUNTERTRANSFERENCE

The basis of objective countertransference is the ability of the therapist to be an open channel of contact in regard to the patient. This means that the therapist is able both to experience the feelings created in him by the patient and to allow them to be present without triggering the therapist's survival mechanisms. To do this the therapist needs to stay grounded in his own reality as an ordinary human being and as such act as a model for the patient. In this open place the therapist will begin to experience, first, how it felt for the patient to be a child in his own family, and second, how it felt to be the patient's parents.

The patient, relating to the therapist from the position of his adaptive self, will demonstrate the way in which he survived in his family. From the position of the negative self, the patient will reject the therapist in the same manner in which he was rejected. This gives the therapist an opportunity to feel what it was like to be the patient as a child. When the patient relates from the contracted self he is forcing the therapist to experience what it was like to be the patient's parents. That is, he will contract and render the therapist helpless. He may also attempt to get the therapist to reject him in the same manner his parents did.

In this way the therapist is able to use his body as a resonating instrument upon which the "music" of the patient is played. This resonance is what the patient did not have from his own family and it now becomes the foundation for the healing of the narcissistic wound. The therapist is now able to trust his intuitive response and is less likely to fall into the narcissistic traps laid by himself and the patient. When this resonance is present, the therapist is much freer to be confrontive without being sadistic and loving without being sentimental. All of this is conditioned upon the therapist having experienced this same kind of resonance for himself and thereby being aware of its healing effects. Having laid this foundation, the patient will experience more safety in risking the exposure of the real self. Since the characterological self of the therapist is now more ego dystonic he will be able to help the patient understand those characteristics toward which he was drawn and how they fit into his early family history. This way the therapist is able to use his characterological self as another powerful tool in the transference-countertransference process.

The countertransference process through which the therapist must move for his own healing is exactly the same as the transference process for the patient. The patient–child is in a constant process of healing the therapist-parent in order that he himself may be healed. As I stated at the end of chapter 7, "Your clients and children will cure you if you give them a chance."

PART III

LEGAL AND ETHICAL CONSIDERATIONS

12

Documentation:
The Therapist's Shield

O. Brandt Caudill, Jr.

DOCUMENTATION HAS BECOME
IMPORTANT TO THERAPISTS

There is a continuing misperception on the part of psychotherapists as to whether notes should be taken during therapy. While the degree of documentation may be left to the individual therapist's judgment, to some extent both the standard of care and various laws and regulations require that notes be taken and records be kept. Thus, the individual therapist who does not take notes because of a philosophical bias against note taking is operating at his or her peril and in ways that can result in significant adverse consequences.

For members of the American Psychological Association, the question is foreclosed by 2.3.3 of the "Specialty Guidelines for the Delivery of Services by Clinical Psychologists," which explicitly requires that adequate notes be taken. A similar provision is found in the "Specialty Guidelines for Counseling Psychologists," and similar guidelines have been developed for other groups of therapists. Since most state licensing boards use either the APA ethical principles or similar principles developed by other professional groups as a basis for disciplinary action, a failure to keep notes could subject a therapist to both ethical complaints before his or her own professional organization and discipline by the state licensing board.

KEEPING ADEQUATE THERAPY NOTES

California Health and Safety Code Section 1795 et sec. requires mental health professionals to provide records to patients if the patient complies with the provisions of the code section. Similar codes exist in other jurisdictions. Obviously, the provisions of this code section contemplate that records will exist. This same code requires records be maintained a minimum of seven years following the discharge of a patient (except in the case of minors where the records shall be kept at least one year after the minor has reached the age of 18, but in no case less than seven years). The code further permits therapists to provide a patient with a summary of the records instead of a copy of the records if certain conditions are met. The code section defines what the summary should contain. That list of items is a good starting point to determine what information should be contained in a patient's file:

1. the chief complaint or complaints;
2. the findings from any consultations or referrals to other health care providers;
3. the diagnosis, if one has been determined;
4. the treatment plan;
5. the progress of treatment;
6. the prognosis, including any significant continuing problems;
7. reports of any diagnostic procedures and all discharge summaries; and
8. any objective findings from a physical examination, although such an examination would not be conducted by the therapist.

DOCUMENTATION AND THE STANDARD OF CARE

Experience also dictates that certain information must be in a patient's notes to meet the standard of care and to adequately protect the interests of both the patient and the therapist. Initially, a pre-printed form should be completed by the patient indicating background and history. While many therapists will take a history on an ad hoc basis, our experience has shown that the presence of a form, which the patient is required to fill out, can be extremely significant if key information is later determined to be missing or false. At a minimum the intake form should ask about the following:

1. family history of depression, suicide, alcohol or drug abuse, or other major mental illness;
2. the patient's prior history of psychological treatment;
3. major physical problems the patient has;
4. name and address of patient's medical doctor and any prior psychotherapists;
5. primary reason the patient is seeking treatment; and
6. prior history of psychological testing.

If the patient identifies prior psychological treatment, then the case law suggests that a therapist attempt to obtain such prior psychological records (*Jablonski by Pahls v. United States* 1983). Therefore, it will be necessary to at least document the request that the patient provide a release for obtaining the records of a prior mental health professional. A very practical reason for obtaining those records is that, if the patient has a borderline personality or other significant personality or thought disorder, the therapist will generally find that the records of prior treatment will contain extremely valuable information that may help to avoid some pitfalls. It is not uncommon to find that the prior therapy records contain information that is inconsistent with the patient's current assertions.

NOTING SEXUAL, VIOLENT, AND SUICIDAL IDEATION

There are no set guidelines on what should be contained in notes of individual sessions. However, if there is any mention by the patient of sexual attraction to the therapist, a comment needs to be noted as close to verbatim as possible. In addition, the therapist should note what was done about the comments. It is not sufficient to say "Patient expressed transference." The patient's words *must* be recorded. It will be difficult at a later point to recall what an ambiguous note about transference was specifically regarding to. If the patient starts to express sexual fantasies and dreams about the therapist, these must be noted as well. If there is any discussion of countertransference issues, the discussion should be spelled out in the notes. If the patient expresses any thoughts of violence toward him/herself or toward others, the notes must reflect those comments and what the therapist did to assess the seriousness of the matter. With some particularly manipulative patients, these types of comments are made so frequently that many practitioners do not note them in the record. However, this is an unwarranted risk. Generally, the one time that the note is not taken is the one time that the patient follows up on the expression of suicidal or homicidal thoughts.

Any discussion of the countertransference that might have occurred needs to be noted. Here again, simply saying "countertransference discussed" is too ambiguous and will not be helpful at a later point to ascertain what was actually said. Notes do not need to be particularly detailed, but they do have to reflect whether the patient has a plan, the means to effectuate the plan, and the level of seriousness that the therapist ascribes to the patient's condition. If a warning to a third party is required, then a copy of the written warning (for example, as required by California Civil Code Section 43.92) should be included in the file. Such warning letters should be sent by certified mail, return receipt registered, or hand delivered by a service so there is proof of delivery.

ADDITIONAL AREAS FOR DOCUMENTATION

It is critically important that any documents authored by the patient and provided to the therapist be kept and maintained in the file. It is particularly tragic to have a therapist state that the patient, who is now suing him or her, had previously sent a series of letters, which were thrown away, lauding the therapist's abilities. Any correspondence, greeting cards, poems, journal entries, or other written documentation provided by the patient must be maintained in the file. Copies should be kept of all documents that are returned to the patient.

Any telephone messages that are taken by the therapist or staff personnel should also be maintained in the file.

When the therapy terminates, there should be a note of the circumstances of termination and what steps, if any, the therapist took regarding the termination (e.g., referring the patient to others, recommending that the patient continue in therapy with someone else, etc.).

A new requirement in California that would be wise to heed elsewhere is that where services are being provided by a psychological assistant (intern, student, etc.), the supervisor is required to provide the patient with notice in writing that the assistant or trainee is unlicensed and is under the direction and supervision of the supervisor as an employee (California Code of Regulations, Title 16, Section 1391.6). A copy of the written notice to the patient should be contained in the file in every instance where an unlicensed person is providing services.

In addition, there should be a written contract with the patient that spells out, among other things, the limitations of confidentiality and the patient's obligation to pay for services rendered (particularly dealing with the specific hourly rate and cancellation policy).

BILLING/INSURANCE PRACTICES

A final area that causes a substantial number of problems is the correlation between the therapist's billing records and notes. There must be at least some correlation between the dates upon which notes are taken and the dates for which bills are submitted for payment. Further, it is not acceptable to bill third-party payers for sessions on days the patient was not actually seen; generally the rationale is that there was an administrative oversight or the session was two hours long instead of one hour, so it made sense to bill two separate sessions instead of one two-hour session. However, this is likely to be seen as fraud, even if the total number of hours of service is accurate.

In addition, the law does not recognize the common practice of using one diagnosis for insurance purposes and another for other purposes. Whatever diagnosis is used with the insurance carrier must be accurate and must be the operative diagnosis for treatment. While there may be some therapeutic validity to the concept that a less-restrictive diagnosis is more beneficial to the patient, such a practice can be characterized as insurance fraud and create extremely difficult problems in the event of litigation.

PROTECTING YOURSELF AND YOUR PATIENT

The criteria set forth above will make it easier for therapists to provide quality care to patients and protect themselves in the process. The additional time and energy required to maintain carefully documented files from beginning to end of treatment is likely to pay off not only in terms of enhancing the therapist's thinking about the patient, but in terms of providing a safety net to protect both therapist and patient from costly and unnecessary litigation.

13

Can Therapists Be Vicariously Liable for Sexual Misconduct?

O. Brandt Caudill, Jr.

On October 9th, and 10th, 1992, the Second National Conference on Sexual Misconduct by Clergy, Psychotherapists, and Health Care Professionals took place in Minneapolis, Minnesota. That conference featured presentations suggesting that therapists who are not themselves engaged in sexual misconduct may become targets of civil suits where individuals whom they are alleged to be responsible for have engaged in sexual misconduct. These suggestions have in fact been implemented and vicarious liability suits have become a major area of sexual misconduct litigation. The original wave of litigation over sexual relationships with patients generally focused on the individual therapist accused of sexual interaction with the patient.[1] As a reaction to that wave of liti-

---

1. In addition to the cases discussed here, some cases alleging sexual relationships between therapists and patients include *Speiss v. Johnson* 748 P.2d 1020 (Ore.App. 1988); *Roy v. Hartogs* 81 Misc.2d 350, 366 N.Y.S.2d 297 (N.Y. 1985); *DiLeo v. Nugent* 592 A.2d 1126 (1990); *Mazza v. Huffaker* 61 N.C.App. 170, 300 S.E.2d 833 (1983); *Horak v. Biris* Ill.App.3d 140, 474 N.E.2d 13 (1985); *Richard H. v. Larry D.* 198 Cal.App.3d 591, 243 *Cal.Rptr.* 807 (1988).

gation, insurance carriers drafted strong policy exclusions limiting or denying insurance coverage to the person accused of such conduct. This has created a situation where a patient alleging such a claim has an economic interest in targeting insurance coverage that would not be subject to such a limitation.[2]

Where a therapist is engaged in a sexual relationship with a patient it is possible for his or her supervisor, partners, and employers to become targets of litigation. There are two types of liability: direct liability and vicarious or indirect liability. Direct liability is an individual's liability for his or her own acts or omissions, while vicarious liability is where an individual is liable for the acts of others because of their relationship. Most states have adopted the Uniform Partnership Act, or equivalent legislation, which makes each partner jointly and severally (i.e., individually) liable for the acts of all other partners, within the scope of partnership business. However, a partner's acts in a purely personal context, such as a domestic dispute, would not give rise to joint and several liability. In some instances these theories may overlap, such as alleging that a partner had a duty to prevent another partner from acting in a particular manner. By the same token, traditionally an employer may be held liable for the negligent acts of an employee where the employee acts within the scope and course of his or her authority from the employer. This doctrine is referred to as *respondeat superior*.

Most therapists are still completely unaware that they may be at risk for sexual misconduct by their partners, supervisees, and employees. Thus most therapists are not adequately investigating the background of potential employees or partners. To limit vicarious liability, a therapist must perform a thorough background investigation focused on whether that individual has been involved in sexual misconduct or is currently at risk for sexual misconduct.[3]

Most therapists would assume that a sexual relationship with a client is outside the scope of normal business, and therefore could not lead to liability to partners, supervisors, and employers. However, a review of the cases indicates a conflict in authority. This issue was specifically con-

---

2. See "Therapist-Patient Sexual Exploitation and Insurance Liability" by Jorgensen et al., *Tort & Insurance Journal*, Vol. 27 No. 3 Spring 1992.

3. An extended discussion of this and a check list can be found in chapter 36, page 453 through 461 of the book *Psychotherapists' Sexual Involvement With Clients: Intervention and Prevention* by Schoener et al; Walk in Counseling Center, 1989.

sidered by a New York Court in *Noto v. St. Vincent's Hospital* (1988), where a patient who had been in a hospital setting for depression, drug, and alcohol dependency developed a posttermination sexual relationship with a psychiatric resident. The plaintiff sought to impose liability on the hospital based on the doctrine of vicarious liability. The Court concluded that the resident's actions clearly exceeded any authority granted by the hospital, and were not a natural incident to his employment duties. The Court determined that plaintiff could not assert a claim against the hospital. However, in *Simmons v. United States* (1986) the question came up in the context of whether the United States Government could be liable for a sexual relationship between a mental health counselor and a patient. The issue of whether the sexual relationship was within the course and scope of employment was critical to reach before finding that a claim could be asserted against the United States. After reviewing the law of Washington, the Ninth Circuit Court of Appeals concluded that the mental health counselor, Mr. Kammers, was acting within the scope of his employment in providing mental health counseling to Ms. Simmons, and that his sexual relationship with her was unprofessional conduct in providing services within the scope of his employment. The court noted that while the counselor was not authorized by the government to become sexually involved with clients, the sexual contact occurred in conjunction with his legitimate counseling activities, and thus within the scope of his employment. The court also made analogies to a series of cases where appellate courts found that sexual relationships between therapists and patients came within the scope of professional malpractice policies even though the conduct was admittedly unethical and unprofessional.[4]

The Ninth Circuit concluded that an abuse by the therapist, Mr. Kammers, of transference was within the scope of his employment. This was found to be true even though the majority of the acts of sexual misconduct occurred during out-of-town trips, not during therapy sessions in the office. In that case the court also concluded that a basis existed for supervisory negligence because the relationship continued for over a year after Mr. Kammers' supervisor was advised of the situation.

---

4. *Vigilant Insurance Co. v. Employers Insurance of Wausau* 626 F.Supp. 262 (S.D.N.Y. 1986); *Zipkin v. Freeman* 436 S.W. 2d 753 (Mo. 1968); *L.L. v. Medical Protective Co.* 362 N.W.2d 174 (1984); *Cranford v. Allwest Insurance Co.* 645 F.Supp. 1440 (N.D. Cal. 1986); *Aetna Casualty Co. v. McCabe* 556 F.Supp. 1342 (E.D. Pa. 1983).

In *Marston v. Minneapolis Clinic of Psychiatry and Neurology* (1983), the Minnesota Supreme Court held that it was a question of fact for a jury to decide whether the conduct of a therapist in pursuing sexual relations with a patient was sufficiently related to his employment as to make a clinic vicariously liable. The court rejected the argument that the plaintiff also had to establish that the employee was acting in furtherance of the employer's interests before a liability could be imposed on the clinic. The court noted that there was testimony that sexual relations between a therapist and a patient was a well-known hazard, and thus to a degree a foreseeable risk of employment. To the same effect is *Trotter v. Okawa* (1994).

The California Supreme Court considered this issue in context of two mothers' claims against a clinic for negligent infliction of emotional distress directed against a psychotherapist who had molested their sons while in treatment (*Marlene F. v. Affiliated Psychiatric Medical Clinic, Inc.* (1989)). In that case the court cited the *Simmons* and *Marston* cases referred to above, and concluded that the question of the viability of claims that the clinic was liable for the psychotherapist's acts of sexual molestation was an open question in California. The court noted that one of the claims was negligence in hiring and supervising the psychotherapist based on the fact that he had allegedly molested another child, and seeking to impose vicarious liability on *respondeat superior, supra,* at Footnote 3, 48 Cal.3d 588.

In *Evan F. v. Houghson United Methodist Church* (1992), a California appellate court noted that there was a split nationally as to whether an employer can be liable to a third person for negligently hiring an employee, particularly where the acts the employee is accused of involve sexual misconduct or intentional tortuous acts. In California, and a number of other jurisdictions, an employer may be liable to a third person for negligently hiring an incompetent or unfit employee.

Given the current state of the law, it seems clear that therapists must assume that they may be sued if a partner, employee, or supervisee engages in a sexual relationship with a patient, because it appears that the courts are moving to the position that a sexual relationship between a therapist and a patient is a recognizable risk of employment that would be within the scope of the employer-employee relationship. With regard to supervisees, the therapist's liability potential is even greater because of the fact that supervisees cannot function without the requisite supervision. Thus, the liability of a therapist for acts of a supervisee is probably more akin to that of a partner, although the relationship is substantially different.

The liability of training schools has been raised in several civil suits in which I have represented individual therapists who are graduates of the schools. Professional schools have been widely perceived as having done a poor job of training therapists on how to deal with questions of sexual relationships with patients, and what to do when experiencing an attraction to a patient.[5] However, while training institutions may ultimately be required to defend their programs, the more immediate concern is the potential liability of the private practitioner who is employing, supervising, or in partnership with other psychotherapists.

There are several ways to limit the potential exposure presented by this situation. One is to investigate every potential employee, supervisee, and partner thoroughly to ensure that they have the caliber of training and character to avoid such situations. However, even the best, brightest, and most well investigated person can fall into a sexual relationship, so this will not by itself preclude potential liability. Employees, supervisees, and partners should be encouraged to freely discuss with peers their attraction to patients, with a goal of ensuring that the feelings are not acted on. This can take the form of supervision sessions, presentations, or informal discussions. Also, it should be made clear to all employees, partners, supervisees, and patients that sexual relationships are unethical and will not be tolerated. As to patients, a statement to this effect should be found in the patient's contract, and a sign should be posted in the waiting room stating that sexual relationships are unethical. While this may seem to be an extreme position, it is an unequivocal statement that will make it hard, at a later date, for vicarious liability to be asserted against the employer, supervisor, or partner. Further, the contracts of each employee, supervisee, and any partnership agreement must state clearly and explicitly that sexual misconduct is beyond the scope of employment, is unethical and unacceptable, and will lead to immediate termination of employment or the partnership agreement. Finally, therapists should consider having their professional associations promulgate legislation to foreclose these types of suits.

---

5. See Pope, Tabachnick and Keith-Spiegal, "Ethics of Practice: The Beliefs and Behaviors of Psychologists as Therapists." *American Psychologist*, Vol. 43 pages 993–1006.

14

The Mind Business

O. Brandt Caudill, Jr.

Over the years of representing psychotherapists, one of the things that has been most apparent is that many of the best therapists are poor business managers and do not take steps to protect themselves from possible litigation. In today's increasingly litigious times therapists must be cognizant of those areas in which they face possible litigation, and the methods of minimizing those risks. A key to minimizing risks is having adequate forms and contracts to govern the different relationships that a therapist will enter into in a business context. The most important contractual relationships are those with patients, employees, trainees, supervisees, and other owners of the practice. I will deal with critical considerations in each of these types of contracts. While managed care contracts are also extremely important, the issues relative to them warrant separate attention and will only be touched on briefly here.

CONTRACTS WITH PATIENTS

The requirement that a therapist have a contract with a patient is ignored by many practicing therapists. The purpose of the contract is to clarify the relationships and the compensation. Certainly under the APA Ethical Principles and the view taken by most state licensing boards, it is the responsibility of the therapist at the inception of the relationship to ensure that the fee arrangements are clear to the patient. Any uncertainty in this regard will be interpreted adversely to the therapist and, depending on the magnitude of the discrepancy, may even rise to the level of an ethical violation.

All contracts discussed in this chapter must be in writing. The fee that is to be received must be clearly spelled out together with the extent to which the therapist will look to an insurance carrier for payment. Where an insurance carrier is to pay a percentage of the fee, it is important to stress that the copayments must actually be made by the patient. Some carriers have taken the position that where a therapist routinely waives a copayment, the actual fee is the amount that the therapist has been receiving from the insurance company and a percentage of that fee is therefore reduced to reflect the absence of a copayment.

The patient agreement should also reflect whether interest will be charged and under what circumstances the account might be referred to a collection agency. We generally strongly advise against the use of collection agencies or of letting fees get high enough to warrant such collection efforts. If a matter is referred to a collection agency and a collection action is filed, the patient typically files a cross-action for professional malpractice. The claim then has to be submitted to the therapist's malpractice carrier and it ends up costing far more than the amount due. The way to avoid this system is not to allow patients to carry high fee balances.

While interest can be charged, therapists must be cognizant that they cannot charge credit card interest rates without running afoul of usury laws. The best guide is to use the then prevailing rate of interest set by the law for court judgments.

The contract must also set forth the mutual expectation with regard to whether sessions canceled within 24, 48, or 72 hours will be billed. The therapist cannot assume the patient understands he or she will be billed for missed sessions. The lack of such a provision has caused a number of problems for clients in the past.

The limitations of confidentiality must be spelled out in a patient contract (see APA Ethical Principle 5.01, 5.02). While it is possible to assume that the patient should be cognizant of the limitations, the fact is that the number of different exceptions to confidentiality has increased dramatically, and patients may not be aware of the situation. At a minimum, the contract should include references to the following situations where confidentiality may be waived:

1. child abuse reporting;
2. elder abuse reporting;
3. a threat of violence made by the patient against a third party that triggers a duty to warn (see as California Civil Code section 43.92);
4. the patient has pursued civil litigation and waived or tendered his/her emotional condition.

An additional provision that could be added is that the psychotherapist/patient privilege cannot be used to shield the planning of a crime or a tort (as in California Evidence Code section 1018). While this may seem like an unnecessary inclusion, some of the issues raised in the Menendez brothers' criminal trial suggest that it may be prudent to use it. In this regard, there is a clear distinction between a discussion with a patient of a past crime, which is protected from disclosure, and a patient's discussion of an anticipated crime, which is not protected by the psychotherapist/patient privilege (or the attorney-client privilege in similar circumstances).

With the proliferation of lawsuits against therapists on a vicarious basis for sexual misconduct of their employees, all patient contracts should contain an express statement that sexual relations with a psychotherapist is against the law and is against the policy of the psychotherapist or clinic. This is necessary so that if an employee engages in acts of sexual misconduct with a patient, the employer can say that such acts were beyond the scope of employment and that the patient was expressly advised of the unethical nature of such acts.

There are two provisions that have not historically been used in therapist contracts with patients that might be incorporated in contracts in the 1990s in an attempt to limit exposure to litigation. These are arbitration clauses and limitation of liability provisions. Many hospital and HMO contracts include mandatory arbitration provisions. There is no reason why a therapist could not utilize such a procedure, assuming that it is done at the inception of the relationship. The question in terms of enforcing arbitration clauses is whether there was arms-length negotiation. At the inception of a psychotherapeutic relationship there is clearly a different level of interaction because the trust relationship essential for therapy has not yet developed. To attempt to introduce an arbitration clause or limitation of liability language in the middle of the therapeutic relationship would probably not be upheld by the court. However, case law suggests that an arbitration clause agreed to at the inception of the relationship would be upheld. The reason is simply that the court system is so overburdened that arbitration is highly favored. If a contract has a mandatory arbitration clause, a simple petition to the Superior Court generally will lead to enforcement of that clause. Arbitration offers a significant cost savings over lawsuits in Superior Court. Further, with arbitration one can select the decision maker and the rules to be applied in making the decision. In Superior Court the parties are generally stuck with the judge that they happen to get, unless they have grounds to assert bias.

Limitation of liability clauses are prevalent in the construction field and have not historically been applied to therapists or other mental health professionals. There is, however, no conceptual reason why such clauses could not be used in a therapist contract. A recent California Appellate Court case called *Markbourough California Inc. v. Superior Court* (1991) upheld an architect's limitation of liability clause that provided that in the event of litigation the maximum that the client could recover was $50,000 or the architectural fees paid, whichever was greater. Litigation ensued with the client attempting to assert a claim against the architect for over a million dollars. The court determined that the limitation of liability clause was legal and did limit the client's claim to $50,000 or the greater of the fees paid. A similar provision could be utilized in therapist/patient contracts. While it might take a number of years before such a clause would be tested and enforceability upheld, the *Markbourough* case offers a sound legal basis to assert it as a viable clause. As a practical matter, the presence of such a clause in a contract may lead a plaintiff's attorney to advise the patient that it would not be feasible to file a lawsuit because of the limited amount recoverable.

Less certain is the extent to which a limitation of liability clause would cut off the exposure for intentional misconduct, such as sexual relations with a patient, as opposed to more general malpractice, such as failure to diagnose and competently treat, breach of confidentiality, and so on. However, it is my belief that at this point in the process, therapists must become creative in trying to stem the rising tide of litigation.

As with the other contracts discussed below, it is important to realize that any patient contract must have certain standard language to minimize disputes over its meaning. First there should be what is called an integration clause. This clause states that all of the negotiations of the parties have been reflected in the written documents and that there are no agreements except for those contained in the written documents. This effectively precludes someone from contending that the therapist agreed to provide other services, or services under different circumstances than in the written agreement. The contract must specify that no modifications can be made, except in writing signed by both parties. This precludes someone from contending that the contract was orally modified. This type of clause is sometimes referred to as an equal dignities clause, because it requires that a change to the contract have the same level of formality as the original agreement itself. The agreement must also specify whether or not attorney's fees are recoverable in an action to enforce the contract. Most therapists think of attorney's fees clauses only in the context of their fees if they have to bring a collection action to obtain payment. However, to be enforceable an attorney's fees clause must provide that the prevailing party in litigation gets attorney's fees, not just the therapist. The attorney's fees clause therefore has the potential to be a two-edged sword if the therapist is the one sued. Generally, since it is more likely that the litigation will be brought by the patient we would recommend against an attorney's fees clause, unless it is tied to the prevailing party in the mandatory arbitration, in which case it would be feasible to include.

CONTRACTS WITH EMPLOYEES AND SUBORDINATES

The next most important contract from the therapist's perspective is the contract with professional employees or subordinates, such as other trainees, interns, and psychological assistants. For a number of years it was a typical practice to call relationships with psychological assistants and interns independent contractor relationships, although such a label was not legally correct because of the requirement of continuing supervision. Currently, both sound practice and some state board regulations require that contracts with unlicensed individuals be employee contracts with W-2 wage payments. The California Psychology Board's regulations (16 CCR section 1391.10) specifically require written evidence of employment of a psychological assistant to be submitted annually. This regulation specifically refers to an employment contract or a letter of agreement as being such documentation.

With the exception of the payment provisions and the supervision requirement, the differences between the employee and the independent contractor agreements are small. Both types of contracts require equal dignities and integration clauses. Both types of contracts specify the services to be provided, the compensation to be paid, and the areas in which the professional employee or independent contractor is to perform. The major difference is the independent contractor can select his or her methods and manner of performance and is not supervised. It is critically important to include an express statement that sexual misconduct with patients is grounds for termination and beyond the scope of employment (see, for example, Noto v. St. Vincent's Hospital (1988). Similarly the agreement should state that social or business relationships with patients are outside the therapeutic one and can be grounds for termination. Here again, while this may seem obvious, the reality is that many employers of psychotherapists have been sued vicariously over the sexual misconduct of their employees and independent contractors, as in, for example, Marston v. Minneapolis Clinic of Psychiatry and Neurology (1983), Noto v. St. Vincent's Hospital (1988), Simmons v. United States (1986), and Trotter v. Okawa (1994).

The agreement should specify that the employee or independent contractor is required to obtain and maintain insurance and provide the psychologist with a certificate of insurance; the amounts of insurance required should be specified. If the psychologist is going to cover the interns or psychological assistants on his or her policy, then that should be spelled out in the agreement as well. If the psychologist is not going to cover these individuals on his or her policy, then that should be stated in the agreement.

The agreement should state that the employee or independent

contractor is representing that he or she has the requisite education, training, and license or certificate status to provide the services specified.

The agreement should state that interns and psychological assistants are not allowed to receive money directly or to provide services off site, and that doing so will be grounds for termination of the agreement.

The agreement should specify that the intern, psychological assistant, or licensed therapist is required to meet the ethical standards of his or her particular profession, such as the American Psychological Association Ethical Principles or whatever other codes apply.

Additionally, it is important to have the employee represent in the contract that all information provided about his or her qualifications are accurate and truthful and that if it is determined that the information is not accurate or truthful that the contract can be terminated.

The contracts should also contain a provision that the duties contained therein are not assignable without the employer's written consent.

CONTRACTS WITH BUSINESS PARTNERS

The next most important form of agreement is between co-business owners. This can take a number of different forms depending upon whether the business is a partnership or a professional corporation. Generally mental health practices are operated by sole practitioners, professional corporations, or partnerships. The advantages of each business form must be discussed with a competent lawyer or tax advisor. Historically there were tax benefits to a professional corporation that have since been limited by IRS regulations. Generally, partners are jointly liable for the acts of each other, while co-owners of a corporation would not be jointly and severally liable. Many psychologists are not aware that professional corporations do not offer the same level of protection from suit as general corporations. As a general proposition, professional corporations may offer psychologists the opportunity to limit liability for general tort claims, such as a slip and fall on the office premises. However, a professional corporation will not limit a psychologist's exposure for malpractice claims.

However, under both a corporate and partnership agreement such litigation is generally protected against by purchasing premises and general liability insurance policies. Each form of business has its own advantages and disadvantages. However, under either form there must be a written agreement between the co-owners of the business specifying how business interest can be bought and sold and restricting an individual's ability to use a business interest as collateral for a loan. Also if there are going to be any differences in ownership interests based on the fact that one person may bring to the business more clients and sources while another might bring more cash, those should be dealt with in the initial agreement. Agreements between co-owners of businesses must also specifically indicate what the scope of the business is so that the co-business owners are only liable within the scope of the joint enterprise. For example, if two psychologists are partners and one operates a copying service on the side, the partnership agreement should clearly specify that the partner's copying business is outside the scope of the partnership endeavor. However, partners might want to preclude outside business that could create image problems for the therapy practice, such as ownership of a bar featuring nude dancers. Additionally, where there are outside interests, the partnership agreement should specify how much of each partner's time is to be devoted to the business.

Partners are fiduciaries as between each other and owe each other duties that shareholders of corporations do not.

Buy/sell agreements also address what happens in the event of divorce, death, bankruptcy, or mental incompetency. It is particularly ironic that therapists who routinely deal with mental instability and incompetency rarely address the effects of such a condition as to their business co-owners. It is not uncommon to have insurance purchased on co-business owners that is used to fund the acquisition of business interests in the event of death, dissolution, or transfer.

A practical provision is to limit the ability of any individual partner to commit or expend more than a certain dollar amount without the expressed consent of the other business owners.

In both leases and managed care contracts (and sometimes in partnership or buy/sell agreements), the issue of indemnity clauses arises. Indemnity is a legal concept of shifting of responsibility. Essentially, an indemnity clause allows the person who has had to pay some amount, or becomes legally obligated to pay some amount to shift that obligation to the person who is actually at fault.

There are two major types of indemnity: express contractual indemnity and implied indemnity. Express contractual indemnity exists where there is a contractual relationship providing for indemnification. The benefit of such a clause is that it may allow the person entitled to the indemnity to recover amounts of attorney's fees that would not otherwise be recoverable. It may also be somewhat easier to enforce because the rights of the parties to indemnification are spelled out clearly and not left to resolution by court. Implied indemnity is equitable in nature and does not arise from a contractual relationship, but from the relative fault of the parties. As an example, if a psychologist were sued by a patient over an injury due to a defective condition on the premises that was actually due to neglect on the part of a landlord, then the psychologist could sue the landlord for indemnity for any amount that the psychologist had to pay or became obligated to pay. As a general rule, a person cannot agree to be indemnified against his or her own negligence because it is against public policy. However, different states have limitations on indemnity and each state's laws governing individuals must be checked before underwritten clauses are agreed to.

In many instances, standard-form leases contain clauses requiring a psychologist or other tenant to indemnify the landlord. Although your bargaining power in such a circumstance may not be very real, it is worth an attempt to eliminate the indemnity provisions from the agreement. By the same token, many managed care contracts contain indemnification provisions, and it would be wise to delete them if it is possible. However, if the contractual provisions are not actually the subject of negotiation but presented to the psychologist on a take it or leave it basis, then an argument can be made against the enforcement of the indemnity provision on the grounds that it is a contract of adhesion. Under California Civil Code section 1670.5, a court can refuse to enforce such a contract in its entirety, refuse to enforce a part of the contract, or limit the part of the contract that is unfair. Most states have similar statutes. In short, the law recognizes that in some circumstances the actual bargaining power of a psychologist or other business person is very small. In fact, a routinely cited example is the actual language of insurance policies, which is dictated by the carrier and not subject to negotiation by an individual therapist applying for insurance. As a practical matter, indemnity is something that psychologists should always avoid agreeing to provide, but should always seek to be provided. Not surprisingly, the lawyers for other parties give them the same instruction, so its not uncommon to have conflicting indemnity provisions apply. The reality is, however, that an indemnification provision can be invaluable in litigation because it may allow cost of defense to be shifted to another party, as well as any ultimate judgment.

CONCLUSION

It should be clear that in approaching the business of minds, psychotherapists need to be conscious of the various ways that contracts impinge upon them, and can protect or disadvantage them. Simply put, the absence of an adequately drafted contract addressing the various points set forth above can put a psychotherapist in a position where his or her livelihood is threatened, when that result could easily have been avoided.

PART IV

THERAPISTS AT RISK

15

False Accusations Against Therapists: Where Are They Coming from, Why Are They Escalating, When Will They Stop?[1]

Lawrence E. Hedges

Over the past five years I have reviewed more than forty psycho-therapy cases in which serious accusations have been made by clients against their therapists. Since in most instances the therapists sought consultation after the disaster had occurred, I could only empathize with them, offer some possible explanations for what had gone wrong, and wish them luck in their ongoing struggle to survive the damaging ravages of the accusatory process.

The majority of these therapists had already had their licenses revoked or suspended by the time I saw them and many had been through lengthy and costly litigation. Others were dealing with losing their jobs and professional standing as well as their homes and personal investments. Malpractice insurance, which therapists carry, does not cover the enormous expenses involved in fighting an accusation at the

---

1. This chapter was first published in *The California Therapist*, 1995, and is reprinted with permission.

level of a licensing board, a state administrative court, an ethics committee, or a civil case in which an allegation of sexual misconduct is involved.

Most of the therapists whom I met with were seeking to gain some clarification as to what had happened to them. Many had read "In Praise of the Dual Relationship"[2] (Hedges 1993) in which I had written about the emergence of the transference psychosis in which the client loses the ability to reliably tell the difference between the perpetrator of the infantile past and the present person of the treating therapist. After the publication of that article, twenty-two therapists from five states told me about the disastrous experiences that had befallen them and asked if I could shed light on what had gone wrong. Many accused therapists expressed the hope that I would pass their stories on to other therapists, advising them of the serious dangers currently facing us. I recently published a series of these frightening vignettes in a book addressed to therapists on the subject of memories recovered in psychotherapy, *Remembering, Repeating, and Working Through Childhood Trauma* (Hedges 1994b).

"IT CAN'T HAPPEN TO ME"

My main business for many years has been working with therapists from many different orientations. Much of my time is spent hearing difficult cases in which transference and countertransference problems have developed. It is clear to me that most therapists are living in denial of the severe hazards that surround them in today's psychotherapy marketplace. Often when I have raised a word of caution regarding the potential dangers of a hidden psychotic reaction emerging and becoming directed at the therapist I hear, "I'm not at all worried about this person suing me, we've been at this a long time and we have a really good relationship." I find this attitude totally naive and dangerous. No one knows how to predict the nature and course of an emergent psychotic reaction and no one can say with certainty that he or she will not be its target.

Each therapist who told me about a disaster in his or her practice took great pains to tell me about the essentially good relationship they

2. Chapter 10 contains the main ideas of the three part article.

had succeeded in forming with the client. Repeatedly I heard how in the face of very trying circumstances the therapist had "gone the second mile" with the client, had done unusual things in order to be helpful to the client. I frequently heard how a therapist had made special concessions because the client had "needed" this or that variation or accommodation "to stay in therapy." In almost every case I heard that for perhaps the first time in this client's life he or she had succeeded in forming a viable relationship with another human being, the therapist. I was invariably told how, right at the moment of growing interpersonal contact or just when the relationship was really getting off the ground, "something happened" and "the client inexplicably turned against me." Or, "an accidental outside influence intervened and the therapeutic relationship was destroyed," resulting in a serious accusation being hurled at the therapist. Is there a pattern in these apparently false accusations of therapists? If so, what is it and how can we learn from it?

THE PROBLEM OF CONSIDERING ACCUSATIONS FALSE

To speak of "false accusations" is to take a seemingly arbitrary point of view regarding an event that is happening between two people. One person points the finger and says, "In your professional role of therapist I trusted you and you have misused that trust to exploit and damage me." The accused may be able to acknowledge that such and such events occurred, but not be able to agree on the meanings of those events or that exploitation or damage was involved. If we had a neutral or objective way of observing the events in question and the alleged damaging results, we might indeed see a damaged person. But would we be able to agree beyond the shadow of a doubt that the observable damage is a direct causal result of exploitative acts by the accused?

In the type of allegation I am defining as "false accusation," it is not possible to establish a direct causal link between actions of the therapist and the damage sustained by the client. Nor is it possible to establish beyond the shadow of a doubt that the activities of the therapist in his or her professional role were exploitative. I am aware that in certain ways this definition may beg the question of what is to be counted as "false" when separate points of view are being considered.

But I also believe that accusations as serious as professional misconduct carry a heavy burden of proof so that the question of true or false requires the establishment of a satisfactory standard of evidence—a standard that frequently seems to be lacking in accusations against therapists. My position, drawn from impressionistic experience, is that there are many therapists who are currently being accused of damage they are not responsible for. So what is the nature of the damage being pointed to and where did it come from?

PHILOSOPHICAL BIAS OR A PERSONAL BLIND SPOT?

Many therapists for a variety of reasons have developed a personal or philosophical bias in their work against systematically considering the concepts of transference, resistance, and countertransference. In choosing to disregard these complex traditional concerns and to embrace more easily grasped popular therapeutic notions, a therapist may unwittingly be setting up his or her own demise. All schools of psychotherapy acknowledge in one form or another the transfer of emotional relatedness issues from past experiences into present relationships. Resistance to forming a living recognition of the influence and power of transference phenomena is also widely understood. And countertransference reactions to the client and to the material of the therapy are universally recognized. The personal choice involved in not noticing and studying what may be happening in these dimensions of therapeutic relatedness does not make them cease to exist. It simply means that one is using personal denial or rationalization for keeping one's head buried in the sand and remaining oblivious to what dangers may be approaching as the relationship deepens.

THE BROADER CONTEXT: MEMORIES
OF ABUSE AND PSYCHOTHERAPY

The problem of false accusations made against psychotherapists is perhaps best understood when considered within the broader context of false accusations that arise from memories "recovered" in the course of psychotherapy. Elsewhere I have written on the importance of taking recovered memories seriously and have reviewed a century of research and study on the problem (Hedges 1994b,d). Some key ideas will be included in the discussion that follows.

Accusations against therapists are usually carried out in confidential settings—administrative hearings, ethics committees, and civil cases that are confidentially settled—so that the process and the outcome of these accusations is still largely a matter of secrecy, with the result that therapists do not yet know where the danger is coming from or what its nature is. A state and national grass roots movement has begun on a large scale that aims to bring into the light of day many miscarriages in justice for therapists.

There are clearly many issues to sort out in the recovered memory accusation crisis before we can regain our individual and collective sanity on this subject. In *Remembering, Repeating, and Working Through Childhood Trauma*, I review the research on the phenomenon of memories recovered in therapy, concluding that if these memories are not taken seriously in the context in which they emerge then we will indeed have a disaster on our hands.

PSYCHOTIC ANXIETIES AND RECOVERED MEMORIES

I relate a large class of recovered memories to primitive or "psychotic" anxieties that I assume to be operating to a greater or lesser extent in all people. My basic thesis is that, while we are now aware of much more real abuse than has ever been acknowledged before, this widely reported class of memories surfacing in psychotherapy today is not new. Psychotherapy began more than a century ago based on the study of recovered memories of incest. Clearly the client has experienced some terrifying and traumatic intrusions—often in the earliest months of life, perhaps even without anyone really being aware that the infant was suffering subtle but devious forms of cumulative strain trauma. Memories from this time cannot be retained in pictures, words, and stories; rather the body tissue itself or the characterological emotional response system retains an imprint of the trauma. Psychotherapy provides a place where words, pictures, and somatic experiences can be creatively generated and elaborated for the purpose of expressing in vivid metaphor aspects of early and otherwise unrememberable trauma.

Psychoanalytic research since 1914 (Freud) has shown how "screen" and "telescoped" memories condense a variety of emotional concerns in a dream-like fashion. "Narrative truth" which allows a myriad of emotional concerns to be creatively condensed into stories, images, somatic sensations, and cultural archetypes, has been well studied (Schafer 1976, Spence 1982) and understood to be the way people are able to present in comprehensible form memories from early life that could otherwise not be processed in therapy. All of these different types of constructed memories have been long familiar to psychoanalysts and serve as expressional metaphors for deep emotional concerns that are otherwise inexpressible.

Memories recovered during the course of psychotherapy need to be taken seriously—considered and dealt with in thoughtful and responsible ways by therapists, not simply believed in and acted upon. I maintain that a therapist who takes a simplified recovery approach of "remember the abuse, be validated by being believed, and then confront the abusers," is not only involved in a devious and destructive dual relationship but is actively colluding in resistance to the emergence of developmentally early transference experiencing and remembering with the therapist.

TRANSFERENCE REMEMBERING

The most powerful and useful form of memory in bringing to light those primordial experiences is reexperiencing in the context of an intimate and emotionally significant relationship with the psychotherapist the traumatic patterns of the early experience. I call the earliest level of transference experiencing with the psychotherapist the "organizing transference" (Hedges 1983, 1992, 1994a,c,d) because the traumas occurred during the period of life when an infant is actively engaged in organizing or establishing physical and psychological channels and connections to his or her human environment. Other psychoanalytic researchers speak of the "psychotic transference" or the "transference psychosis," which frequently appears in the therapy of people who are basically nonpsychotic.

Given the intensity of the primitive organizing or psychotic transference that is brought to the psychotherapy situation for analysis and the dangers to the therapist that this kind of work entails, it is not difficult to understand (1) why many counselors and therapists without training or experience in transference and resistance analysis are eager to direct the intense sense of blame away from themselves and onto others in the client's past, (2) why so many therapeutic processes end abortively when transference rage and disillusionment emerge and psychotic anxieties are mobilized, and (3) how therapists can so easily become targets for transferentially based accusations of abuse. If personal responsibility for ongoing internal processes cannot be assumed by the client and worked through, then the blame becomes externalized onto figures of the past or onto the therapist of the present. Continuing externalization of responsibility for feeling victimized and/or not adequately cared for is the hallmark of therapeutic failure.

FOUR KINDS OF REMEMBERING AND "FORGETTING"

Psychoanalysts and psychologists have no viable theory of forgetting, only a set of theories about how different classes of emotional events are remembered or barred from active memory. "Forgetting impressions, scenes, or experiences nearly always reduces itself to shutting them off. When the patient talks about these 'forgotten' things he seldom fails to add: 'As a matter of fact I've always known it; only I've never thought of it'" (Freud 1914, p. 148). Of course, there are many things around us which we do not notice and therefore do not recall. Further, much of our life's experience is known but has never been thought about. Much of this "unthought known" (Bollas 1987) can be represented in stories, pictures, and archetypes of the therapeutic dialogue and understood by the client and the therapist. Even if sometimes "a cigar is just a cigar," psychoanalytic study has never portrayed the human psyche as anything so passive as to be subject to simple forgetting. How then do analysts account for what appears to be "forgotten" experience? Based on a consideration of the development of the human relatedness potential psychoanalysts have evolved four viable ways to consider personality structure and to understand the different kinds of memories associated with each.

FOUR DEVELOPMENTALLY BASED
LISTENING PERSPECTIVES

To discuss the nature of the primitive mental processes at work in false accusations I need to establish a context by reviewing briefly the four developmental listening perspectives that have evolved in psychoanalysis for understanding four distinctly different types of transferences, resistances, and countertransferences (Hedges 1983). These listening perspectives are most often spoken of as four developmental levels, stages, or styles of personality organization, although we understand that every well-developed person may be listened to with all four perspectives at different moments in the therapeutic process. These four stages are described in Chapter 2. In considering false accusations against therapists our attention will be drawn to the fourth or earliest developmental form of transference remembering.

At the level of neurotic personality organization *secondary repression* is brought about by self instruction against socially undesirable, internal, instinctually driven thoughts and activity. Note that the definition of repression does not include externally generated trauma but only applies to overwhelming stimulation arising from *within* the body.

At the narcissistic level *dissociation* operates, in which certain whole sectors of internal psychic experience are (defensively) walled off from conscious awareness in the main personality because they cannot be integrated into the overall span of the main personality. Dissociated aspects of self experiences are not forgotten and are not considered unconscious. Rather their presence in immediate action and consciousness is dependent on the interpersonal situation present at the moment.

At the symbiotic or borderline level *ego-affect splitting* operates in which mutually contradictory affect states give rise to contrasting and often contradictory self and other transference and resistance memories that are present or not depending on the interpersonal context. The split-affect model of early memory used in understanding symbiotic or borderline personality organization postulates the presence in personality of mutually denied contradictory ego-affect states, which represent specific transference paradigms based on internalized object relations (Kernberg 1975). Whether a split ego state is or is not present in consciousness is dependent upon the way the person experiences the current interpersonal relationship situation. This means that what is remembered and the way it is recalled is highly dependent upon specific facilitating aspects of the relationship in which the memory is being recalled, expressed, or represented. As such, transference and resistance memories represented in split ego-affect states are always complete and subject to distortions by virtue of the lack of integration into the overall personality structure.

At the organizing developmental level *primary (neurologically conditioned) repression* (Freud 1895) acts to foreclose the possibility of reengaging in activities formerly experienced as overstimulating, traumatic, or physically painful. It is the organizing level of transferences, resistances, and countertransferences that usually gives rise to false accusations.

Primary repression characteristic of the organizing period of human development is a somatic event based on avoidance of experiences that are perceived as potentially painful (Freud 1895). McDougall (1989) points out, "Since babies cannot use words with which to think, they respond to emotional pain only psychosomatically. . . . The infant's earliest psychic structures are built around nonverbal 'signifiers' in the body's functions and the erogenous zones play a predominant role" (pp. 9–10). Her extensive psychoanalytic work with psychosomatic conditions shows how through careful analysis of manifestations in transference and resistance the early learned somatic signifiers can be brought from soma and represented in psyche through words, pictures, and stories. McDougall illustrates how body memories can be expressed in the interpersonal languages of transference, resistance, and countertransference.

Bioenergetic analysis (Lowen 1971, 1975, 1988) repeatedly demonstrates the process of bringing somatically stored memories into the here and now of transference and resistance in the therapeutic relationship. In bringing somatically stored memories out of the body and into psychic expression and/or representation, whether through psychoanalytic or bioenergetic technique, considerable physical pain is necessarily experienced. The intense physical pain encountered is usually thought of as resulting from therapeutically "breaking through" long-established aversive barriers to various kinds of physical experiencing that have previously proven frightening and were then forsaken. That is, the threshold to more flexible somatic experience is guarded by painful sensations

erected to prevent future venturing into places once experienced as painful by the infant or developing toddler. The therapist who tells me, "these
memories must be true because of the physical context" (e.g., vomiting,
shaking, convulsing) seems not to realize that it is the physical manifestations that *are* the memory from infancy—not the images or stories that
the client generates in order to metaphorically express or represent what
that trauma was like to her or his infant self.

FOUR DEVELOPMENTALLY DETERMINED
FORMS OF MEMORY

Childhood memories recovered in the psychoanalytic situation fall
into four general classes that correspond to the four types of personality organization just discussed (Hedges 1994b,d):

1. *Recollections* of wishes and fears of oedipal (triangular, 4- to 7-
   year-old) relating, which take the form of words, pictures and
   stories;
2. *Realizations* of self-to-selfobject (3-year-old) resonances, which
   take the form of narcissistic (mirroring, twinning, and idealization) engagements with the therapist;
3. *Representations* of self and other (4- to 24-month old) scenarios,
   in both passive and active interpersonal replications, which take
   the form of actual replications of mutual emotional engagements with the therapist;
4. *Expressions* of the search for and the rupture of potential channels or links to others (4 months before and after birth), which
   take the form of emotional connections and disconnections. It
   is this last class of memories that interests us in considering the
   problem of false accusations against therapists.

THE RUPTURE OF CONNECTIONS TO THE OTHER

The earliest transference and resistance memories are those from the
"organizing" period of relatedness development (Hedges 1983, 1992,
1994a,b,c,d). In utero and in the earliest months of life, the fetus and

neonate have the task of organizing channels to the maternal body and mind for nurturance, evacuation, soothing, comfort, and stimulation. Infant research (Tronick and Cohn 1988) suggests that only about 30 percent of the time are the efforts made by an infant and mother successful in establishing that "rhythm of safety" (Tustin 1986) required for the two to feel satisfactorily connected. The many ways in which an infant fails in securing the needed contact from its (m)other become internalized as transference to the failing mother. These disconnecting transference modes become enacted in the relationship with the therapist.

Because the biological being of the baby knows (just as every mammal knows) that if it cannot find the maternal body it will die, any serious impingement on the infant's sense of continuity of life, of "going on being" (Winnicott 1965) will be experienced as traumatic. An internalized terror response marks once-failed channels of connection with a sign that reads, "never reach this way again." Such traumatic organizing level transference memories are not only presymbolic, but preverbal and somatic. Resistance to ever again reexperiencing such a traumatic, life threatening breakdown of linking possibilities is *expressed* in somatic terror and pain, which mark "where mother once was and where I must not go again."

Winnicott (1965) points out that early impingements on the infant's sense of continuity with life oblige the infant to react to environmental failure before the infant is fully prepared to begin reacting and thinking. The result of premature impingement is the formation of a primary persecutory mode of thought that forms the foundation of subsequent thought processes. That is, traumatic impingement on the infantile (omnipotent) sense of "going on being," ensures that the first memory that is destined to color all later memories is "the world persecutes me by intruding into my mental space and overstimulating (traumatizing) me. I will forever be on guard for things coming at me that threaten to destroy my sense of being in control of what happens to me." As a lasting imprint this earliest memory is essentially psychotic or unrealistic because the world at large offers many kinds of impingement. And searching the environment tirelessly for the particular kind of primary emotional intrusion that once forced the infant to respond in a certain way not only creates perennial paranoid hazards where there may be none, but causes the person to miss other realistic dangers that are not being scanned for because of this prior preoccupation of the sensorium. A person living out organizing states will do so without her or his usual sense of judgment, perception, or reality testing capabilities so that inner fears and preoccupations cannot be reliably distinguished from external features or forces; thus, the person may be temporarily or perennially living in frames of mind that are in essence psychotic in nature, although this may not be obvious to others.

FEAR OF BREAKDOWN

Winnicott (1974) has shown that when people in analysis speak seriously of a fear of a breakdown or a fear of death, they are projecting into future time what has already been experienced in the infantile past. One can only truly fear what one knows about through experience. Terrifying and often disabling fears of breakdown and death are distinct ways of remembering traumatic experiences that happened in a person's infancy. What is dreaded and feared as a potentially calamitous future event is the necessity of experiencing through the memory of the evolving psychoanalytic transference the horrible, regressive, and once death-threatening breakdown the person experienced in a dependent state in infancy.

The fear of breakdown (from the infant's view) manifests itself in many forms as resistance to reexperiencing in transference the terror, helplessness, rage, dependency, and loss of control once known in infancy. Therapists and clients alike dread disorganizing breakdowns during the therapeutic process so that there are many ways in resistance and counter-resistance that the two can collude to forestall the curative experience of remembering by reliving the breakdown experience with the therapist. One way for a therapist to collude with resistance to therapeutic progress is to focus on external perpetrators or long-ago traumas to prevent having to live through deeply distressing and frightening breakdown re-creations together in the here-and-now therapeutic relationship.

The breakdown fear a person felt in infancy lives on as the somatic underpinning of all subsequent emotional relatedness but cannot be recalled because (a) no memory of the experience per se is recorded—only a nameless dread of reexperiencing the dangers of infantile dependence and breakdown, (b) the memory of the breakdown experience itself is guarded with intense pain, somatic terror, and physical symptoms of all types, (c) the trauma occurred before it was possible to record pictures, words, or stories so it cannot be recalled in ordinary ways, but only as bodily terrors of approaching breakdown and death. But massive breakdown of functioning is not the only kind of trauma known to occur in infancy. Masud Khan's (1963) concept of *cumulative trauma* as discussed in chapter 2 adds a new set of possibilities to those already discussed. The person with vulnerabilities left over from infantile cumulative strain trauma "can in later life break down as a result of acute stress and crisis" (p. 56). Many symptoms and/or breakdowns in later life, occasioned by conditions of acute living stress, have their origins in infancy. The adult experience of believing that one has suffered a vague, undefinable, and/or forgotten earlier trauma is attributable to the cumulative effects of strain in infancy caused by environmental failure to provide an effective stimulus barrier during the period of infantile dependency. There may have been no way at the time of knowing what kinds of stimuli were causing undue strain on the infant because they were not gross and they were operating more or less silently and invisibly.

In expressions of searching for and breaking off (*primary repression of*) the possibility of contact with others, the early traumatic ways the nurturing other ruptured or failed to sustain contact live on as transference and resistance memories that interfere with subsequent attempts to make human contact which would lead toward full emotional bonding. Organizing (or psychotic) transference memory involves the search for connection *versus* a compulsion toward discontinuity, disjunction, and rupture of connections. The resistance memory exists as the person's automatic or inadvertent reluctance to establish and/or to sustain consistent and reliable connection to the other (which might serve to make interpersonal bonding of these somatic experiences a realistic possibility).

CASE ILLUSTRATION: SWITCHING PERSONALITIES

It is this organizing experience and the reluctance to permit or to sustain here-and-now connectedness experience that I and my clinical colleagues have researched and written about extensively. A brief example of what an organizing level transference disconnect might look like in a clinical situation suggests a direction for consideration.

A therapist working with a multiple personality presents her work to a consultant. After an overview of the case is given, the consultant asks for the therapist to present "process notes" (event by event) of a recent session for review. The therapist begins reading the process notes, telling how her client, Victor, began the hour and how the client gradually zeroed in on a particular emotional issue. The therapist hears the concerns and very skillfully empathizes with the client's thoughts and feelings. Suddenly "little Victoria, age 4" appears in the room. The "switch" is significant in all regards and the therapist now listens to what the alter, Victoria, has to say. The consultant asks how the therapist understands what has just happened. The answer is that Victor felt very understood in the prior transaction, and in the safety of the presence of the understanding therapist a more regressed alter (Victoria) can now appear. This kind of event is ubiquitous in the treatment of organizing experiences—an empathic connection is achieved by the therapist and there is a seemingly smooth and comfortable shift to another topic, to a flashback memory, or to an alter personality. The therapist had to work hard to achieve this connection and feels gratified that his or her interpretive work has been successful. The therapist feels a warm glow of narcissistic pleasure that is immediately reinforced by the client's ability to move on to the next concern.

Wrong! When organizing or psychotic issues are brought for analysis, what is most feared on the basis of transference and resistance is an empathic interpersonal connection. This is because in the infantile situation the contact with the (m)other was terrifying in some regard. A more viable way of seeing the interaction just cited is to realize that *the successful empathic connection was immediately, smoothly, and almost without notice ruptured with the shift!* The therapist may fail to see what happened for perhaps several reasons: (a) the therapist is a well-bonded person and assumes unwittingly that empathic connection is experienced as good by everyone; (b) the therapist doesn't understand how organizing transference and resistance operate and so is narcissistically pleased by the apparent connection he or she has achieved; (c) the client is a lifetime master at smoothly and efficiently dodging interpersonal connections—across the board or only at certain times when organizing issues are in focus; (d) a subtle mutual seduction is operating in the name of "recovery" in which resistance and counterresistance are winning the day, with both parties afraid of personal and intimate connectedness presumably because of its intense emotional demands; (e) the personality switch, sudden flashback, or change of subject focuses both on the historical causes of the dissociation or some other red herring; or (f) the search for memories and validation forecloses the possibility of here-and-now transference experiencing of the emotional horror of infantile trauma and breakdown and how the connection with the therapist is stimulating its appearance. In all of these possibilities the tragedy is that the very real possibility of bringing to life and putting to rest traumatic memory is lost by the therapeutic technique being employed.

I hope I have succeeded in drawing attention to how precarious our current situation is. We have learned how to follow people deep into their infantile psychotic anxieties in order to provide an opportunity for reliving and therapeutic mastery of the problem of emotional contact in the context of an adult psychotherapy relationship. But the possibility of a negative therapeutic reaction looms large. In *Working the Organizing Experience* (Hedges 1994c), I specify a series of features that characterize the development of the transference psychosis, elaborate on common subjective concerns of the person living an organizing experience, and provide a series of technical issues to be considered by therapists choosing to do long-term, intensive psychotherapy. The companion casebook, *In Search of the Lost Mother of Infancy* (Hedges 1994a), provides a theoretical and technical overview of working the organizing experience as well as lengthy and difficult in-depth case study reports of long-term work with organizing transferences reported by eight psychotherapists. The working through of the organizing transference or transference psychosis is demonstrated when it exists as the pervasive mode of the personality as well as when it exists only in subtle pockets of otherwise well-developed personalities.

Clients who were traumatized early in life are at risk for the development of a negative therapeutic reaction in the form of a transference psychosis that can be suddenly, surprisingly, and destructively aimed at the person of the therapist. False accusations against therapists will not stop until therapists become knowledgeable about how to work with the primitive processes of the human mind!

16

Therapists at Risk

Virginia Wink Hilton
Robert Hilton
Lawrence E. Hedges

The authors of this book have presented a series of psychodynamic, personal, legal, and ethical issues that face therapists today. On many fronts we are beset with dangers that threaten to undermine the practice of psychotherapy in various ways. The consequences of failing to be attentive to these dangers are great. We often hear protests and cries of discouragement from our colleagues to the effect that therapy as we once knew it can no longer be practiced. The authors of this book, however, believe that these dangers create a challenge for psychotherapy which ultimately benefits therapists and clients alike.

Psychotherapy clients today are far less likely than in the past to accept that "the doctor knows best." Unethical or substandard treatment is no longer tolerated or hidden to the degree that it once was. The pressure for higher standards is good news for the profession. But other forces which are at work in the culture at large and within the individual person create dangers for the practicing clinician. The prevalence of the so-called victim mentality, the need to find quick answers, the wish to shift responsibility and to assign blame, the readiness to litigate—these and other factors play a role in creating a climate wherein false memories and false accusations produce fears, constriction, and even paranoia among clinicians. It is our belief that these trends and these times force us into close scrutiny of ourselves.

As we work with those who seek our help it becomes more important than ever before that we face our own deepest psychic issues. The dictum, "Physician, heal thyself" is more relevant now than ever. The present climate requires us to understand more clearly how we heal, grow, and expand ourselves through our encounters with our clients. It is only when we understand the depth of our own emotional involvement in the therapeutic process that we can be fully responsible, fully attentive clinicians, open and able with bounded clarity to accompany our clients on their unique and personal journeys.

References

Abramowitz, S. I., Abramowitz, C. V., Roback, H. B., et al. (1976). Sex-role related countertransference in psychotherapy. *Archives of General Psychiatry* 33:71–73.

Alexander, F. (1961). *The Scope of Psychoanalysis*. New York: Basic Books.

Appelbaum, P., and Jorgenson, L. (1991). Psychotherapist-patient sexual contact after termination of treatment: an analysis and a proposal. *American Journal of Psychotherapy* 148(11):1466.

Auden, W. H. (1948). Age of Anxiety. In *Collected Works, Poems*. New York: Random House, 1991.

Axelrod, S., and Brody, S. (1968). *Infant Feeding at Six Weeks*. Film available from the Southern California Bioenergetic Society Library Catalog, No. 1.

Bacal, H., and Thompson, P. (1993). *The psychoanalyst's selfobject needs and the effect of their frustration on the treatment: a new view of countertransference*. Paper presented at the 16th annual conference on Psychology of the Self, Toronto, October.

Balint, M. (1949). Changing therapeutical aims and techniques in psycho-analysis. In *Primary Love and Psycho-Analytic Technique*, ed. M. Balint. New York: Liverright, International Psycho-Analytical Library, 1953, pp. 221–235.

Bates, C. M., and Brodsky, A. (1989). *Sex in the Therapy Hour: A Case of Professional Incest*. New York: Guilford.

Belote, B. (1974). *Sexual intimacy between female clients and male therapists: masochistic sabotage*. Unpublished doctoral dissertation, California School of Professional Psychology, Berkeley.

Bibring, G. (1936). A contribution to the subject of transference resistance. *International Journal of Psycho-Analysis* 17:181–189.

Bird, B. (1972). Notes on transference: universal phenomenon and the hardest part of analysis. *Journal of the American Psychoanalytic Association* 20:51–67.

———— (1972). Notes on transference: universal phenomenon and hardest part of analysis. In *Classics in Psycho-Analytic Technique*, ed. R. Langs. New York: Jason Aronson, 1981.

Blum, H. J. (1973). The concept of eroticized transference. *Journal of the American Psychoanalytic Association* 21:61–76.

Bollas, C. (1979). The transformational object. *International Journal of Psycho-Analysis* 59:97–107.

———— (1983). Expressive uses of the countertransference. In *Shadow of the Object: Psychoanalysis of the Unthought Known*, pp. 200–236. London: Free Association Press, 1987.

———— (1987). *The Shadow of the Object: Psychoanalysis of the Unthought Known*. London: Free Association Press.

Bouhoutsos, J. (1984). Sexual intimacy between psychotherapists and clients: Policy implications for the future. In *Women and Mental Health Policy*, ed. L. Walker, pp. 207–227. Beverly Hills, CA: Sage.

Bouhoutsos, J., Holroyd, J., Lerman, H., et al. (1983). Sexual intimacy between psychotherapists and patients. *Professional Psychology: Research and Practice* 14(2):185–196.

Breuer, J., and Freud, S. (1893–95). Studies on Hysteria. *Standard Edition* 2.

Brown, L. S. (1988). Harmful effects of post-termination sexual and romantic relationships with former clients. *Psychotherapy:* 25, 249–255.

Buckley, P., Karasu, T. B., and Charles, E. (1981). Psychotherapists view their personal therapy. *Psychotherapy: Theory, Research, and Practice* 18(2):99–305.

Butler, S. (1975). *Sexual contact between therapists and patients.* Unpublished doctoral dissertation, California School of Professional Psychology, Los Angeles, CA.

Butler, S., and Zelen, S. L. (1977). Sexual intimacies between therapists and patients. *Psychotherapy: Theory, Research, and Practice* 139:143–144.

Carlson, R. (1986). After analysis: a study of transference dreams following treatment. *Journal of Consulting and Clinical Psychology* 54:246–252.

Cheatham v. Rogers 824 S.W. 2d 231 (1992).

Chesler, P. (1972). *Women and Madness.* New York: Avon.

Clavreul, J. (1967). The Perverse Couple. In Schneiderman's *Returning to Freud: Clinical Psychoanalysis in the School of Lacan.* New Haven: Yale University Press, 1980.

D'Addorio, L. (1977). *Sexual relationships between female clients and male therapists.* Unpublished doctoral dissertation, California School of Professional Psychology, San Diego, CA.

Deutsch, H. (1926). Occult processes occurring during psychoanalysis. In *Psychoanalysis and the Occult,* ed. G. Devereaux. New York: International Universities Press, 1953.

DiLeo v. Nugent 592 A.2d 1126 (1990).

Durre, L. (1980). Comparing romantic and therapeutic relationships. In *On Love and Loving: Psychological Perspectives On the Nature and Experience of Romantic Love,* ed. K. S. Pope, pp. 228–243. San Francisco: Jossey-Bass.

Eissler, K. R. (1953). The effect of the structure of the ego on psychoanalytic technique. *Journal of the American Psychoanalytic Association* 1:104–143.

Eliot, T. S. (1950). The Waste Land. In *The Complete Poems and Plays.* New York: Harcourt, Brace.

Ernsberger, C. (1979). The concept of countertransference as a therapeutic instrument: its early history. *Modern Psychoanalysis* 4:141–164.

Evan F. v. Houghson United Methodist Church 8 Cal. App.4th 828 (1992).

Feldman-Summers, S., and Jones, G. (1984). Psychological impacts of sexual contact between therapists or other health care practitioners and their clients. *Journal of Consulting and Clinical Psychology* 52(6):1054–1061.

Fenichel, O. (1945). *The Psychoanalytic Theory of Neurosis*. New York: W. W. Norton.

Ferenczi, S. (1926a). The further development of an active therapy in psycho-analysis. In *Further Contributions to the Theory and Technique of Psycho-Analysis*, pp. 198–217. London: Hogarth.

——— (1926b). Contra-indications to the active psycho-analytical technique. In *Further Contributions to the Problems and Methods of Psycho-Analysis*, pp. 156–167. London: Hogarth.

——— (1933). Confusion of tongues between adults and the child. In *Final Contributions to the Problems and Methods of Psycho-Analysis*, pp. 126–142. London: Hogarth Press, 1955.

——— (1952). *First Contributions to Psycho-Analysis*, compiled by John Rickman. New York: Brunner/Mazel.

——— (1955). *Final Contributions to the Problems and Methods of Psycho-Analysis*. New York: Brunner/Mazel.

——— (1962). *Further Contributions to the Theory and Technique of Psycho-Analysis*. New York: Brunner/Mazel.

Ferenczi, S.; and Rank, O. (1923). *The Development of Psychoanalysis*. New York and Washington: Nervous and Mental Disease Publishing Co., 1925.

Fredrickson, R. (1992). *Repressed Memories*. New York: Simon and Schuster.

Freedman, L., and Roy, J. (1976). *Betrayal*. New York: Stein and Day.

Freud, A. (1951). Observations on child development. In *Indications for Child Analysis and Other Papers*, pp. 143–162. New York: International Universities Press, 1968.

——— (1952). The role of bodily illness in the mental life of children. In *Indications for Child Analysis and Other Papers*, pp. 260–279. New York: International Universities Press, 1968.

——— (1958). Child observation and prediction of development. In *Research at the Hampstead Child-Therapy Clinic and Other Papers* (1970), pp. 102–135. Taken from Khan, M. M. R. (1974). *The Privacy of The Self*. New York: International Universities Press.

Freud, S. (1895a). Project for a scientific psychology. *The Complete Psychological Works of Sigmund Freud. Standard Edition* 1:283–397.

—— (1905). Fragment of an analysis of a case of hysteria. *Standard Edition* 7:3–124.

—— (1905). Three essays on the theory of sexuality. *Standard Edition* 7:125–244.

—— (1910). The future prospects of psychoanalytic therapy. *Standard Edition* 1:141–151.

—— (1912a). Papers on technique: the dynamics of transference. *Standard Edition* 12:92–108.

—— (1912b). The dynamics of transference. In *Classics in Psycho-Analytic Technique*, ed. R. Langs. New York: Jason Aronson, 1981.

—— (1914). Recollecting, repeating, and working through (further recommendations on the techniques of psycho-analysis II). *Standard Edition* 12:145–156.

—— (1915). Observations on transference love (further recommendations on the technique of psycho-analysis III). *Standard Edition* 12:159–171.

—— (1915). Observations on transference love. In *Collected Papers*, vol. 2, ed. E. Jones, pp. 377–391. New York: Basic Books.

—— (1918). An infantile neurosis. *Standard Edition* 17:1–124.

—— (1920). Beyond the pleasure principle. *Standard Edition* 18:3–64.

—— (1923). The ego and the id. *Standard Edition* 19:3–68.

—— (1925). An autobiographical study. *Standard Edition* 20:75–77.

—— (1933). New introductory lectures on psycho-analysis. *Standard Edition* 22:1–184.

—— (1937). *The Ego and the Mechanics of Defense*. New York: International Universities Press.

Gabbard, G., ed. (1989). *Sexual Exploitation Within Professional Relationships*. Washington, D.C.: American Psychiatric Association.

Gabbard, G., and Pope, K. (1988). Sexual intimacies after termination: clinical, ethical, and legal aspects. *Independent Practitioner* 8(2): 21–26.

Gartrell, N., Herman, J., Olarte, S., et al. (1986). Psychiatrist-patient sexual contact: results of a national survey. I: prevalence. *American Journal of Psychiatry* 143:1126–1131.

—— (1987). Reporting practices of psychiatrists who knew of sexual misconduct by colleagues. *American Journal of Orthopsychiatry* 57 (2): 287–295.

Gorkin, M. (1987). *The Uses of Countertransference*. New York: Jason Aronson.

Green, A. (1986). The dead mother. In *On Private Madness*. London: Hogarth.

Green, T. A. (1992). *Satan and Psyche: The Ego's Encounter with Evil*. Unpublished manuscript.

Greenacre, P. (1954). The childhood of the artist: libidinal phase development and giftedness. *Psychoanalytic Study of the Child* 47–72. New York: International Universities Press.

——— (1958). Towards the understanding of the physical nucleus of some defense reactions. *International Journal of Psycho-Analysis* 39:69–76.

——— (1960). Further notes on fetishism. *Psychoanalytic Study of the Child* 15:191–207. New York: International Universities Press.

Greenson, R. (1965). The working alliance and the transference neurosis. In *Explorations in Psychoanalysis*, pp. 199–225. New York: International Universities Press, 1978.

——— (1978). *Explorations in Psychoanalysis*. New York: International Universities Press.

Gross, J. (1994). Suit Asks, Does "Memory Therapy" Heal or Harm? *The New York Times*, April 8.

Guntrip, H. (1964). *Healing and the Sick Mind*. New York: Appleton-Century.

Hedges, L. E. (1983). *Listening Perspectives in Psychotherapy*. New York: Jason Aronson.

——— (1989). Working the countertransference. Videotape lecture, May 5, 1989. Orange, CA: Listening Perspectives Study Center.

——— (1992). *Interpreting the Countertransference*. Northvale, NJ: Jason Aronson.

——— (1994a). *In Search of the Lost Mother of Infancy*. Northvale, NJ: Jason Aronson.

——— (1994b). *Remembering, Repeating, and Working Through Childhood Trauma*. Northvale, NJ: Jason Aronson.

——— (1994c). *Working the Organizing Experience*. Northvale, NJ: Jason Aronson.

——— (1994d). Taking recovered memories seriously. *Issues in Child Abuse Accusation* 6(1):1–30. Northfield, MN: Institute for Psychological Therapies.

Hedges, L. E., and Coverdale, C. (1985). Countertransference and its relation to developmental concepts of empathy and interpretation. Unpublished manuscripts. Orange, CA: Listening Perspectives Study Center.

Heimann, P. (1950). On countertransference. In *Classics in Psychoanalytic Technique*, ed. R. Langes. New York: Jason Aronson.

Herman, J. (1981). *Father-Daughter Incest*. Cambridge, MA: Harvard University Press.

Herman, J., Gartrell, N., Olarte, S., et al. (1987). Psychiatrist-patient sexual contact: results of a national survey, II: psychiatrists' attitudes. *American Journal of Psychiatry* 144(2):164–169.

Hilton, R. (1990). Physical contact in psychotherapy: the transference and countertransference implications. Paper presented at the California Association of Marriage and Family Therapists Conference, May.

——— (1993). Ending with an open heart. Paper presented at the Pacific Northwest Bioenergetic Conference, Whistler, British Columbia, August.

Hilton, V. W. (1987). Working with sexual transference. *Journal of Bioenergetic Analysis* 3(1):77–88.

——— (1989). Sexual countertransference. In *Training Manual*. Pacific Northwest Bioenergetic Conference.

——— (1993). When we are accused. *Journal of Bioenergetic Analysis* 5/2:45–51.

——— (1994). The Devil in America. *The California Therapist*, Vol. 6 Issue 1, Jan/Feb 37–41.

Holmer, N. M., and Wassen, H. (1947). *Mu-Ingala or the Way of Muu, a Medicine Song from the Cunas of Panama*. Goteborg. (Quoted in Levi-Strauss 1949.)

Holroyd, J. C. (1983). Erotic contact as an instance of sex-based therapy. In *The Handbook of Bias in Psychotherapy*, ed. J. Murry and P. R. Abramson, pp. 285–308. New York: Praeger.

Holroyd, J. C., and Bouhoutsos, J. (1985). Sources of bias in reporting effects of sexual contact with patients. *Psychotherapy: Research and Practice* 16:701–709.

Holroyd, J. C., and Brodsky, A. M. (1977). Psychologists' attitudes and practices regarding erotic and nonerotic psychical contact with patients. In *American Psychologist* 32:843–849.

Horney, K. (1950). Neurosis and Human Growth. In *Collected Works of Karen Horney*, vol. 2. New York: W. W. Norton.

Horak v. Biris 130 Ill. App. 3d 140, 474 N.E. 2d 13 (1985).

Jablonski by Pahls v. United States 712 F.2D 39 (9th Cir. 1983).

Jacobson, E. (1964). *The Self and the Object World*. New York: International Universities Press.

James W. v. Superior Court 17 Cal. App. 4th 246 (1993).

Journal of Psychohistory (Spring 1994). 21(4).

Kardener, S., Fuller, M., and Mensh, I. N. (1973). A survey of physicians' attitudes and practices regarding erotic and nonerotic contact with patients. *American Journal of Psychiatry* 130(10):1077–1081.

Kenworthy, T. A., Koufacos, C., and Sherman, J. (1976). Women and therapy: a survey on internship programs. *Psychology of Women Quarterly* 1:125–137.

Kernberg, O. F. (1965). Notes on countertransference. *Journal of American Psychoanalytic Association* 13:38–56.

——— (1975). *Borderline Conditions and Pathological Narcissism*. New York: Jason Aronson.

——— (1980). *Internal World and External Reality*. New York: Jason Aronson.

Khan, M. M. R. (1963). The concept of cumulative trauma. *Psychoanalytic Study of the Child* 18:286–306. New York: International Universities Press.

Kitchener, K. (1988). Dual relationships: What makes them so problematic? *Journal of Counseling and Development* 67:217–221.

Klein, M. (1946). Notes on some schizoid mechanisms. *International Journal of Psycho-Analysis* 27:99–110.

Kluft, R. (1992). Lecture given at "Advanced Treatment of Personality Disorders Conference," Westword Institute, El Cerrito, CA.

Kohut, H. (1971). *The Analysis of the Self*. New York: International Universities Press.

——— (1977). *The Restoration of the Self*. New York: International Universities Press.

——— (1984). *How Does Analysis Cure?* Chicago: University of Chicago Press.

Kris, E. (1951). Some comments and observations on early autoerotic activities. *Psychoanalytic Study of the Child* 6:95–116. New York: International Universities Press.

——— (1956a). The personal myth. *Journal of the American Psychoanalytic Association* 4:653–681.

——— (1956b). The recovery of childhood memories in psychoanalysis. *Psychoanalytic Study of the Child* 11:54–88. New York: International Universities Press.

Landis, C. E., Miller, H. H., and Wettstone, R. P. (1975). Sexual awareness training for counselors. *Teaching of Psychology* 2:33–36.

Langs, R. (1975). Therapeutic misalliances. *International Journal of Psychoanalytic Psychotherapy* 4:77–105.

——— (1976a). *The Therapeutic Interaction*, vol. 2. New York: Jason Aronson.

——— (1976b). *The Bi-Personal Field*. New York: Jason Aronson.

——— (1979). *The Supervisory Experience*. New York: Jason Aronson.

——— (1980). *The Therapeutic Environment*. New York: Jason Aronson.

——— ed. (1981). *Classics in Psychoanalytic Technique*. New York: Jason Aronson.

——— (1983). Countertransference and the process of cure. In *Curative Factors in Dynamic Psychotherapy*, ed. S. Slipp. New York: McGraw-Hill.

Lanning, K. (1992). *Investigator's Guide to Allegations of "Ritual" Child Abuse*. Quantico, VA: Science Unit, National Center for the Analysis of Violent Crime, Federal Bureau of Investigation, FBI Academy.

Lester, E. (1982). *The female analyst and the eroticized transference*. Paper presented at the American Psychological Association.

Le Vey, A. (1969). *The Satanic Bible*. New York: Avon.

Levi-Strauss, C. (1949). The effectiveness of symbols. In *Structural Anthropology*, vol. 1, pp. 186–205. New York: Basic Books, 1963.

Lewis, R. (1988). Exhibitionism. *Journal of Bioenergetic Analysis* 3(2).

Little, M. (1981). Counter-transference and the patient's response to it. In *Transference Neurosis and Transference Psychosis*. New York: Jason Aronson.

——— (1990). *Psychotic Anxieties and Containment: A Personal Record of an Analysis with Winnicott*. Northvale, NJ: Jason Aronson.

Loewald, H. W. (1960). On the therapeutic action of psycho-analysis. *International Journal of Psycho-Analysis* 41:16–33.

Loftus, E. (1993). The reality of repressed memories. *American Psychologist* 48:518–537.

Loftus, E., and Waters, E. (1994). *Making Memories.*

Lowen, A. (1971). *The Language of the Body.* New York: Collier.

———— (1975). *Bioenergetics.* London: Penguin.

———— (1988). *Love, Sex and Your Heart.* New York: Macmillan.

Markbourough California Inc. v. Superior Court 227 Cal. App. 3d 705 (1991).

Marlene F. v. Affiliated Psychiatric Medical Clinic, Inc. 48 Cal. 3d 583, 257 Cal. Rptr. 298, 770 P.2d 278 (1989).

Marmor, J. (1972). Sexual acting-out in psychotherapy. *American Journal of Psychoanalysis* 22:3–18.

Marston v. Minneapolis Clinic of Psychiatry and Neurology 329 N.W. 2d 306 (Minn. 1983).

Masters and Johnson Report 2(1): Summer, 1993.

Mathis v. Morrissey 11 Cal. App. 4th 332 (1992).

Mazza v. Huffaker 61 N.C. App. 170, 300 S.E.2d 833 (1983).

McDougall, J. (1989). *Theaters of the Body.* London: Free Association Press.

Miller, A. (1981). *Prisoners of Childhood,* trans. R. Ward. New York: Basic Books.

Miller, W. A. (1981). *Make Friends with Your Shadow.* Minneapolis: Augsberg.

Milner, M. (1952). Aspects of symbolism in comprehension of the not-self. *International Journal of Psycho-Analysis* 33:181–195.

Modell, A. H. (1976). "The holding environment" and the therapeutic action of psychoanalysis. *Journal of the American Psychoanalytic Association* 24:285–308.

Money-Kyrle, R. E. (1956). Normal counter-transference and some of its deviations. *International Journal of Psycho-Analysis* 37:360–366.

Montoya v. Bebensee 761 P.2d 285 (Cal. App. 1988).

Natterson, J. (1991). *Beyond Countertransference. The Therapist's Subjectivity in the Therapeutic Process.* Northvale, NJ: Jason Aronson.

Newman, W. A. (1974). *Dorland's Medical Dictionary,* 25th ed. Philadelphia: W. B. Saunders.

Norman, H., Blacker, D., Oremland, J., and Barret, W. (1976). The fate of the transference neurosis after termination of a satisfactory analysis. *Journal of American Psychoanalytic Association* 24:471–498.

Noto v. St. Vincent's Hospital 142 Misc. 2d 292 (1988).

Ofshe, R. (1992). Inadvertent hypnosis during interrogation: false confession due to dissociative state, misidentified multiple personality, and the satanic cult hypothesis. *International Journal of Experimental Hypnosis* 40:125–156.

Ofshe, R., and Watters, E. (1994). *Making Monsters: Repressed Memories, Satanic Cult Abuse and Sexual Hysteria.* New York: Simon and Schuster.

Oremland, J., Blacker, K., and Norman, H. (1975). Incompleteness in successful psychoanalysis: a follow-up cast study. *Journal of American Psychoanalytic Association* 23:819–844.

Orr, D. W. (1954). Transference and countertransference: a historical survey. *Journal of American Psychoanalytic Association* 2:621–671.

Person, E. S. (1985). The erotic transference in women and in men: differences and consequences. *Journal of American Academy of Psychoanalysis* 13(2):159–180.

Pfeffer, A. (1963). The meaning of analysis after analysis. *Journal of American Psychoanalytic Association* 11:229–244.

Plasil, E. (1975). *Therapist.* New York: St. Martin's/Masek.

Pope, K. S. (1987). Preventing therapist-patient sexual intimacy: therapy for a therapist at risk. *Professional Psychology: Research and Practice* 18(6):624–628.

——— (1988). How clients are harmed by sexual contact with mental health professionals: the syndrome and its prevalence. *Journal of Counseling and Development* 67:222–226.

——— (1990). Therapist-patient sexual involvement: a review of the research. *Clinical Psychology Review* 10:477–490.

Pope, K. S., and Bouhoutsos, J. C. (1986). *Sexual Intimacy Between Therapists and Patients.* New York: Praeger.

Pope, K. S., Keith-Spiegel, P., and Tabachnick, B. G. (1986). Sexual attraction to clients: the human therapist and the (sometimes) inhuman training system. *American Psychologist* 147–157.

——— (1987). Ethics of practice. *American Psychologist* 42:993–1006.

Pope, K. S., Levenson, H., and Schover, L. (1979). Sexual intimacy in psychology training: results and implications of a national survey. *American Psychologist* 34:682–689.

Pope, K. S., Sonne, J. L., and Holroyd, J. (1993). *Sexual Feelings in Psychotherapy.* Washington, D.C.: American Psychological Press.

Racker, H. (1957). The meaning and uses of countertransference. In

Transference and Countertransference. New York: International Universities Press, 1968.

———— (1953). Countertransference neurosis. In *Transference and Countertransference.* New York: International Universities Press, 1968.

Reich, A. (1951). On countertransference. *International Journal of Psycho-Analysis* 32:25–31.

Richard H. v. Larry D. 198 Cal. App.3d 591 (1988).

Robertiello, R., and Schoenewolf, A. (1987). *101 Common Therapeutic Blunders.* Northvale, NJ: Jason Aronson.

Rogers, M. L. (1992). Evaluating adult litigants who allege injuries from sexual abuse. *Journal of Psychology and Theology* 20:3.

Roy v. Hartop 81 Misc. 2d, 366 N.Y.S.2d 297 (NY1985).

Rutter, P. (1989). *Sex in the Forbidden Zone.* Los Angeles: Jeremy P. Tarcher.

Sanford, John A. (1981). *Evil, The Shadow Side of Reality.* New York: Crossroads.

Schafer, R. (1976). *A New Language for Psychoanalysis.* New Haven, CT: Yale University Press.

Schover, L. R. (1981). Male and female therapists' responses to male and female client sexual material: an analogue study. *Archives of Sexual Behavior* 10:477–492.

Schwaber, E. (1979). Narcissism, self psychology and the listening perspective. Pre-presentation reading for lecture given at the University of California, Los Angeles Conference on the Psychology of the Self-Narcissism, October.

———— (1983). Psychoanalytic listening and psychic reality. *International Journal of Psycho-Analysis* 10:379–391.

Searles, H. (1959/1965). Oedipal love in the countertransference. In *Collected Papers on Schizophrenia and Related Subjects,* pp. 284–303. New York: International Universities Press.

———— (1979a). Countertransference and theoretical model. In *Countertransference and Related Subjects.* New York: International Universities Press.

———— (1979b). The countertransference with the borderline patient. *In Advances in Psychotherapy of the Borderline,* ed. J. Leboit, and A. Capponi. New York: Jason Aronson.

Silverburg, W. V. (1918). The concept of transference. *Psychoanalytic Quarterly* 17:309–310.

Simmons v. United States 805 F.2d 1363 (9th Cir. 1986).

Smith, M. (1993). *Ritual Abuse*. New York: HarperCollins.

Sonne, J., Meyer, C. B., Borys, D., and Marshall, V. (1985). Clients' reaction to sexual intimacy in therapy. *American Journal of Ortho-psychiatry* 55:183–189.

Speigs v. Johnson 748 P.2d 1020 (Ore. App. 1988).

Spence, D. (1982). *Narrative Truth and Historical Truth*. New York: W. W. Norton.

Stern, D. N. (1985). *The Interpersonal World of the Infant*. New York: Basic Books.

Stone, L. G. (1980). *A study of the relationships among anxious attachment, ego functioning, and female patients' vulnerability to sexual involvement with their male psychotherapists*. Unpublished doctoral dissertation, California School of Professional Psychology, Los Angeles.

Strachey, J. (1934). The nature of the therapeutic action of psycho-analysis. *International Journal of Psycho-Analysis* 15:117–126.

Strausburger, L. H., Jorgenson, L., and Sutherland, P. (1992). The pre-vention of psychotherapist sexual misconduct: avoiding the slip-pery slope. *American Journal of Psychotherapy* 46(4):544–554.

Sullivan, H. S. (1953). *The Interpersonal Theory of Psychiatry*. New York: W. W. Norton.

Sullivan v. Cheshier (N.D.Ill 1994) 846 F. Supp. 654.

Swartz v. the Regents of the University of California 226 Cal. App. 3d 149.

Terr, L. (1994). *Unchained Memories: True Stories of Traumatic Memory Loss*. New York: Basic Books.

Thompson, C. (1946). Transference as a therapeutic instrument. In *Current Therapies of Personality Disorders*, ed. B. Gluck, pp. 194–205. New York: Grune & Stratton.

——— (1950). *Psychoanalysis: Evolution and Development*. New York: Hermitage House.

Tomm, K. (1991). The ethics of dual relationships. *The Calgary Par-ticipator: A Family Therapy Newsletter* 1:3. (Reprinted in *The Cali-fornia Therapist* Jan./Feb., 1993.)

Tower, L. E. (1956). Countertransference. *Journal of the American Psy-choanalytic Association* 4(2):224–255.

Tronick, E., and Cohn, J. (1988). Infant-mother face-to-face commu-nicative interaction: age and gender differences in coordination and the occurrence of miscoordination. *Child Development* 60:85–92.

Trotter v. Okawa 145 S.E.2d 121 (Va. 1994).

Tustin, F. (1981). *Autistic States in Children*. London: Routledge and Kegan Paul.

———— (1986). *Autistic Barriers in Neurotic Patients*. New Haven, CT: Yale University Press.

Vinson, J. S. (1987). Use of complaint procedures in cases of therapist-patient sexual contact. *Professional Psychology: Research and Practice*:18, 159–164.

Walker, E., and Young, T. D. (1986). *A Killing Cure*. New York: Henry Holt.

Warren, J. (1994). Trial Focuses on Validity of Recovered Memories. *Los Angeles Times*, April 6.

Wink, W. (1986). *Unmasking the Powers*. Philadelphia: Fortress Press.

Winnicott, D. W. (1947). Hate in the countertransference. In *Through Paediatrics to Psycho-Analysis*. New York: Basic Books.

———— (1949). Birth memories, birth trauma, and anxiety. In *Through Paediatrics to Psycho-Analysis*, pp. 174–194. New York: Basic Books.

———— (1954). Metapsychology and classical aspects of regression. In *Through Paediatrics to Psycho-Analysis*, pp. 278–294. New York: Basic Books.

———— (1958). *Through Paediatrics to Psycho-Analysis*. New York: Basic Books, 1975.

———— (1971). *Playing and Reality*. London: Tavistock.

———— (1974). Fear of breakdown. *International Review of Psycho-Analysis* 1:103.

Wolowitz, H. (1972). Hysterical character and feminine identity. In *Readings on the Psychology of Women*, ed. R. Bardwick, pp. 307–314. New York: Harper and Row.

Wright, L. (1993). Remembering Satan. *The New Yorker*, May 17 (Part I) pp. 60–81, May 24 (Part II) pp. 54–76.

———— (1994). *Remembering Satan*. New York: Knopf.

Yapko, M. (1994). *Suggestions of Abuse*. New York: Simon and Schuster.

Index